LAP

THE COMPLETE IDIOT'S GUIDE® TO

Fortune Telling

by Diane Ahlquist

ALPHA

A member of Penguin Group (USA) Inc.

This book is dedicated to the memory of Ernest Sekunna, of Cassadaga, Florida, who predicted my publications as well as many other aspects of my life that are now meeting with success.

ALPHA BOOKS

Published by the Penguin Group

Penguin Group (USA) Inc., 375 Hudson Street, New York, New York 10014, U.S.A.

Penguin Group (Canada), 10 Alcorn Avenue, Toronto, Ontario, Canada M4V 3B2 (a division of Pearson Penguin Canada Inc.)

Penguin Books Ltd., 80 Strand, London WC2R 0RL, England

Penguin Ireland, 25 St Stephen's Green, Dublin 2, Ireland (a division of Penguin Books Ltd.)

Penguin Group (Australia), 250 Camberwell Road, Camberwell, Victoria 3124, Australia (a division of Pearson Australia Group Pty. Ltd.)

Penguin Books India Pvt. Ltd., 11 Community Centre, Panchsheel Park, New Delhi—110 017, India

Penguin Group (NZ), cnr Airborne and Rosedale Roads, Albany, Auckland 1310, New Zealand (a division of Pearson New Zealand Ltd.)

Penguin Books (South Africa) (Pty.) Ltd., 24 Sturdee Avenue, Rosebank, Johannesburg 2196, South Africa

Penguin Books Ltd., Registered Offices: 80 Strand, London WC2R 0RL, England

Copyright © 2006 by Diane Ahlquist

International Standard Book Number: 1-59257-539-0
Library of Congress Catalog Card Number: 2006924213

08 07 06   8 7 6 5 4 3 2 1

Interpretation of the printing code: The rightmost number of the first series of numbers is the year of the book's printing; the rightmost number of the second series of numbers is the number of the book's printing. For example, a printing code of 06-1 shows that the first printing occurred in 2006.

Printed in the United States of America

Note: This publication contains the opinions and ideas of its author. It is intended to provide helpful and informative material on the subject matter covered. It is sold with the understanding that the author and publisher are not engaged in rendering professional services in the book. If the reader requires personal assistance or advice, a competent professional should be consulted.

The author and publisher specifically disclaim any responsibility for any liability, loss, or risk, personal or otherwise, which is incurred as a consequence, directly or indirectly, of the use and application of any of the contents of this book.

Most Alpha books are available at special quantity discounts for bulk purchases for sales promotions, premiums, fund-raising, or educational use. Special books, or book excerpts, can also be created to fit specific needs.

For details, write: Special Markets, Alpha Books, 375 Hudson Street, New York, NY 10014.

Publisher: *Marie Butler-Knight*
Editorial Director: *Mike Sanders*
Managing Editor: *Billy Fields*
Senior Acquisitions Editor: *Randy Ladenheim-Gil*
Development Editor: *Lynn Northrup*
Senior Production Editor: *Janette Lynn*
Copy Editor: *Krista Hansing*

Cartoonist: *Chris Eliopoulos*
Book Designers: *Trina Wurst/Kurt Owens*
Cover Designer: *Kurt Owens*
Indexer: *Angie Bess*
Layout: *Chad Dressler*
Proofreaders: *Aaron Black/Mary Hunt*

Contents at a Glance

Part 1:   **Optimizing Your Success**   1

   1   Get Ready ... Get Set ... Start Your Psychic Engine!   3
Invoke your inner power with concentration and focus.

   2   The Best Times and Places for Fortune Telling   17
Timing can make the difference in the accuracy of a reading.

   3   Readings for Others   31
Reading for another person or in a group.

   4   Set the Scene   43
A little preplanning can produce a lot of results.

Part 2:   **Interpreting Images**   57

   5   Reading Tea Leaves and Coffee Grounds   59
These messages are good to the last drop.

   6   Ice Rendering   75
Snow, icicles, and ice cubes can tell you a lot.

   7   Spondanomancy   81
From yesterday's ashes come tomorrow's messages.

   8   Divining by Sand and Smoke   89
Writing in the sand and gazing at candle smoke is no joke.

   9   Candle Wax Divination   99
Wax drippings create a story for your future.

Part 3:   **Fortune Telling with Games**   107

  10   Ouija Boards: The Directions You Won't Find
in the Box   109
Circle around the board for answers spelled out in letters.

  11   Cartomancy   121
It's all in the cards ... past, present, and future.

  12   Dominoes and Dice: Not Just Games!   137
A flip of a tile or a throw of the dice can reveal your destiny.

  13   Knife Prophecies   149
Spin a knife and get a message.

14 Tablets of Fate   161
    What's your fate for today?

Part 4:   Seeing into Your Future   173

15 Reading Facial Features and Bumps   175
    It's written all over your face—literally.

16 Cloud Prophecies   191
    Look to the sky for pictures in the clouds that can guide you.

17 Crystal Gazing and Scrying   199
    It's clear that you can "see" images in clear objects.

18 Palmistry   213
    It's all there in the palm of your hand.

19 Signs and Symbols   229
    *Those little notes we suddenly see or hear really mean some-
    thing.*

Part 5:   Methods of the Ancients   239

20 Runes   241
    Pick a stone, see a symbol, and find your way.

21 Pendulums and Dowsing   255
    Vibrations are the keys to helpful insights.

22 The *I Ching*   267
    A philosophy and a form of divination all in one.

Appendixes

    A Glossary   287

    B Resources   293

    C Fortune-Telling Journal   297

       Index   305

Contents

Part 1:   **Optimizing Your Success**   **1**

  1   **Get Ready ... Get Set ... Start Your Psychic Engine!**   **3**

Find Your Inner Power 4

  Keep Positive 5

  Connect Your Mind, Body, and Soul 5

  Use Discretion 6

Now Concentrate! 7

  Concentration: The Card Game 7

  Concentrating on an Object 8

Protecting Yourself 9

Track Your Progress: Keeping a Journal....................................10

Practice, Practice, Practice! 13

  Making a Living 14

  Before You Begin 14

  Compare Different Methods 14

  2   **The Best Times and Places for Fortune Telling**   **17**

Different Days for Different Ways 18

What Questions on What Days? 19

Going Through Phases with the Moon 21

  New Moon...21

  Waxing Moon 21

  Full Moon 22

  Waning Moon 22

  Dark Moon 22

Full Moon Seasons 23

  January—Full Wolf Moon 24

  February—Full Snow Moon 24

  March—Full Worm Moon 24

  April—Full Pink Moon 24

  May—Full Flower Moon 24

  June—Full Strawberry Moon 24

  July—The Full Buck Moon 25

  August—Full Sturgeon Moon 25

  September—Full Harvest Moon 25

  October—Full Hunter's Moon 25

  November—Full Beaver Moon...25

  December—The Full Cold Moon 26

Environment Counts 26
The Great Outdoors 26
The Inner Sanctum 27
Compass Directions...27

3 Readings for Others   31

One-on-One Readings 32
Readings Just for Fun 32
Going the Serious Route 32
Knowing When You're Ready 33
Do the Right Thing..34
How Long Is a Reading? 35
Questionable Questioning 36
Specific and General Readings 36
Fair Exchange 37
When Disappointment Strikes 37
Group Participation in Telepathic Experiments.................38
Things You Will Need 39
Fun with Telepathy 39
Group Participation in Psychometry 40

4 Set the Scene   43

The Magic of Salt 44
Salty Qualities 44
Techniques for Salt Protection 45
Color Your World 46
Candles, Music, and Incense 48
Light My Fire 48
Candles Light the Way 49
Carve a Thought 49
Candle Blessing 50
Create Your Own Oil..50
Mood Music 51
Incense That Makes Scents 52
Gemstones and Their Attributes 53

Part 2:   Interpreting Images   57

5 Reading Tea Leaves and Coffee Grounds   59

How Did This Art Begin?..60
The Cup, the Coffee; the Tea, the Brewing 61
Selecting the Right Cup 61
A Cup of Prophecy 62
Selecting and Brewing Tea 63

Let's Read Tea Leaves and Coffee Grounds...............................64

The Actual Reading 64

Past, Present, Future 65

Interpretations of Shapes and Images 65

General Shapes 66

Letters 66

Numbers and Numerology 66

Interpretations of Symbols...68

Sample Readings 72

6 Ice Rendering **75**

Baby, It's Cold Outside 75

Frosty, the Fortune Teller 76

What You'll Need...76

The Cold and Simple Facts..77

The Big Meltdown 78

Icicles 78

Ice Cubes 78

Reading the Watermarks..79

7 Spondanomancy **81**

The Ashes of Time 82

Method One—Blowing in the Wind 82

Let's Make Ashes 83

Safety Warnings...83

How to Do a Reading...84

Method Two—Letters in the Ashes 85

Cinder Ceremonies 87

8 Divining by Sand and Smoke **89**

Circles in the Sand..89

Sand or Smoke: It's All Concentration and Intuition...........90

Meditation Technique Before Divining 91

Time to Get Moving 92

How to Do a Sand-Sational Reading 92

Sand Marks and More...93

The Sands of Time...94

Where There's Smoke, There Are Visions...........................95

When Smoke Gets in Your Eyes, You Can "See" Better.......95

Let's Get Smokin' 96

9 Candle Wax Divination **99**

Lighting the Fires of Time 100

Burning Hot for the Optimum Reading.................................100
  Color Your Wax *100*
  You Need a Nice Shape..*101*
  That Smells Good...*101*
New Moon Candle Ritual 102
Two Methods of Reading Wax 102
  A Mess Can Be Good *102*
  Who Says Water and Fire Don't Mix?...........................*104*

Part 3:   Fortune Telling with Games   107

10   Ouija Boards: The Directions You Won't Find in the Box   109

Portal to the Unknown? 110
Making Your Own Board 111
When and Where to Ouija 111
  Night Fright *112*
  Other Times..*112*
  A Safe Place...*113*
The Traditional Way to Use the Ouija Board 113
  Getting Ready *114*
  Asking Questions *115*
Three or More Participants 116
The Solitary Method 117
Ouija Wisdom 118

11   Cartomancy   121

Cards as a Form of Divination 122
  On a Personal Note *122*
  Using Thirty-Two Cards *123*
  Choosing a Deck of Cards.....................................*123*
Meanings of the Cards 124
  Hearts *124*
  Diamonds *125*
  Clubs *126*
  Spades *126*
Cards in Sequence 127
Card Spreads 128
  One-Month Spread *129*
  Sample Reading for First Week of a One-Month Spread..........*129*
  One-Question Card Spread *130*
What Are You Thinking? 132

12 Dominoes and Dice: Not Just Games! **137**

Roll Those Bones 138
Roll Into Method One...138
   Shaking Things Up *139*
   A General Reading *140*
Roll Into Method Two...140
What the Numbers Mean 140
Dominoes Have a History, Too 142
Finding a Set 143
What Do the Dots Mean for You? 143
   The Western System...*144*
   Interpretations for the Western System *145*
   Doubles Are Special *145*
   The Eastern System *146*
   Interpretations for the Eastern System *146*

13 Knife Prophecies **149**

An Amusing Pastime 150
Tools You Will Need 150
How to Proceed 151
Body, Mind, and Spirit Prophecies 151
   Health *152*
   Education..*152*
   Spiritual Messages *153*
Lifestyle 154
   Job/Career *154*
   Money *155*
   Social Life *156*
Matters of the Heart 156
   Love/Romance *157*
   Family...*157*
   Marriage/Partnerships...*158*

14 Tablets of Fate **161**

What in the World Are Tablets of Fate? 162
Get Permission from the Sphinx Before You Begin....................163
The Sphinx Card 163
   Well, Sphinx, What Do Ya Say?...*164*
   The Sphinx Number Meanings *165*
Other Tablets of Fate..166
   Venus Numbers: All About Love...*166*
   Sun Numbers: Timing Is Everything *168*
   Celestial Numbers: Answers to General Questions....................*170*

Part 4:   Seeing into Your Future   173

15   Reading Facial Features and Bumps   175

Is It Scientific or Just Woo-Woo?....................................176
Studying the Face 176
Forehead 177
Ears...178
Eyes 179
Eye Color 179
Eyebrows 180
Nose...181
Chin 182
Mouth 182
Lips 183
Face Time 183
The Bumpy Roads of the Past 184
The Head Divided...184
Don't Get Stumped by Bumps 186
Feelings 186
Sentiments 187
Intellectual Faculties 188

16   Cloud Prophecies   191

Look Up to See Your Future...192
Types of Clouds 192
Cumulus 193
Stratus..193
Cirrus 193
Nimbus 193
Questioning the Heavens 194
The Nine Muses and Cloud Divination 194
A Cloudy Message 196

17   Crystal Gazing and Scrying   199

Answers Under Glass?...200
Clairvoyance...200
Nostradamus' Gift 201
The Most Common Scrying Tools..202
Crystals 202
Crystal Shopping 203
Clearing Your Crystal 203
Charge Your Crystal..204
Black Mirrors 204
Finding a Black Mirror (or Creating Your Own) 205
In the Dark 205

Gaze Patiently 206

Plan Ahead 206

Session One 207

Session Two 209

Asking "Yes" and "No" Questions 210

General Questions 210

A Phone Call Without a Phone 211

18 Palmistry **213**

Give Our Ancients a Hand 214

Take My Hand 214

What's Your Size? 214

Palms Away 215

I Have to Hand It to You 216

The Fickle Finger of Fate 218

Here's a Tip 219

Nice Joint You Have There 219

Let's Get Connected 220

My Fingers Have Names 220

Thumbs Up 221

Nailing the Process 222

Major Highways of the Hand 222

Life Line 223

Head Line 224

Heart Line 225

Fate Line 225

Love Affair Lines 226

Other Marks on the Hand.............................227

19 Signs and Symbols **229**

Is It Just Coincidence or Is That a Real Sign? 230

The Physical Evidence 232

Pick Your Own Sign.....................................232

Recognizing a Sign.......................................232

I Never Looked at It That Way 233

Those Who Have Passed to the Other Side 234

Signs from the Spirit World.........................235

Dreams 236

Face West for a Psychic Telephone Call 236

Part 5: Methods of the Ancients **239**

20 Runes **241**

The Tradition Behind Runes 241

Obtaining Your Runes 242
  Buy 'Em 242
  Make 'Em 242
  Stones or Shells Work Well 243
  Wooden, Nut, Bean, or Seed Runes 245
Rune Definitions 246
  Fehu 246
  Uruz 246
  Thurisaz 246
  Ansuz 247
  Raidho 247
  Kenaz 247
  Gebo 247
  Wunjo 247
  Hagalaz 248
  Nauthiz 248
  Isa 248
  Jera 248
  Eihwaz 248
  Perthro 249
  Algiz 249
  Sowilo 249
  Tiwaz 249
  Berkano 249
  Ehwaz 250
  Mannaz 250
  Laguz 250
  Ingwaz 250
  Dagaz 250
  Othala 251
Laying Out the Truth 251
  Single Rune: Pick a Rune, There's Your Answer 251
  Three Runes: Three Different Methods 252
  Five Runes: Cross 252

21 Pendulums and Dowsing **255**

Getting Into the Swing of Things 256
  Making a Pendulum 256
  Yes/No or More? 256
Using a Pendulum 257
  Basic Method 258
  Advanced Method 260
The Art of Finding Things 260
  How Does Dowsing Actually Work? 262
  Dowsing Equipment 262

A-Dowsing We Will Go!..263
   Y-Rods *264*
   L-Rods *264*
   Map Dowsing with a Pendulum *264*

22   The *I Ching*   267

What Is the *I Ching?* 268
Hexagrams—Not Something Witches Send 268
The *I Ching* as an Oracle..270
   Pennies from Heaven *270*
   Heads or Tails? *270*
   Shake, Rattle, Roll, and Draw *271*
Interpretation Key for the Sixty-Four Hexagrams................272
   1. Ch'ien—The Creative *272*
   2. K'un—The Receptive *273*
   3. Chun—Difficulty at the Beginning *273*
   4. Mêng—Youthful Folly *273*
   5. Hsu—Waiting (Nourishment) *273*
   6. Sung—Conflict *274*
   7. Shih—The Army..*274*
   8. Pi—Holding Together (Union) *274*
   9. Hsiao Ch'u—The Taming Power of the Small *274*
   10. Lu—Treading (Conduct) *274*
   11. T'ai—Peace *275*
   12. P'i—Standstill (Stagnation)................................*275*
   13. T'ung Jên—Fellowship with Men *275*
   14. Ta Yu—Possession in Great Measure *275*
   15. Ch'ien—Modesty *275*
   16. YuYü—Enthusiasm *276*
   17. Sui—Following *276*
   18. Ku—Work on What Has Been Spoiled (Decay) *276*
   19. Lin—Approach *276*
   20. Kuan—Contemplation (View) *276*
   21. Shih Ho—Biting Through *277*
   22. Pi—Grace *277*
   23. Po—Splitting Apart..*277*
   24. Fu—Return (The Turning Point) *277*
   25. Wu Wang—Innocence (The Unexpected) *277*
   26. Ta Ch'u—The Taming Power of the Great............*278*
   27. I—The Corners of the Mouth (Providing Nourishment) *278*
   28. Ta Kuo—Preponderance of the Great *278*
   29. K'an—The Abysmal (Water) *278*
   30. Li—The Clinging, Fire *278*
   31. Hsien—Influence (Wooing) *279*

32. Hêng—Duration 279
33. Tun—Retreat...279
34. Ta Chuang—The Power of the Great....................279
35. Chin—Progress 279
36. Ming I—Darkening of the Light 280
37. Chia Jên—The Family (The Clan) 280
38. K'uei—Opposition 280
39. Chien—Obstruction 280
40. Hsieh—Deliverance 280
41. Sun—Decrease...281
42. I—Increase...281
43. Kuai—Break-Through (Resoluteness) 281
44. Kou—Coming to Meet 281
45. Ts'ui—Gathering Together (Massing) 282
46. Shêng—Pushing Upward...282
47. K'un—Oppression (Exhaustion) 282
48. Ching—The Well...282
49. Ko—Revolution (Molting) 283
50. Ting—The Caldron 283
51. Chên—The Arousing (Shock, Thunder) 283
52. Kên—Keeping Still, Mountain 283
53. Chien—Development (Gradual Progress) 283
54. Kuei Mei—The Marrying Maiden...........................284
55. Fêng—Abundance (Fullness) 284
56. Lu—The Wanderer 284
57. Sun—The Gentle (The Penetrating, Wind) 284
58. Tui—The Joyous, Lake 284
59. Huan—Dispersion (Dissolution)............................285
60. Chieh—Limitation..285
61. Chung Fu—Inner Truth 285
62. Hsiao Kuo—Preponderance of the Small...............285
63. Chi Chi—After Completion 285
64. Wei Chi—Before Completion 286

Appendixes

A Glossary   287

B Resources   293

C Fortune-Telling Journal   297

Index   305

Introduction

Whether they are believers or not, most people are fascinated by fortune telling. But few really want to try to practice this type of art any more. But because you are reading this book, you most likely have a sincere interest in pursuing this craft.

Fortune telling dates back before recorded history. There is much evidence of it in places such as ancient Egypt, China, and Greece, to name only a few. This comes in forms of drawings and artifacts that were deemed tools of divination.

It appears that every culture had its own methods of foretelling events and situations that would lie ahead. It is still simple human nature that sparks most of us to want to know what the future will bring. Times change, technology advances, and logical scientific methods abound. Regardless, insights into the unknown still expand. Hopefully, the searching for answers beyond the physical will stay undiminished.

The methods discussed in this book are introductory and presented in a beginner's format. Some are more primitive techniques from days of yore, while others represent more current, sophisticated practices. I attempted to present a sampling of various methods to satisfy every mystic taste. Tally one method against the other and make your own determinations.

What You'll Find in This Book

This book is divided into five parts:

Part 1, "Optimizing Your Success," shows you how to develop your psychic senses and the most productive times and places to conduct fortune telling. Reading for others can be tricky and is addressed in this segment. The use of candles, salt, music, gemstones, and incense is discussed—these items can put you in a mode that is conducive to successful divination.

Part 2, "Interpreting Images," gives you the how-tos of reading tea leaves, watermarks from ice cubes, ashes, smoke, sand, and wax. There isn't much left after this group of image-making elements is discussed. Some methods offer specific definitions of shapes and symbols, while others prompt you to use your personal psychic impressions to come to conclusions.

Part 3, "Fortune Telling with Games," tells you how common items like dice and cards can be used to divine your destiny. Other not-so-common items, such as tablets of fate that you can make yourself, and Ouija boards are covered as well. Here you will find new twists to old games.

Part 4, "Seeing into Your Future," discusses some forms of prophecy that may already be familiar to you, including reading palms, gazing into crystal balls, and determining the meanings of signs and symbols. This part also covers a few forms you may not know about, such as cloud prophecies and reading bumps on a person's head.

Part 5, "Methods of the Ancients," tells you about the old and tested methods of looking into what the future may hold. In this part, you uncover the methods of crafting or buying your own runes, dangling a pendulum, and consulting the *I Ching* to get answers to questions.

Extras

Throughout this book you'll find four types of sidebars that offer tips, definitions, quotations, and related bits of information to help you understand more about fortune telling:

Visionary Insights

Here you find tips to help you with the fortune-telling process, to save you time or to answer questions you may have.

def•i•ni•tion

Check these boxes for definitions of words or phrases that may be new to you.

Notions Through Time

These insightful quotes, some amusing and some serious, encourage you to reflect on a given subject.

Enlightening Extras

These boxes offer miscellaneous bits of information that help make the trek through this book more understandable.

Acknowledgments

No book is usually the effort of one single person, and this one is no exception. So there are many people to whom I am grateful.

To my agent, Jacky Sachs, for having the confidence that I could tackle this project. To Randy Ladenheim-Gil and Lynn Northrup, my extraordinary and talented editors, who put up with my humor, not to mention those smiley faces often embedded in the body of my e-mails. Also, thanks to all the other special individuals at Alpha Books who brought this book to a professional status.

A heartfelt thank you to three special ladies who helped make this book shine: Susan Dobra, Ph.D., for her editorial advice that came with professionalism, and for her conscientious efforts; Sandra Gentile, who helped with research, edited drafts, and acted as my daily sounding board; and Patty Volz, a friend I love dearly, for her illustrations, knowledge, and contributions to the output of this book.

Let's not forget my loving family: My mother, Rosemarie, for her support and love, as always. My beautiful sister (inside and out), Marie Frenden, who was there with her insights at the click of an e-mail message. Bob Irwin, who believes there is more in life beyond the five senses. John and Kiki Frenden, who have climbed mountains to find a better view. Daniel, Lori, and Joshua Frenden, for their long-distance energy.

My husband, Adrian Volney, for learning the meaning of the words "frozen entrees" and "take-out," and for mastering the washing machine. What a guy—can't wait till he buys the book.

Myka, Shane, and Bron Volney, for their enthusiasm.

Mike Seery: For years you have supported my literary pursuits and anything I do or attempt to do. I don't care what they say about your ponytail … I like it.

Joe Lubow: Without your efforts years ago, the magick of my literary endeavors would not have come to fruition.

Nicki Dodd: My deep appreciation for your interest and concern in the process of this book. You truly are not only a radiant friend, but a sweet spirit.

Jeralyn Sheldon: Your sincere excitement and support touched my heart.

I do not want to forget my lovely neighbors Pat and Steve Samuels and Linda and Jerry Mroczlowski, who always took the time to ask if I needed anything to help the advancement toward my deadlines. They made me laugh in between chapters, not to mention a glass of Chardonnay here and there … don't tell!

Brenton Ver Ploeg: My favorite skeptic, pantheist, and friend, for keeping me on my toes when matters of scientific thought meet the mysterious. If we can get along with our compatible differences, there is still hope for all the other believers and nonbelievers on the planet to form a convergence!

Trademarks

All terms mentioned in this book that are known to be or are suspected of being trademarks or service marks have been appropriately capitalized. Alpha Books and Penguin Group (USA) Inc. cannot attest to the accuracy of this information. Use of a term in this book should not be regarded as affecting the validity of any trademark or service mark.

Part 1

Optimizing Your Success

Fortune telling is not like the drive-up window at a fast-food restaurant. "I'll take two low-fat answers about my boyfriend, one insight about that girl next door, and three soft-shell predictions about my career. Thanks!"

Some people want to get right to the art of fortune telling. They don't care about the roads they should travel to get there. They want a jet to drop them off at the end. The thoughts and ideas before getting started may be irrelevant to many, but they are very important.

Setting the scene with enhancements to put you in a better state of mind, properly centering yourself, being diplomatic with others, and timing considerations are important parts of the process and should not be neglected.

Get Ready ... Get Set ... Start Your Psychic Engine!

In This Chapter

◆ Invoking your inner power

◆ Tips for improving your concentration

◆ Using white light to protect yourself

◆ Keeping a journal of your progress

◆ Practice makes perfect!

Fortune telling can be great fun. It can also help you or whoever's fortune you are telling make decisions about the future. Even if you don't think it's a good idea to plan your career on the basis of what some tea leaves say, it's always nice to have the option.

It's not really difficult to learn how to do fortune telling well, but if you can start the journey by developing your psychic sensitivity, you'll move forward much faster. You may not want to take the time to learn these beginning techniques because you want to skip right to the fortune-telling methods. And that's okay! But do come back to this information if you really want to hone your skills. Increased psychic awareness enhances your ability to read fortunes because it's not just what the signs say—it's what you read into them. I can't guarantee you will become Madame (or Mister) ZaZa in one day, but you will be well on your way!

So get yourself in your most receptive state of mind: we begin by helping you learn how to focus, invoke your own psychic powers, and practice concentration techniques before you start to use these methods. You'll want to keep a journal of your progress, too. I can see into your future … and you're going to become a great fortune teller!

Find Your Inner Power

An ancient story about an argument between the sun and the wind goes like this: The sun and the wind decided to have a competition. When they saw a man walking down the street one day, they seized the opportunity to test their powers. They agreed to see which one could get the man to remove his coat. The sun told the wind to try first. The wind started with a huge gust, taking the man by surprise. The man's coat was nearly blown off, but not quite. So the wind continued to blast, wail, and swirl in all directions. But the harder the wind blew, the tighter the man held on to his coat. Eventually, the wind tired and gave up.

Next, it was the sun's turn. The sun surprised the man also, but not with a sudden blast of heat. Instead, it came out slowly from behind a cloud. The man smiled, welcoming its warmth. The sun smiled with the man and continued to shine as the man strolled on. After a while, the man began to get warm. He decided to remove his coat and carry it over his shoulder. The sun had won, using the "me with you" approach, which worked better than the wind's "me against you" approach.

The same is true of invoking inner power. If you can relax and work *with* your psychic intuitions rather than trying to wrestle them out of the airwaves, you will find that they begin to come willingly. Try not to act hastily or get agitated because you are not getting the results you want with a certain form of *divination*. Allowing insight to come to you is a type of power you can develop with patient practice. Don't work against it—work *with* it.

Start by finding a quiet place where you won't be disturbed. Sit down, close your eyes, and breathe deeply, filling your belly with air and your body with energy. Now imagine your skin becoming translucent and the energy from your body moving out through your skin and into the space around your body. Feel this *energy body* as a receptive "outer skin," able to sense in its own way, through emotions and fleeting impressions. Simply experience these, without needing to hold on to them or act on them in any way. Just breathe and notice your thoughts and feelings. Find a little time to do this every day, even if only for 15 minutes. Then tune in to your energy body at different times and places during the day.

After a while, tuning into your energy body will become a habit—and a good one, at that. You will be able to use the sensitivity and awareness you develop to enhance your fortune-telling skills. As you practice invoking your psychic energy, you will feel more confident and more empowered to become a better fortune teller.

def•i•ni•tion

Divination is another word for fortune telling. **Divining** means to be actively using a fortune-telling method, as in "I was divining my future using a pendulum." Your **energy body** is the area around your body into which life force radiates. It is thought by some to be the source of the "sixth sense" of psychic awareness.

Keep Positive

Another way of invoking inner power is through cultivating positive attitudes toward others and the fortune-telling techniques in this book. A relaxed, receptive state of mind is best for receiving psychic insights. Anger, stress, and impatience deplete our psychic powers. Cultivate an attitude of calm awareness, not too passive or too aggressive, to allow information to come *to* you from the psychic realms. Being a good friend, a trustworthy member of your community, and a decent human in general will help you tune in to the subtle realms. Nothing clears the psychic pathways like good old heart energy—and nothing blocks them like fear or self-doubt. If you start with the attitude that you will never be able to predict your future, you will prove yourself right. Remain open-minded and confident, and you'll open yourself up to psychic success.

Some fortune-telling methods will be easier for you than others. But just because a particular method doesn't work well for you doesn't mean that it doesn't work at all. Try a little of everything and see what "comes through" for you.

Connect Your Mind, Body, and Soul

If you're in good health mentally and physically, not to mention spiritually, you've got a great power source. This may sound more medical than cosmic, but if you are strong in mind, body, and spirit, you are in harmony with all things.

If you are going to practice telling prophecies—which means to predict future events—take care of yourself. This will open your psychic channels more easily. Someone who is sick, depressed, or spiritually void will not have the presence of mind to make these modes of psychic interpretation work.

Perhaps you think invoking the power within means calling on magical entities or sorcerers. But it's all about using the insight and love with which we were all born. And that's the strongest power of all.

> **Enlightening Extras**
>
> To enhance your psychic powers ...
> ◆ Learn something new every day.
> ◆ Cultivate love in your life.
> ◆ Maintain your physical well-being with preventative methods, and get regular medical check-ups.
> ◆ Pay attention to your physical appearance, which promotes self-confidence.
> ◆ Practice some type of spirituality, whether it is organized religion or your personal idea of being a spiritual person.

Use Discretion

Be careful who you share your new interest with. Some people may think fortune telling is fascinating, while others may think it's not proper. When I was a little girl, my mother wouldn't let my sister and me use a Ouija board in the house, so we hid it in the attic. (To us, that wasn't really the house.) Mom felt that using a Ouija board was not a nice thing for little girls to do (and perhaps it was even a little dangerous). She certainly wouldn't have wanted the neighbors to find out that her daughters were speaking to spirits! (I tell you all about using a Ouija board in Chapter 10.)

Test the waters when you're not sure how someone feels. Try a quick comment, such as, "Some of that fortune-telling information seems interesting, but I don't really know. What do you think?" If you get a positive response, you have a source of conversation—and you may even find someone you can team up with for a card *reading* at a later time. If you get a response such as "I think it's the work of the devil," it's best to say something like, "Oh, I just see so much of it around these days—one can't help being curious. So, how 'bout those White Sox?"

def•i•ni•tion

A **reading** is another name for the practice of divination or fortune telling, as in "She did a reading for me with her Tarot cards."

If you associate yourself with someone who does not approve of such things, that person can deplete your power, so change the subject rather than open yourself up to negativity. Don't attempt to shove your beliefs down someone else's throat; either, people are entitled to their opinions, as you are to yours.

Now Concentrate!

When developing psychic abilities, you must increase your ability to concentrate. How many times do you suddenly do something incorrectly that you've been practicing for years? It could be missing your exit off the interstate or forgetting to close the salad dressing bottle before you shake it. You will most likely think or say, "I *never* do that. I just wasn't concentrating." The reason is that you allowed your mind to wander off, thinking about other things. When you really concentrate, you center your mind on one single concept.

Focusing on one main factor, such as the question you are asking, is important when it comes to reading past, present, or future events. You need time to focus accurately. Don't think that you do not have good concentration just because you may find it difficult at times. Have you ever been so engrossed in a television program that you didn't hear the phone ring or see someone walk through the door? That is an example of focused concentration.

Concentration: The Card Game

You can increase your concentration in many simple ways. The most familiar is the card game called Concentration, which you may have played when you were a child. Concentration is a memory game in which you match cards that are similar or exactly the same. As simple as it sounds, this game can assist you in your concentration techniques as an adult. These decks can be found in the toy department of any discount store or in any toy store. Also, the Internet has Concentration card game sites where you can click on cards and try to find the match. However, if you are not computer savvy or you don't want to brave the toy section at a store, you can create your own using a regular deck of playing cards and a clock or timer.

You will be using only 26 cards of the original deck. Separate out all the red cards: the hearts and diamonds suits, including 2 kings, 2 queens, 2 jacks, 2 tens, 2 nines, 2 eights, 2 sevens, 2 sixes, 2 fives, 2 fours, 2 threes, 2 twos, and 2 aces. This is a total of 26 cards. Set the rest of the deck aside. Shuffle the cards and lay them out, face down, six across by four rows down. The two remaining should form row number five.

Watch the clock and time yourself, starting with perhaps 15 minutes and gradually reducing the time. To play, turn over any two cards. If they match, remove the cards.

If they do not match, turn them back over and try again. You can never have three cards or more turned over at a time. The challenge is to find all the sets of matching cards, leaving none remaining on the table. Try to beat your own best time. But remember, shuffle the cards each time you begin a new session before laying them out again. You will notice that the more you play, the better you become. You'll increase your concentration and have fun doing it.

Two or more people can play this game, and whoever ends up with the most pairs wins. I wouldn't normally recommend gambling, but laying a little wager might motivate you to improve your concentration faster!

Concentrating on an Object

Select a piece of fruit, an object such as a faceted crystal wine glass, or anything that has markings or patterns. Even a piece of fabric such as a pillowcase or scarf would work.

In a quiet space where you will be undisturbed, start to focus on the object. Examine it from all sides and angles. Hold it in your hand if you need to.

You will find that your mind starts to wander while doing this. You may think about the day you bought that scarf or think that it is out of style. Regardless, acknowledge those thoughts and get right back to concentrating on the object itself. See it, smell it, touch it. Notice if it has a tear or flaws or special coloring.

After you have studied the object, close your eyes and try to visualize it. On what side was that apple bruised? Where was the chip on the wine glass?

Attempt to see a well-defined image. If you become frustrated and can't remember much about the object, don't fret. Merely open your eyes and look at the object again; then close your eyes and start over.

After a while, you will get the concept of concentration. Not only will this prepare you for fortune telling, but it also will help you in school, work, and other activities such as sports or hobbies.

Whatever the occupation, anyone who has achieved any type of success in life uses concentration. Being able to focus is the key to living consciously in the world. When you learn to become more conscious, you will find yourself being less frustrated. You won't misplace your wallet as easily or forget to take out the trash. You will be expanding your mind. Your self-confidence will increase, and you will be able to function on a daily level more easily.

Enlightening Extras

Concentration is different from meditation. When you concentrate, you are focusing on an external object and seeing it in a physical form. In meditation, you may start by concentrating, but you often go beyond that and focus your consciousness on things not physical. Thoughts and messages may come to you from a higher power through meditation. Meditation is something you may want to investigate in the future. Many good books are written about the subject, including *The Complete Idiot's Guide to Meditation, Second Edition* (see Appendix B).

It's amazing how a few simple exercises that don't cost you anything can do so much. Set aside time daily to do some type of concentration-building exercise.

In my experience, these simple techniques increased my concentration, thus increasing my psychic abilities. To this day, I play Concentration with cards, concentrate on crystals and trees, and even focus on cereal boxes, trying to recall where each cornflake is located. Okay, cornflakes can be a bit tough, but visualizing a nice box of Lucky Charms can be great fun!

Start using these techniques today to increase your concentration. You could take a few minutes right now by putting down this book and concentrating on its cover. You can focus on any object. It is how you recall the detail that is significant. Good luck!

Protecting Yourself

The most important part of doing any form of divination is what you do before you begin. You are inviting into your psychic space all manner of information, vibrations, and perhaps even entities from other dimensions of existence. Most of these cannot cause you harm, but a little psychic safety net never hurt anybody. Start any divination session with a protection technique of using white light.

When you are in the place where you will be conducting your session, get comfortable and visualize a cloud of bright light encompassing you, at least 2 feet out, from your head to your toes. If you are working with other people, they should do the same thing.

Next, put together your index and middle fingers, forming a type of pointer. Pointing down, draw an imaginary circle of white light around yourself, your companions, and any materials you will be using. In fact, you can make the circle as large as the entire room. To do this, you will have to turn in a 360° circle clockwise with your fingers pointed downward. If you are working with another person, only one person needs to create the circle. After you create your general circle around yourself and other participants, including helpers or observers, draw another etheric circle around the divination materials themselves for extra protection.

Visionary Insights

If you're planning a short session, use an easy protection technique by counting down from four. Sitting in a comfortable position, start counting backward from four, visualizing a white light coming up from the ground, up through your body at the speed you want (four, three, two, one) until it moves to a few inches above your head. The light should now encompass your entire body. Doesn't that feel good?

When the session is over, visualize the circle lifting into the air through the ceiling, through the roof, and into the atmosphere. Wash your hands after your consultation, feeling yourself to be clear and refreshed. If water is not available, you can shake your hands as a way of clearing yourself.

If you have to leave your circle before your consultation is complete, draw an imaginary door or arch with the same fingers you used to create your circle. Open it so you can leave and then close it behind yourself. To re-enter, open and close as before and continue your session.

Track Your Progress: Keeping a Journal

If you intend to practice fortune telling, you should create a journal to keep track of your progress. You can think of it as your "Divination Diary." Write in it every time you do a reading, if you can, and record your thoughts, goals, successes, and failures. Later, when you go back and read your entries, you'll be able to tell what worked and what didn't, and start to figure out why.

Let your journal be a private place where you can indulge your most secret ideas about the art of fortune telling and what you want to achieve with it. You can write about which modes of fortune telling you have mastered and which ones you may not be drawn to. You could even create your own "Madame ZaZa" alter ego there! Don't allow anyone else to see your journal unless they are very special, are understanding about your practices, and respect your interests.

The first thing you need is a something to write in. I recommend purchasing a three-ring binder so it's easy to remove and add pages. Consider one with inside pockets for miscellaneous items. Any book with blank pages will also work. Elaborate types of portfolios are available, but I suggest something plain so you can decorate and personalize it. This is where you can use your creative talents.

If you are not artistic, don't worry. You can simply cover it in cloth—something soft but durable. This will make it more special, alive, and magical.

If you choose, you can adorn your journal with stickers, drawings, pictures, leaves, feathers, or anything that means something to you. Consult your psychic intuition to get ideas.

If you're not excited about decorating your journal, you might want to buy a blank notebook with a cover that appeals to you. I've seen some lovely ones, from simple handmade paper to leather-bound ones with beaded decorations. The idea is to make *you* feel as if your journal is special. If you are better at the art of shopping than arts and crafts, that doesn't make you a bad person. Go buy something beautiful!

My journal is covered in brown fabric, which signifies learning and stability. I merely attached the fabric with spray glue. It's not perfect, but neither am I, so it seemed to be appropriate!

Here are some other colors you might consider, along with what each represents. (You'll find more about colors in Chapter 4.)

Blue	Peace and tranquility
Yellow	Increased confidence
Green	Success and prosperity
Orange	Self-control and organization
Red	Passion, physical strength, and capability
White	Originality, purity, and peace
Purple	Divination, wisdom, and success
Black	Psychic powers, vision, and divination

After you have prepared your journal, your pilgrimage can begin. Here are some ideas for what you can write in it:

- Date the top of the page.

- Describe the type of weather you had for that day.

- Explore how you were feeling.

- Record what type of divination you were using: Tarot, cloud interpretations, pendulums, and so on.

- Write down the questions you asked that day.

◆ Tell what your results were. Be honest. If you just couldn't interpret an answer or had trouble, say so.

◆ Write your thoughts about what you saw, thought, felt, or sensed; what you think it might have meant; and what you'd like to try next time.

As an example, I will share a few pages from my personal journal:

September 26, 2005

Today there is a hurricane approaching Florida. This has caused me to relocate from the east coast of Florida where I was visiting, back home to the west coast. I am feeling a little stressed and tired.

It's windy, and intermittent rain followed me as I drove down Alligator Alley.

When I finally arrived home feeling safe but tired, I took out my tarot cards to see the outcome of an article I submitted to a magazine. These cards tell me the article will be rejected, but it's for the best. Hmmm … who likes rejection? But I can deal with it if it's "for the best." I will wait to see the results, which I will get in a few days.

September 29, 2005

The weather is still rainy and gloomy, but not too bad.

I feel okay but not into doing any type of readings for myself or other people. I think I will relax.

Got an e-mail. My article WAS accepted and is due by November 1. My reading on September 26 was totally wrong!! Oh well, no one is perfect. I might not be concentrating enough. I better work on that.

October 13, 2005

The weather is great and I am feeling good.

The magazine that accepted my article just went out of business. Had I completed it and sent it to them, I would never have gotten paid. Too bad for them. But at least my reading of September 26 was right after all. Whew!!!

I think I will leave these cards alone for a while and do a little tea-leaf reading.

Okay, I just did my tea-leaf reading and it shows a canceled trip. That's interesting because I have no plans on going anywhere in the next week. Wonder what that's about. Once again I have to wait and see. By the way, what's the big deal about green tea? This stuff tastes terrible.

You need to write in your journal only when you do a reading for yourself or someone else; it is not necessary to do it every day. But do write at least a few lines after every reading so you start to develop the habit of writing in your journal. Don't think of it as a chore, but rather as a tool for empowering yourself. Write on!

Notions Through Time

The truly valuable thing is the intuition.

—Albert Einstein, U.S. physicist

If you have a computer, you might want to keep your journal on your computer. It's clear, typed, and, if you use your spell checker, free of typos. This is a personal choice, of course. If putting pen to paper makes it more personal and traditional for you, that is the avenue you should travel. If tapping your keyboard makes it easier for you, then follow the sound of that drummer.

Always bear in mind that the reason you are keeping a journal is so you can go back and check to see why some days your readings were better than others. Are you more accurate when it's raining and you're blue? Or do you seem to nail those predictions on sunny days when you just had a bowl of ice cream? After a while you will see how your moods, conditions, and the things that surround you make the difference.

No one is alike when it comes to the reason why we can divine better under certain conditions than others. Your journal will help you to discover what works best for you.

After approximately three weeks, you will have enough information to judge what makes you more precise and what doesn't work for you. In other words, if you know that on sunny days after you eat chicken fajitas, you never do good readings, then wait for a day when it's raining and you said no to Mexican food!

Practice, Practice, Practice!

Unlike practicing something you don't like, practicing fortune telling is fun. You can work with a different type of divination every day—one day it may be reading coffee grounds (see Chapter 5), and the next it may be ice cube rendering (see Chapter 6).

For some methods, you obviously need much more training than for others. The trick is not to strain yourself to the point that it just isn't fun anymore. When it stops being fun and becomes a chore, that's when it's time to put things away for a while and go back to it when you are more in the mood. On the other hand, if you enjoy a daily routine of fortune telling as a hobby, then do it as often as you like. Remember, there are no quizzes and there's no passing or failing here.

Making a Living

Put fortune telling in perspective. This is something you should see as a pastime to begin with. True, some people can make a living at it. These individuals, if they are honest and not phonies, have studied years and have achieved professional stature. If you feel you have a talent above others, keep practicing. But before you can become a professional, you need to know in your heart that your accuracy is at least in the 90 percent range.

Before You Begin

When starting any of the fortune-telling procedures, remember the importance of concentration. Laughing and joking have their time and place in these endeavors. But when you are first starting out, you need to keep the giddiness out of the sessions. When you can focus without much effort, you can be more light-hearted.

Compare Different Methods

This book enables you to try different methods and compare them to each other. When practicing, try asking the same questions using the different fortune-telling methods discussed in this book. For example, look at the clouds and ask your questions. Write down your answer in your journal. Then go to the Ouija board, and ask the same question and record that answer. Finally, try your chance at the cards and see what kind of response you get from them. Write that down in your journal as well.

When you go back to see how well you did a few days (or maybe even weeks) later, it will give you a good barometer of what form of fortune telling works best for you.

> **Visionary Insights**
>
> Start simply. Don't try to compare more than three forms of fortune telling at first; it is just too confusing. However, as time goes on, you can start to do more complex comparisons.

After lots of experimenting, you will find a special niche that suits you. If you do have a flair for one type of divination, you may want to really elaborate on that one and use the others for a little distraction or something different on a rainy day. The only way to find out your particular specialty is to practice, practice, practice.

It is admirable to try to teach yourself a skill and routinely practice it. One way to help remember details and try out new ideas is to teach other people. Teaching others what you know instills it even better in your mind. Let people who are really interested know that you are just beginning and are a student yourself, but that you would like to share your experiences and knowledge thus far. By trying to educate others, you become inspired to recall all the information you have gathered because others are counting on you for guidance. Never pretend that you are an expert at something when you are not. However, it never hurts to say, "You might find this fun. I'll do the best I can to show you, but remember, I'm just learning myself. I might still have to look up a few things or research it with you."

The Least You Need to Know

- True power comes from within. Work *with* your intuition rather than trying to force it.

- Increasing your level of concentration will increase your psychic abilities.

- Keeping a journal of your successes and disappointments will help you learn.

- Try all the forms of divination, and then focus on your favorite.

- Nothing happens overnight. Keep practicing, and you will see results!

The Best Times and Places for Fortune Telling

In This Chapter

♦ What days go with what fortune-telling ways

♦ Your day for answers

♦ Harmonizing with the phases of the moon

♦ Synchronizing with the seasons

♦ Finding the right environment

Finding a special time or place for fortune telling allows you to get in synch with the flow of energy on the planet. Certain days, moon phases, and environments result in more fortune-telling accuracy than others. Many of our ancients, who were more connected to nature and the elements than we are, conducted their lives according to the conditions they saw around them. Therefore, much of the information in this chapter is drawn not only from personal experience, but also from the perceptions and insights of oracles, soothsayers, and other "Merlin the Magician" types who came before us. Call them what you will—they studied their craft intently, experimented throughout the ages, and performed their magic, which gave us modern-day fortune tellers a foundation on which to build.

That does not mean they were always right. But they did somehow manage to pass on to generations their methods and their understanding of things beyond the physical world to us. If they hadn't, perhaps you wouldn't be reading this book right now.

Different Days for Different Ways

From ancient times, there has been an understanding that different days of the week have different energies. This was probably learned by trial and error through long experience by magical practitioners of all kinds. It has been passed down to us by the keepers of this knowledge, and I pass it on to you as my teachers passed it on to me. By choosing to conduct your fortune-telling techniques on a particular day of the week, you add the energy of that day to your craft.

Each day of the week has its own magical correspondence that relates to the planet that rules that day, as shown in the following table.

Day of the Week	Ruled By	Planet Correspondence(s)
Sunday	Sun	Leadership, vitality, ambition, recognition
Monday	Moon	Inspiration, psychic powers, feminine interaction, creativity
Tuesday	Mars	Progress, activity, courage, independence
Wednesday	Mercury	Awareness, communication, balance, eloquence
Thursday	Jupiter	Abundance, optimism, reverence, honor
Friday	Venus	Love, romance, sex, artistry
Saturday	Saturn	Learning, wisdom, stability, endurance

The energy of these planets, studied by astrologers and other diviners, guides us to what types of questions will be most successful on what days. For example, Venus rules Friday, so that is a good day to ask questions about matters of the heart. Saturday is ruled by Saturn, the planet that rules the removal of things. So Saturday is a good day to ask questions about how to release things, such as "How can I stop eating so much?"

The energy of each day of the week also corresponds well with the different methods of divination. The following table lists the different fortune-telling methods that I discuss in this book, along with their corresponding days.

Method of Divination	Best Days to Practice It
Coffee grounds/tea leaves	Monday, Tuesday, Wednesday
Ice cube rendering	Monday, Tuesday, Wednesday
Spondanomancy (reading ashes)	Friday, Saturday, Sunday
Divining by sand	Monday, Saturday, Sunday
Candle wax divination	Monday, Tuesday, Wednesday
Ouija boards	Monday through Saturday
Cartomancy (reading playing cards)	Any day of the week
Dice	Thursday through Sunday
Dominoes	Thursday through Sunday
Knife prophecies	Friday, Saturday, Sunday
Tablets of fate	Thursday through Sunday
Bumps, face readings, and palmistry	Any day of the week
Cloud prophecies	Any day of the week
Crystal gazing/scrying	Monday, Thursday, Saturday, Sunday
Signs and symbols	Any day of the week
Runes	Friday, Saturday
The *I Ching*	Any day of the week
Pendulums/dowsing	Tuesday, Wednesday, Saturday, Sunday

Some of these correspondences were passed down to me from my mother and to her from her mother. They've come down through the generations to me and, through me, to you. Everything works differently for different people, though, so experiment on your own and see what days work best with what ways for you!

What Questions on What Days?

Certain days of the week may be more suited for certain types of questions than others. Although I can't completely explain why, some insights seem to come through better on some days than others. For example, on Monday, Tuesday, and Wednesday, tea leaves often tell about travel. (The leaves make the shape of little planes and birds. You'll learn more about reading tea leaves in Chapter 5.) That doesn't mean you can't ask questions any time of the week; these are merely suggestions of times when you may find you receive specific answers more clearly.

Notions Through Time

Monday's child is fair of face,
Tuesday's child is full of grace,
Wednesday's child is full of woe,
Thursday's child has far to go.
Friday's child is loving and giving,
Saturday's child works hard for a living,
But the child born on the Sabbath Day,
Is fair and wise and good and gay.
—"Monday's Child" (A Mother Goose nursery rhyme)

You can also find out if you resonate strongly with the psychic realms on the day that corresponds with the day of the week you were born. If you don't know what day that was, it should be on your birth certificate (or try asking your mother or other close relative). You can also go to Internet sites by typing into the search engine, "What day of the week were you born?" These sites have calendars that will help you figure it out. Once you have it, try doing your readings on the day corresponding to the day you were born, to see if you have a special connection to that day of the week.

The following table lists some of the issues you might find particular clarity about on a particular day of the week.

On This Day of the Week ...	Ask Questions About ...
Sunday	General healing, decision making, problem solving, spirituality, employment, money
Monday	Reincarnation, animals, divine messages, children, home, women's issues
Tuesday	Romantic endeavors (especially those involving lust), athletic events, legal issues, shopping, disagreements, breaking bad habits
Wednesday	Intellectual objectives, travel, self-improvement, career/job, education, creativity
Thursday	Finances, legal insights, employment, gambling, health, spiritual development
Friday	Matters of the heart, cosmetic makeovers, fidelity, artistry, fertility, nature
Saturday	Releases of all kinds, such as extra weight, poor relationships, bad habits, commitments of any kind, past lives

Going Through Phases with the Moon

We all know that we are affected by the moon. In fact, the word *lunacy* was derived from the word "lunar," which stems from the Latin and Italian "luna," meaning moon. It was through folklore that people associated madness with the phases of the moon. The moon affects the tides here on Earth, and our bodies are 55–70 percent water, so it's obvious that the moon affects us as well. The energy of the moon also affects the results of divination.

Visionary Insights

Add to your journal the days of the week you conduct your fortune-telling methods, the moon phases, and the places in which you perform these esoteric ventures for future referral. This will enable you to track your success according to these different factors. See if you find any patterns in what works best for you.

New Moon

The new moon is also called the crescent moon or sickle moon. Barely visible as a sliver of light in the sky, the new moon is the next phase after the dark moon, which is when you cannot see the moon at all. As the new moon appears to increase each night, it is an excellent time to ask questions that deal with beginnings. Questions about new relationships, ventures, jobs, and creative ideas can be more powerful at this moon phase. This is also a time to think about promoting anything you want magnified. In addition to fortune telling about finances, business dealings, and popularity, it is an excellent time to take action toward improving these things in your life.

Waxing Moon

The waxing moon seems to be increasing in size and is on its way to becoming full again. This is an appropriate time to query your chosen form of fortune telling about creating abundance. You will want to inquire about subjects that deal with improved finances, good health, relationships of any kind, and bringing in more of anything.

Full Moon

The full moon is the prime period to really test your psychic abilities. You might have heard how police reports and hospital records show that people go a little crazy during a full moon. That same energy can work to your advantage. Harness that lunacy! Your powers of divination are at their peak during this time. Ask for guidance as you plot your future and seek fulfillment. Take inventory and recommit to those things or people who are important.

This is a time for fulfilling dreams, if you can deal with the power of our round celestial friend. For some people, it is too powerful; when they attempt any kind of divination, their level of concentration becomes strenuous because they cannot focus. If that is the case for you, opt for a waxing moon and leave the full-moon activities for a time when you are more confident.

Don't forget to ask your romantic questions at this time. All senses are heightened under a full moon. So bring on the sex and romance questions!

Waning Moon

The waning moon is a time for endings. You can get good insight during this phase for when it is time to end a relationship, a friendship, a job, or anything else that has come to its natural completion for you. Look at the inventory you took at the full moon and reassess those low-priority people or activities that are consuming your time and energy. Now is the time to use your fortune-telling skills to seek guidance in choosing those you would do best to eliminate from your life.

Ask for guidance in banishing those energy vampires and negative influences, losing those bad habits, and releasing yourself from dead-end relationships and jobs that are going nowhere. Use the energy of the waning moon to show you where your boundaries need to be.

Dark Moon

On the average wall calendar, the dark moon is indicated by a black circle and is called a new moon. However, for our purposes, we make a distinction between the dark moon and the new moon: the term "new moon" has the energy of beginning, while the dark moon is more of a time for stillness and meditation.

The dark moon takes place two or three days after a waning moon. The waning moon appears smaller and smaller, and all of a sudden, poof—you can't see the moon at all. Its lack of visibility has nothing to do with clouds or weather—it's actually because the earth has moved between the sun and the moon. So for those few days right before a new moon or crescent moon starts to appear, the night sky is dark.

The dark moon is a good time for contemplation, giving yourself the time you need to recharge your energy. You may want to reaffirm answers you got from the forms of divination you did while under a waning moon. This generally is not a good time to conduct any fortune-telling techniques because your answers will be vague or inconclusive. The techniques themselves will go smoothly, but the outcome may be frustrating and disappointing. The reason for this is that the energy is flat and not very charged. You might equate it to low lighting, which makes things difficult to see. Take the time to do other things, and give yourself and your magical tools a rest.

Full Moon Seasons

Every month of the year has one full moon, with one exception. Every 2.7 years, when there are two full moons in one single month, that moon is called a blue moon.

Many diviners, including myself, pay attention to how a full moon in any given month of the year might affect the energies of fortune telling.

Connect your concerns with the full moon in a special month and see how accurate your readings in the different lunar seasons are. For example, the full moon in April is also called the full pink moon. It is a time for growing and planting. Therefore, asking questions about new jobs or relationships may give your readings a little extra boost.

This lunar lore of the seasonal full moons is associated with Native Americans who dwelled in cold-weather climates of the United States. These peoples kept track of the seasons by giving names to each full moon based on something that occurred during that time of the year. There was some variation among the tribes, but similar names were shared by the Algonquin tribes from New England to Lake Superior.

Here are their names for each of the months, along with the kinds of fortune-telling issues that correspond to them.

January—Full Wolf Moon

In the frost of winter, when snow was frequently falling in the colder parts of the United States, packs of wolves were hungry. Native Americans could frequently hear the cries of these ravenous animals. Consequently, they named the first full moon after the winter solstice the full wolf moon. This time of year is an excellent time to consider thoughts and ideas about your past, and the mistakes and the accomplishments you made throughout the year.

February—Full Snow Moon

Typically February is the month of year with the most snowfall. Thus, the name for the February full moon is the full snow moon. Use February as a springboard to reflect about what will come in the future as the snow melts and you start anew.

March—Full Worm Moon

When the earth begins to thaw, the worms begin to awaken. They churn up the soil, letting us know that spring is just ahead. Brainstorming about business, school, or future vocations is the key to this period. Full worm moon is a great time to meet with others to conduct readings.

April—Full Pink Moon

Pink wildflowers grace the ground and are one of the first signs of spring. Think romance, love, and relationships while requesting information from your fortune-telling methods.

May—Full Flower Moon

Flowers are everywhere, and the landscape can be breathtaking. Money and finances should be considered during this cycle. It's all about abundance, growth, and prosperity.

June—Full Strawberry Moon

Strawberries are harvested during the month of the summer solstice. Balancing of the body and mind is the mantra for this month. Be light-hearted in your queries, and don't dwell too much on complex issues.

July—The Full Buck Moon

The new antlers of deer bucks start to appear at this time of year; hence, Native Americans named this time the full buck moon. This moon is also referred to as a full thunder moon because of the thunderstorms that commonly occur at this time of year. Spiritual goals and insights are key in July. This is also an excellent time for increasing your psychic abilities and working with the forms of divination you would like to improve.

August—Full Sturgeon Moon

Sturgeons are large freshwater fish that were easily caught around this period. Ask for guidance and general messages from the universal life force. Your answers may be plentiful.

September—Full Harvest Moon

This is a time when food such as pumpkins, corn, and beans are gathered. Even Europeans call this the harvest moon. Query your fortune-telling devices about changes that involve learning and further education.

October—Full Hunter's Moon

Hunting at this cycle was easier because the trees had fewer leaves and fields had been cleared. This made it simpler to spot animals. If you enjoy working with your Ouija board, this is a good time to do it. The veil of energy between earth and the other side is at its thinnest, making communication easier with those who have passed over.

November—Full Beaver Moon

Beavers zestfully prepare for the coming winter during this time. The full beaver moon is a good time to consult your favorite mode of divination about things that make you happy. This is the time to call in material things that you want to come into your life.

Visionary Insights

Because it is not always possible to take the time from your busy schedule to perform a reading on the exact night of a full moon, one or two days before can work as well, but not afterward. Have fun with the full moons. If you are a "lunar type," you will have great success and enjoyment with this phase of the moon.

December—The Full Cold Moon

The origin of this full moon name is quite obvious: it's just plain cold out! Use this time of year to do readings for others. In addition, consider artistic and creative ideas that you have been putting off. For those who are in the arts, it is a great time to see where your future is leading you.

Environment Counts

Where you carry on your divination practices is very important. You need to be in a place where you can be undisturbed yet inspired, somewhere that feels comfortable yet enables you to be attuned to everything around you. It's important to think about the benefits and drawbacks of any given locale. Think about an area before you decide to do your fortune telling; you do not want to have to relocate in the middle of a reading because it just isn't working.

The Great Outdoors

Outdoor fortune-telling sessions, with nature surrounding you, are fantastic. Nevertheless, be practical. Think about the consequences of divining outside in your environment.

The most important thing is safety. If you live in the middle of New York City, standing on the corner with your pendulum will simply not work. Realize that doing energetic work will attract people—and it's not always in your best interest to attract this kind of attention. Besides, there are too many distractions in a busy city and too much energy swirling all around you to get a clear reading.

Outdoor work should be done in a place that is comfortable and that has no traffic rushing by. It also should be in a location where no people will be walking past or watching you. Sometimes even your own backyard won't work if Mrs. Busy-Body next door keeps gawking at you and nudging her husband.

Find a secluded place in a comfortable natural setting. Tune in to the sounds of nature around you and, when you feel safe, expand your energy body into the surrounding environment. You'll often find that being close to nature will heighten your sensitivity and put you more in tune with your feelings and intuition. If you are a city-dweller and are fortunate enough to have even a small balcony with plants, that is a very workable situation. Daytime is probably the best time for outdoor readings. To be outside alone at night with a candle or flashlight trying to conduct dowsing, for example, is not wise. In addition, think about the elements such as the wind. The wind could blow out a candle, move a Ouija board pointer, or sweep away your cards in a moment. Use common sense at all times.

But in good weather, with like-minded friends, in a quiet and secure area, you can get really good results. Give it a try!

> **Notions Through Time**
>
> Go forth under the open sky, and list To [sic] Nature's teachings.
> —William Cullen Bryant, U.S. poet and journalist

The Inner Sanctum

It's great if you have a private place, such as your room, where you can conduct your readings and divination experiments. Clearly, this is the most sensible place to practice. You have everything available that you may require. Plus, you do not need to battle with unpleasant temperatures and other weather conditions. You're in a place where you feel safe and where everything is familiar. This will reduce distractions while you practice the concentration needed to get a good reading. Remember to turn off any electronic devices that may be distracting, such as phones, fax machines, televisions, security alarms, and so on. If you would like a view of the moon or the night skies, you should try to sit by a window or glass door. This could give you the security of being indoors while still enabling you to commune with the natural realm.

Doing readings in public places such as restaurants, waiting rooms, or libraries is in poor taste and could peg you as a person who is looking for attention. Avoid it.

Similarly, it may be tempting to practice some form of divination on planes, trains, or buses because you might get bored while traveling. But attempting to divine in these places usually won't get the job done. Use your judgment. A sight-seeing boat would not be fitting, whereas a private craft, such as a sailboat, small fishing boat, motorboat, or canoe anchored on relaxing water might work beautifully.

Compass Directions

When you become more comfortable with your fortune-telling techniques, you may want to consider adding compass directions to your routine. When you face a specific direction—north, south, east, or west—you are using the vibration that direction has to offer.

Each direction has an element associated with it:

- **North = Earth.** North is the most forceful direction. If you are in doubt about what direction to face, choose north because it is grounding and a solid foundation for fortune-telling practices. It corresponds to health-related issues, spirituality, divination, divine messages, and transcending the physical.

- **South = Fire.** South corresponds to matters of the heart, relationships of all types, creativity and artistic endeavors, and all emotional concerns.

- **East = Air.** East corresponds to career pursuits, new business ventures, mental healing, comprehensibility, and anything that is starting anew. As the sun rises in the east, so do new ideas, relationships, and adventures.

- **West = Water.** West corresponds to releasing things that are troubling you; bad habits; cleansing the mind, body, and spirit; and forgiving yourself and others.

> **Enlightening Extras**
>
> It's fun to experiment and see if your "creative juices" flow better when directing your physical self toward different compass points. Use a compass (or the global positioning system—GPS—in your car) to get the direction exactly right. Using a simple form of divination, such as the pendulum, try asking the same question in each of the four directions. See if you can sense any difference. Note it in your journal.

The elements are considered to be the basic components of our planet. They appear in the esoteric teachings of cultures all over the world, from Hawaiian huna to Celtic druidism to medieval alchemy to Siberian shamanism, as the root material of our existence and the key energies of what is sometimes called magic.

As the sun sets, so does our negativity and our attachment to this life. Face the direction west if you are trying to contact a dead loved one. Many feel it is a portal to the other side, the place where the dead pass through.

The Least You Need to Know

- Each day of the week has its own energy and is conducive to certain types of divination and certain kinds of questions.

- The phases of the moon each hold a particular vibration. Each phase is good for a different divination purpose.

- ◆ Each month has its own auspicious character. Understanding what questions are best to ask in each season will increase your accuracy and insight.

- ◆ Your environment affects your reading. Finding the right place for you and even the best direction to face will enhance your readings.

Chapter 3

Readings for Others

In This Chapter

- Reading for someone else
- The ethics of doing readings for others
- Doing telepathic experiments in groups
- Fun with psychometry

You have a secret admirer who thinks you're gorgeous, and ... you will someday be very famous, and ... your home-based business will make a bundle, and ....

Sure, we all want to hear these types of things. (Well, maybe not the famous part. The paparazzi would frazzle you.) Having a friend or acquaintance wish you these generous thoughts in life is one thing. But isn't having someone "see" it in a fortune-telling session better?

Most people, including disbelievers, are curious to know "what's in the cards"—or any type of fortune-telling method, for that matter. That's why doing readings for someone else can be so gratifying. Nonetheless, as with good cooking, there is a knack to reading for other people. You have to include a healthy heaping of ethics, a dollop of honesty, and a dash of humor. Let's take a look at some recipes for success.

One-on-One Readings

Talk about popularity and amusement ... wow! Performing a fortune-telling consultation for someone can be lots of fun and a great way to develop friendships. But it is also something you really need to contemplate before doing. It takes experience, knowledge, and a deep level of concentration.

When you do a reading for someone using any form of divination, you have to think about what the situation actually is. Are you doing this for sport with a close friend, or is someone you don't know as well coming to you for serious advice?

Readings Just for Fun

If this is merely a fun event for two, you should make it known to the recipient that your predictions are not to be taken seriously and that this is merely entertainment.

When doing a one-on-one reading just for fun, it is still good to concentrate the best you can. If the person you are reading for is laughing and joking, don't get upset. That's probably how you approached the process in the first place, right? It's just like playing a game and forgetting about it the next day. In fact, in such a casual setting, if you have to sit with this book in front of you, that's okay, too. There is no pressure on you to perform like a renowned psychic reader, having everything memorized and perfected. You're just a guy or gal with some fortune-telling tools of the trade who is playing. There is nothing wrong with this attitude. It's like any other pastime.

> **Visionary Insights**
>
> Doing a reading can be a unique idea for a date or a get-together with a special friend, if he or she is comfortable with that idea. It allows you to venture out a little beyond the norm and make an impression. Anyone can rent a movie. Be a little unconventional!

Often people have loves and hobbies but don't excel at them—or, on the other hand, are not interested in "going pro." It doesn't mean they can't continue to pursue these things. It just means they won't make a career out of them. There's nothing wrong with that as long as you are doing something that brings you contentment. If you're just having fun with it, "read" away and take pleasure in creating an anxiety-free situation.

Going the Serious Route

If you want to get serious about your readings, that's a whole different level of commitment. Carrying out a fortune-telling reading of significance should be a labor of love and ability. If you have decided you want to move forward in this direction, fortune-telling will take on a whole new meaning.

Taking your fortune-telling talent earnestly means studying, practicing, and believing you have the competence and talent to do so. Reading this book—or any book—once or twice does not make you an expert; it just makes you someone who read a book once or twice.

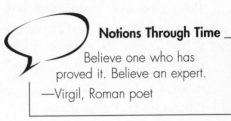

Notions Through Time

Believe one who has proved it. Believe an expert.
—Virgil, Roman poet

However, after simply reviewing this book, you should have a better understanding about whether you would want to pursue fortune telling as a serious trade. Dedication is key to this craft, to really make it work well for other people. Seekers may be counting on you, so you have an obligation to become as proficient at it as you can.

Don't get overconfident too quickly. Making a few fortune-telling predictions for yourself that come true does not make you ready to be Zoltar's associate at the State Fair.

To truly prepare yourself, discover what fortune-telling methods you like best and make them part of your life. Regularly consult the form or forms of divining you most enjoy until you start to discern patterns and develop your personal vocabulary of meanings. For example, you may find that a certain animal or insect will show up from time to time in your readings, and that it always points to some insight about the way events will unfold. Birds come into my readings a lot, and they always indicate some kind of travel. Getting to the point that you recognize this personal symbolism takes lots of time, practice, and careful attention.

Knowing When You're Ready

To determine whether you are truly ready to read for someone else, you have to feel that you have done at least 14 predictions for yourself, of which at least 10 were accurate. This will give you a little less than a 75 percent accuracy level. If you don't have at least 10 accurate readings, you should start from scratch with a new batch of 14. You should be aiming for at least 75 percent accuracy.

Do not do 14 readings in one sitting to try to prove a point or so you can move on quickly. The maximum number of readings for one individual in a day should be three, in response to three different specific questions, or one full reading doing general predications for different aspects of the person's life.

Sometimes "readers" say they cannot read for themselves. If this is the case for you, pick one person who is open to your intent and read for that person at least 14 times. Do not use more than one person; this is too confusing at the start and gets too many people involved.

When you find that one special person who will not judge or criticize you, ask him or her to stay clear of questions you can guess the answers to. Perhaps you were reading for your best friend, and she asked you if you saw travel for her in November. If you know that every Thanksgiving she visits her sister in Ohio, that just isn't a fair reading!

A general reading is simply telling the inquirer what you "see" in his or her future. It might go something like this: "I pick up that you are considering a job change in the next two weeks. I can't be 100 percent sure, but from what I am seeing, it doesn't look good at this time. Consider offers carefully. However, I am not 100 percent accurate, and this is just what I am 'getting.' All decisions need to be made using your best judgment."

Then you might move on to another subject: "Now I get that there is a man with dark hair who is not happy with you and is intentionally not getting in touch. I would recommend not calling him, as I see him getting past whatever the problem may be and calling you in the next four days."

Psychic readers or fortune tellers should be approximately 90 percent accurate if they are taking a fair amount of money for a reading. However, if you are starting out and want people to respect what you are doing, 75 percent accuracy is acceptable. Anyone can have a lucky guess to a yes-or-no question; this is why 50 percent is not adequate.

Do the Right Thing

You want to be treated with respect, so always do the same for others. Some people will have had many readings in their lives, while others will never have had a reading. The latter group may ask you questions such as what they should ask and what to expect. Be patient and tell them to the best of your ability.

Try not to take their skepticism or nervous humor personally. You might even want to give them the opportunity to express their feelings about getting a reading. They may say that they feel silly or that they are afraid of being manipulated or misled. This is good information for you to take in, and it's okay to agree with them about the fact that fortune telling is a very inexact art and should be received in the appropriate balance with other kinds of guidance (such as common sense). Even if you're taking money to do readings, you do not have to—and should not—promise 100 percent accuracy or the "key" to their decision making.

How Long Is a Reading?

Some readers say a reading is as long as they receive messages. That's true, depending upon what form of divination you are using. With scrying or crystal gazing, images come and go, and you don't have much of a choice. With card readings, *I Ching*, runes, and so on, you have more control. So with most forms of fortune telling, when you have charge of your time, I recommend giving it 15 minutes to start and building from there.

After teaching many classes, I have determined that for a beginner, more than 15 minutes is a drain. I know there are exceptions to the rule, and if you are the exception and can focus longer, then go for it. We are all very different. You'll determine your own psychic stamina after the first few readings.

In my own practice, I used to read for an hour. Then I discovered that because I talked so quickly and the information was so dense, 30 minutes was plenty. I never got any complaints. It's all about how much information you give in a certain amount of time. You might want to tape the session so the person you are reading for can listen later and absorb it more.

If you tend to mumble, stumble, and use a lot of silence, it might take you 2 hours to relay the same amount of information that another reader could do in 45 minutes. Don't stall just to fill in time.

People notice readers who artificially stretch time frames. Give them your best, even if it's not as long as *they* think it should be, and use your judgment about how much *information* you've given rather than how much *time* it has taken.

Questionable Questioning

A reader who has to ask too many questions of their guests may immediately be labeled as someone who is not very skilled. Questions at the beginning such as "Do you have a boyfriend?" and "Do you have job?" are not appropriate. You are supposed to be the one who is going to answer the questions, not ask them.

And, of course, be ready for the comedians. While trying to be polite, you may ask someone, "So how are you today?" They may reply "Don't you know? You're the psychic!" That's where you have to chuckle and say, "Oh, that's a good one." After hearing it 100 times, you can just smile at how many times you've heard it. Try not to let them see you roll your eyes. We all like to think we are clever.

Specific and General Readings

When you start a session, you should give the person for whom you are reading a choice of two classifications of readings. Do they have specific questions? Or do they just want a general reading to see what messages you "pick up"? The questions are much easier because you can focus on one concern instead of the person's whole life in general.

If you are asked to give specifics, whether you try to do so depends upon your level of ability. But know that the average reader does not pick up the names of people, addresses, and, most of all, lottery numbers. If someone asks you why not, say you just don't see things that exactly, especially because you are new to this endeavor.

Still, if a name or place does come to mind, share the information. Always reiterate something such as, "I could be wrong on this, but I am picking up the name Michael. Does that mean anything to you?" If the person says "no," do not make excuses for yourself. Just tell the person to keep it in mind, and maybe in the future it will. (And hopefully, it will.)

Fair Exchange

When you first start reading for others, you will find it fun and rewarding. You will get practice and they will also benefit. That's fine for a while, but you may find it tiresome when, every time a friend has a problem or a question, they expect you to conduct a reading of some type.

For this reason, it is wise to always give the honest impression that this is not an easy chore. In fact, there should be a fair exchange of energy in the form of a gift or favor from the person who is accepting your advice. Let your mystic believer know that, even though you are just beginning, the process works better if there is a two-way exchange. In this way, the energy of giving and taking is balanced.

It also puts a little pressure on you to be more accurate. When would you typically work harder, when you are cleaning your own house or when someone was paying you to clean theirs?

Perhaps something as simple as a gallon of ice cream or a bunch of flowers from the person's garden can be offered. Consider having that person do an errand for you that you find disagreeable. And let's not forget spirituality in these material items. If you are of a religious or spiritual nature, think about asking someone to pray for you as reimbursement. Although this sounds good in theory, it can be uncomfortable to come right out and ask for something from a friend. Keep the conversation light and try to come up with a plan in advance. For example, you might say, "Mary, we're doing your reading tomorrow, so in exchange for the reading will you say a prayer tonight that my cat gets better? Is that fair to you?"

If someone offers you cold hard cash, it's up to you whether you are ready to take it. Do so only if you feel quite confident—or take only a small amount for a short reading of 10 or 15 minutes. If you are doing this for a business you need to act like a business professional. If someone asks you for a reading you need to tell him or her that you charge for the readings and what the cost will be. To start to accept money for readings on a regular basis is to start a business as a professional psychic reader. Be aware that in certain states, these things require a business license and other legal necessities. If someone insists on giving you cash, you can say that you think of it as a gift or love offering, not a payment for services.

When Disappointment Strikes

As you read for others, you will experience highs and lows. One person might think you are the *Oracle at Delphi*, and the next might feel that you don't have a clue about what you're doing.

Visionary Insights

Delphi was a city in ancient Greece. The Oracle at Delphi was a priestess named Pynthia. It is said that she got messages from Apollo while sitting on a tripod inhaling fumes that put her into a trance state.

The compliments praising you about your accuracy and the expressions of astonishment such as "How could you have ever have known that?!" may leave you feeling exhilarated and confident. Still, they will be inevitably offset when someone says, "You weren't right about anything." If this happens, use your instinct to decide whether you should return the money or the gift. Both parties should walk away happy. For new readers wanting to bring in a little extra income, good public relations is much more valuable than money or gifts received. Therefore, I recommend giving back a gift or money to unsatisfied customers. Another approach is to ask them if they would prefer to have another reading on another date. This is one of the downfalls of trying to make this a business and perhaps why it is best left to those few who feel this is a real calling.

Group Participation in Telepathic Experiments

Mental telepathy or *telepathic communication* is an awareness. Simply put, it is sending or receiving information from someone else's mind without any type of sensory communication. I'm sure you have had an experience in which you were thinking about someone, and suddenly that person called or e-mailed you. Was that just coincidence, or were you really picking up that person's thoughts a few minutes before he or she began to dial or type? Why does a mother often know when something is wrong with her child? Because she has developed her telepathic skills, in most cases without even being conscious of it. Have you ever said the words "I had a feeling you'd be here?" The list goes on—and it would be very unlikely that someone reading this book has never had a thought or a perception about someone else that came true.

To test this idea, put together a group of two or more people, including yourself. They should be individuals who are like-minded and investigative. This can be an amusing experience but should also be taken seriously. The more relaxed the group, the better the results, so don't make them feel as if they're in school taking an exam.

Hopefully, this activity should also broaden everyone's skills of perception and give them a barometer of how acute they are at *ESP,* or *extrasensory perception.*

The idea behind conducting telepathic experiments is not necessarily to "test" people, but rather to do a form of scientific research in an informal and relaxed atmosphere. Research into paranormal abilities and behavior is being conducted in many institutes, but most of us will never get the opportunity to participate, even as subjects. Doing these tests at home combines curiosity with fun.

Things You Will Need

Be sure you have the following things on hand before you start:

- ◆ Pencils and paper for everyone attending.

- ◆ Clipboards or something they can place their paper on, such as a book or magazine, because they will be writing on their laps. Another alternative is to have a large table or tables where everyone can be seated.

- ◆ If serving refreshments, make sure everyone has what they require so no one will get up and leave the area later, before the experiment is completed.

def•i•ni•tion

Mental telepathy or telepathic communication is the ability to communicate information from mind to mind, without the benefit of any other form of communication. It is one form of extrasensory perception (ESP). ESP is the ability of an individual to perceive someone's thoughts, distant circumstances, or events— sometimes even in the future— without having any sensory communication or physical association.

Fun with Telepathy

Gather your materials and have your group seated. When everyone is situated, one person is appointed as the "sender"; the rest are "receivers." The sender goes into another room with her or his paper and pencil, and draws a picture of anything he or she chooses. (No artistic abilities are necessary.) It can be a picture of a star, a triangle, a cat, or an entire scene with a house, mountains, and trees. There are no rules; it can be absolutely anything! Use a time limit of approximately 1 or 2 minutes for the sender to draw the picture.

After 1 or 2 minutes, the sender stays in the room and concentrates on the drawing. The sender should visualize his or her thoughts going into the minds of the others. During that time, ask the group of receivers to draw what they think the sender drew. Remind them that it can be one single symbol or an elaborate illustration. Give the group approximately 2 minutes to complete their drawings.

Next, have the sender come back into the room and show the group the drawing. How close did the receivers in the group come to accuracy? Who's the most "in tune"?

You can do this again and again, using different senders. When the group starts to appear bored, switch to another experiment. Don't tire out the receivers.

Group Participation in Psychometry

Psychometry is the capability of gaining impressions by tuning in to someone's vibrations. By simply holding in your hand an object that belongs to an individual, you should be able to sense whom the item belongs to and perhaps other information about that person. The person does not have to be present—or even alive, for that matter.

def•i•ni•tion

Psychometry refers to the ability to get information about an object or the people or things connected to it by touching it, holding it, or being close to it.

The best objects are things that the person has an emotional attachment to, such as jewelry, clothing, or personal items. The closer the personal connection to the object, the easier it is to get a "reading" or impression from it.

When you invite your guests, tell them to bring a favorite piece of jewelry. If they do not wear jewelry, have them bring something medium to small, such as a special pen, eyeglasses, the key to something important, or something they have handled quite often.

It is important that the piece they bring belong to them exclusively, without previous owners. For example, Grandpa Ludvik's old watch just won't work.

If you want to make the process more fun, don't tell the guests why they are bringing an item. Also suggest that they not bring something too expensive or too personal. If they lose it, you don't want to feel responsible.

Have each of your guests privately put their personal item on a tray. It is important that no one sees the other person doing this. Gather the group back together, and have each participant pick an item from the tray. Tell the guests that if they recognize something they know belongs to someone else, they should not choose it.

As your guests study the objects they have chosen, they should not try to figure out by any logical means who the objects belong to. For instance, if Becky always wears long, dangly earrings and there is a long, dangly earring on the tray, they shouldn't "guess" that it belongs to Becky.

The visitors should relax and concentrate on the object they are holding in their hands. They should then write down who they feel the object belongs to and any other thoughts they may have. For example: "I think it belongs to Laura. I sense she got this when she was near a train station." Give participants a minute or two to write down their impressions. If you give them longer, they will keep changing and second-guessing, which is not good. Their first guess will be their most accurate. Let them know this.

When everyone has completed their written analysis, have them, one by one, share the information with the rest of the group.

After they give their conclusion, have the person who owns the object tell the rest of the group the history behind the item. It's fun to see how well each person "reads" the item's vibrations.

The Least You Need to Know

- When reading for someone else, determine whether you are doing it just for fun or really seriously.

- There should be a fair exchange of energy for each personal reading.

- Telepathy is "knowing" what someone else is thinking.

- Psychometry is "sensing" whom an object belongs to, and maybe the person's history with it.

Chapter 4

Set the Scene

In This Chapter

◆ Using salt as a magical tool

◆ Adding color to your readings

◆ Set a mood of tranquility with candles, music, and incense

◆ The power of gemstones

"Mind the Threefold Law you should, three times bad and three times good."
This is a rhyme used by some pagan religions to make a point. But you
don't have to be pagan to see the value of this particular philosophy.
Contemplate these words before you start to set up a relaxing fortune-
telling atmosphere. The Threefold Law you should "mind" is that everything you do will come back to you tripled, whether it be good or bad.
That means that if you project kindness (harm no one), it will come back
to you three times over. But if you project hurtful intentions, you will get
back misfortune three times over. Reflect on your intentions. It's amazing
how negative thoughts about a person or situation can yield negativity and
positive thoughts can produce positive outcomes.

Embellishments to your readings such as salt, candles, incense, and gemstones are like sponges: they absorb your negative or positive thoughts and
retain them. Psychic enhancements can be more powerful than you realize, so it's important to choose them with care and treat them with respect.

Colors are also important; each color has a vibration that will affect the nuances of your reading.

These enhancements are all optional and are totally left to your discretion. Only you can decide what works best for you.

The Magic of Salt

The magical use of salt is highly recommended in setting up your fortune-telling session. Salt serves as a form of protection and strengthens your divination methods. It has had powers associated with it since the beginning of time. In his search for food, primitive man followed game trails to salt licks, for his efforts he got both meat and the salt to preserve it. The Chinese had identified 40 types of salt by the year 2700 B.C.E. The Egyptians used salt in their mummification process. The Bible also contains more than 30 references to salt.

Salt was so precious to ancient cultures that it was both used as a monetary measure and worshiped as holy. As a preservative, salt kept meats through the long winters. Without it, food was bland and tasteless. Most relevant of all, humans cannot live without salt; we are, in fact, made out of liquids that are kept in place by the salt in our systems.

> **Enlightening Extras**
>
> One folk tale in which the value of salt is praised appears in fairly consistent form in countries all over the world. As the story goes, a man asks his daughters how much they love him. One daughter says she loves him more than salt and is turned out for belittling her father. Eventually, the opportunity to serve the father an unsalted meal proves that he values salt as well, and the relationship is mended.

Salty Qualities

Salt has been assigned a great many characteristics. Because pure salt is white, it has been associated with innocence, purity, and untarnished character. That and its use as a preservative may be the reasons it has been used to ward off the corrupting effects of evil, negative energy, and demons—obviously, the perfect method of getting rid of those unsavory entities.

Protection of babies and homes from evil seems to have been a source of great concern for people long ago, and salt became a traditional source of peace of mind. Holy water is salt water that has been blessed and is used in the baptism of babies. It is said that using a circle of salt around a bed or crib will ward off evil spirits and protect the occupant within. Small packets of salt were put in cribs at night to protect babies because any evil spirit would have to count every grain of salt before it could hurt the child. It was assumed that spirits would not be able to finish counting by morning, leaving the baby safe.

It was also common to pour a line of salt on the thresholds and windowsills to help keep evil out of the home. Even the dead were considered vulnerable to evil spirits, and it was common practice to place salt in the coffin of a loved one for protection.

The practice of tossing salt over one's left shoulder to protect against bad luck or evil after spilling salt may have originated out of the need to conserve salt, the idea being not to spill it in the first place. The left side was considered the side that harbored man's more sinister elements. Therefore, tossing salt over that shoulder was meant to rein in negative forces all around. Carrying salt in one's pockets was considered beneficial to solidifying business deals. So the next time you're at your favorite fast food place, throw a few of those free salt packets in that Armani business suit pocket. You're all but guaranteed that your next deal will be much more savory.

The use of salt is also common in ceremonies. Gypsy weddings use salt as an element, and some Jews use salt on certain holy days. Some pagan religions also use salt in their rituals. Salt has even been attributed to improving a man's sexual performance. In a poem from the Middle Ages, women are encouraged to use salt on their men for improved performance. Sure, it's a lot cheaper than the latest prescription medicine. Let's just hope they don't have any open cuts ... ouch!

Just as it was valued in the past, it is valued now as a sacred element that provides protection and purity when using any form of fortune telling. You can use salt in any number of ways as part of the ritual and ceremony you create around setting up your fortune-telling sessions.

> **Visionary Insights**
>
> To use table salt or sea salt ... that is the question! Some people use only sea salt or rock salt because of its purity. In spite of that, table salt will work if nothing else is available. If your intention is strong, it really doesn't make a difference.

Techniques for Salt Protection

To make yourself more comfortable with any form of divination, use a pinch of salt. As you sprinkle or place the salt, you can say the following: "May this salt protect, enhance, and persevere." There are several options for using salt:

◆ Sprinkle a little salt in every corner of the room where you will be doing a reading, or create a circle of salt around the table or surface upon which you will be doing your reading. This process will keep out unwanted entities from your space as a form of protection.

♦ Sprinkle salt at the entrance and back door of your home before a reading to keep bad vibrations from entering.

♦ Put salt into a pouch and wear it around your neck during your divination. This process stops any negativity from entering your state of mind while it is open to outside vibrations.

♦ Place a small bowl or plate of salt on the table where you are divining to enhance your vision.

♦ Sprinkle a little salt over your forms of divination, such as cards, Ouija boards, dominoes, and so on. This will preserve the vitality of the tool of divination.

Color Your World

Color is significant in divination. It is an enhancement that carries a vibration. We affiliate feelings with color when we aren't even conscious of it. How many times have you ever said or heard, "I was green with envy," "I was so mad, I saw red," or "I'm feeling in the pink today"?

We associate color not only with moods, but also with how we judge people's attitudes or lifestyles: "She looks too flashy in that red dress." "He's boring. He always wears that same brown suit." "Geez, doesn't she own anything other than black? No wonder she's depressed all the time."

> **Notions Through Time**
>
> Colors, like features, follow the changes of the emotions.
> —Pablo Picasso, Spanish painter and sculptor

We are very conscious of color. When choosing clothing, we all have certain colors that make us "feel better." When you are doing readings for others, you might consider the effects of the colors you choose to wear for the occasion. Do you want to come across as flamboyant or mysterious, secular or spiritual, plain or vibrant? Your choice of colors, textures, and styles will project an image that will help determine how your readings will be received. It does make a difference. That is why it is important to incorporate color into your readings, if possible. It's not only about looking good, but also about feeling emotionally balanced and confident.

Another idea to consider when thinking in terms of color is storing your tools of fortune-telling in a colorful way. If you will put your cards, pendulum, or crystals in a pouch or box, consider the color of the storage component. The energy of the color will infuse your tools of divination.

Use the following list as a general reference for the meanings of different colors. These insights can be used for clothing, candles, gemstones, flowers, and so on. If you intuitively have a different thought about the meaning of a color, go with your instinct. These are only recommendations—nothing is written in stone when it comes to your relationship with color.

Try to remember the significance of each color. The more you put to memory, the easier it will be for you to pursue your fortune-telling studies.

- **Blue**—Peace and tranquility, prophetic dreams and increased psychic power, truth, understanding, health, and spiritual powers

- **Green**—Prosperity and money, fertility, healing, good luck, and generosity

- **Yellow**—Increased confidence and charm, improved memory and concentration, intellect, and creativity

- **Orange**—Energy, concentration, legal negotiations, power, control, and courage

- **Red**—Passion and sexuality, love, energy, will power and strength

- **Pink**—Love, friendship, healing, and morality

- **Purple**—Healing, breaking of spells, divination, ambition, wisdom, and success

- **White**—Purification, consecration, blessings, protection, cleansing, and harmony

- **Brown**—Protection of the home and pets, power of the elements, learning, and the encouragement of others to be helpful

- **Gray**—Neutralizes other forces, counteracts sadness, and cancels effects of other spells

- **Black**—Psychic powers, vision, divination, release, repelling of dark magic, and banishing of negativity

- **Gold**—Protection by the gods or universal life force energy, especially the male aspect; improved psychic powers and intuition

- **Silver**—Stability, warding off evil, invoking a higher power and victory

When working with magic, a color is associated with each compass direction. There are different schools of thought on this, and you will find discrepancies. However, I have found these to be the most reasonable. This information is useful when placing candles and gemstones, which I tell you more about later in this chapter.

- ◆ **East**—Yellow for Air

- ◆ **South**—Red for Fire

- ◆ **West**—Blue for Water

- ◆ **North**—Green for Earth

Candles, Music, and Incense

def•i•ni•tion

An **altered state of consciousness** refers to a deep sense of relaxation or a more profound shift in awareness. One can sometimes be accessed in the time between waking and sleeping, right before drifting off into dreamland. Meditation and hypnosis can also produce an altered state of consciousness.

Light a candle, burn some incense, and put on some music. This sets a mood of tranquility and can advance you into an *altered state of consciousness*. These simple embellishments create a mood of mysticism and promote intuitiveness. They're easy to do, and they can go a long way.

Anything that may help you to relax and release the pressures of your life for a short while will work to put you into an altered state of consciousness conducive to fortune-telling sessions. Of course, we are speaking of all things *legal*, right? Yes, that's right. No marijuana or other drugs! Alcohol is not recommended, either.

Light My Fire

Candles are an important element in rituals and fortune telling, and you will find them very effective for setting a mystical atmosphere. (Just make sure you snuff them out when you're done, and never leave a burning candle unattended!) Candles come in all sizes and colors, of course, but the shape, fragrance, and type of holder need only fit your own personal preference—feel free to shop for candles without any restrictions. Candles in glass containers work well and are also very safe.

The colors of the candles are significant: you will find that using a candle of a certain color for a specific form of divination or question works well. For example, if you are asking questions about health, use candles that are blue and/or purple (refer to the previous list of colors). You can use as many candles as you choose or combine them in any way you like.

You can use multicolored candles with stripes, swirls, and designs that are varied for complex intentions or multifaceted readings. The important aspect is that the variegated candle has all the right hues for all your purposes. Floating candles can be set in a bowl for readings that have to do with aspects of water such as fluidity or cleansing.

Candles Light the Way

Position your candles anywhere you feel appropriate. However, if you want to do it the same way many magical practitioners do, place a candle in each of the four directional points of the room or table. When placing your candles, arrange them in the form of a cross, not in the corners. Place a yellow candle in the east, a red candle in the south, a blue candle in the west, and a green candle in the north.

The correctly colored candle placed in each directional point will add more power to your divination and stabilize your intention. Although this is not necessary, try it at least once. Thereafter, jot down in your journal what your results are with and without the compass placements. This will help you in establishing how and when you want to use candle magic.

Carve a Thought

Candles can also be carved with symbols to increase their power. As they burn, the symbols are released and sent up to the Universe. If this is something that interests you, follow these simple steps for candle etching:

1. Select a knife, toothpick, pen, or anything that can serve as something with which to engrave.

2. With your etching instrument, write on the top of the candle. It can be the initials of someone you are thinking about or the name of a company for which you would like to work. Use your imagination and your logic. If the candle is small and you are going to divine about money, use dollar signs: $$$. Use a heart for love, a clover for luck, and so on. Use only the first letter of each word in a sentence—for example: Will Jeff call me? (W-J-C-M?)

3. Right before you start your divination session, light the candle. As the candle burns down, your symbols will disappear. The faster it melts, the faster your intention ascends to the heavens. This is why we write on the top of the candle,

not on the sides—it's just faster. If you do have a lot of time, writing on the sides and all around the candle is acceptable. It all depends on the size of the candle and the time it takes to burn all the way down.

Candle Blessing

Some people like to do a little ritual and bless and anoint their candles to charge them with additional magical powers. You can make your own magical oil or you can buy store-bought oils. If you are buying store-bought oils, look for the following individually or in blends:

- **Frankincense**—The most sacred oil. It is used for purification and blessings.

- **Sandalwood**—An oil of protection, healing, and psychic vision.

- **Myrrh**—Oil that has a high vibration and is perfect for ceremonies of a spiritual nature. It also purifies, protects, and negates arrows of anger that might be thrown.

Create Your Own Oil

If you are ambitious, try blending your own protection and anointing oil:

- $\frac{1}{4}$ cup cooking oil (any kind)

- $\frac{1}{2}$ tsp. crushed rosemary

- $\frac{1}{2}$ tsp. nutmeg

- $\frac{1}{2}$ tsp. powdered myrrh (also called chervil) or 3 drops of myrrh oil (or other herb such as anise)

This recipe makes about $\frac{1}{4}$ cup of oil. If you are going to anoint several candles, you may want to double or triple these amounts. Save the mixture in a glass jar for use within 30 days.

Mix the ingredients together when the moon is waxing (see Chapter 2). You can strain the mixture through cheesecloth, if you like, but this is not necessary. Keep the mixture in a glass jar for a minimum of 24 hours. This period of time charges the mixture with positive energy.

When you are ready to anoint your candle or candles, dip your fingers into the mixture and rub the candle from the bottom up. As you do this, say: "I consecrate this candle as a magical tool. And so it is."

Feel free to add anything else you feel you want to say. It could be a prayer or a poem. You can also end with "Amen," "Blessed be," or any other closing statement that puts an ending note to the process.

Mood Music

It has been known for centuries that music can advance you into an altered state of consciousness and stimulate your brain. Select music that puts you into a state of mind in which you feel your intuitive senses are heightened.

Musical preference is so personal that it is difficult to suggest what you might want to listen to. In particular, though, including meditative, new age, or classical music as part of your fortune-telling happenings is quite conducive to serenity. This type of music is abundant and can be found at almost any establishment that sells music. Select something you like, but for best results, it needs to be calming. Rock'n'roll won't cut it for this purpose! I recommend that you go into bookstores or music stores that allow you to listen to the music before purchasing it. This may take a while, but the experience is relaxing and can be very rewarding.

Notions Through Time

I think I should have no other mortal wants, if I could always have plenty of music. It seems to infuse strength into my limbs and ideas into my brain. Life seems to go on without effort, when I am filled with music.

—George Eliot (pseudonym of Mary Ann Evans), English novelist

Absorbing yourself in the sounds of tranquil compositions takes your mind off problems and relieves stress. This allows your psychic abilities to flow through more easily.

When you have selected the right music, check in advance of your fortune-telling session to be sure that your playing equipment is functional. It can be frustrating to hit the Play button on your CD player and hear … zippo!

If you are considering listening to a radio station during your divination session, don't. Those pesky commercial breaks can bring you down from your melodic high all too quickly.

Enlightening Extras

Researchers have been studying the therapeutic effects of music for inducing altered states of consciousness, helping with addictions, and even bringing severely disassociated patients back to awareness. One book that gathers much of this research into one place is *Music and Altered States: Consciousness, Transcendence, Therapy and Addictions*, by David Aldridge and Jörg Fachner (Jessica Kingsley Publishers, 2005).

On the other side of the orchestra pit, if you simply don't enjoy listening to tunes or you find them distracting, do not include them. This is all about what makes you happy and what works best for you.

Incense That Makes Scents

As discussed in the section on candles, scents can uplift us, calm us, and heal us—and encourage psychic perceptions. If feasible, consider the use of incense in your prophecy work. Whether you use cones or sticks is up to you. It's the aroma that's meaningful. Experiment with different scents before you include them in any method. Some artificially scented incense can be quite cloying. And once an undesirable stick of incense is burning, it can negate your entire psychic reading. There goes your accuracy! Additionally, that scent can linger in your home for hours.

Choose the incense that seems to suit your needs for your fortune-telling session. Each fragrance has its own objectives. Here are some popular scents. (As with burning candles, never leave burning incense unattended. Although it is not an open flame, it is still a burning element.)

- **Carnation**—Use for healing.
- **Cinnamon**—Use to increase your financial status and gain success.
- **Coconut**—Use for protection and purification from negative vibrations.
- **Frangipani**—Uplifts the energy of your home, and promotes friendships and love interests.
- **Honeysuckle**—Burn for well-being, good luck, and psychic abilities.
- **Jasmine**—Use this popular scent when addressing all matters of the heart.
- **Lotus**—Use for order in all things and harmony of the body, mind, and spirit.
- **Musk**—This scent promotes and increases sexual passion. It also promotes patience and vitality.
- **Passionflower**—This sweet fragrance encourages harmony and stability.
- **Patchouli**—Use for sex, attraction, and love questions.

- ◆ **Pine**—Burn for health and protection from others.

- ◆ **Rose**—Use for love, romance, and finding a mate. It also keeps people around the home calmer.

- ◆ **Sandalwood**—Use to exorcise ghosts, promote healing, and increase psychic abilities.

- ◆ **Strawberry**—Burn for tenderness, luck, and companionship.

- ◆ **Tangerine**—Use for money, money, and more money!

- ◆ **Vanilla**—Burn to increase sex drive and attract lovers.

The sizes, shapes, and colors of incense holders can be anything you find desirable.

Gemstones and Their Attributes

The use of gemstones with fortune telling also can evoke certain attitudes. Gemstones have magical properties that can center and guide energy to a specific intention. Gemstones dispatch vibrations that can surround us with love, comfort, and healing.

Gemstones can be added as an enhancement to any type of divination you select. For example, if you are using a table you can put the stone on the table in front of you. If you are reading cloud formations, you might hold the stone in your hand, wear it, or place it near you. If you want to use several stones you can put them in a circle around your form of divination or at the corners of a table or altar.

When purchasing any stone, touch it, if possible; if you "feel" it is the right one, it is. You should also "clear" the stone. To do this, simply run cold water over the stone in the sink and visualize the negativity from others who came before you and who have handled the stone running down the drain. Then wipe the stones off with a clean paper towel or cloth. This is the easiest and most effective way to work with stones.

Visionary Insights

All of your tools of divination should be cleared of energy from people who may have handled them. There are several ways. One easy method is to blow or wave. To clear any form of divination, face west where negative energy passes into the ethers and dissipates. Simply hold the object and blow over it, visualizing negativity flowing away. Another way is to pass your hand over the object in a swishing motion to the direction west and see the negative energy being swept away.

There is an immense amount of information about the qualities of these varied stones. For our purposes, I have included some of the most commonly used gemstones and their attributes:

- **Agate**—This stone is used for cleansing, stabilizing, and achieving balance emotionally, physically, and mentally. It is said to remove the little things that disturb your ability to think clearly and improve concentration and performance.

- **Amber**—An amulet of amber is used to bring good luck and to ward off evil and danger. Amber brings balance to your energies, facilitates good health, and cleanses your aura. Valued since prehistoric times for its properties, amber was used to help women in childbirth as well.

- **Amethyst**—Amethyst worn or held is said to provide spiritual insight, clarity, and composure. It is said to transform negative energy that is focused on you by repelling it and changing it into light that is absorbed by the cosmos. A very powerful stone for magic and spells, it has been used as an aid to psychics and sorcerers for centuries.

- **Aquamarine**—Attributed to protecting those going into battle, aquamarine is said to assist with quick thinking, good judgment, and physical protection. Traditionally, it has been used to shield its owner from both physical and psychic harm, and speed up the thought processes to allow for quick action. Although it is a good defensive stone, it also promotes compassion and gentleness that encourages peaceful solutions and fairness.

- **Bloodstone**—This stone has been used for centuries to impart courage and strength, providing protection in dangerous situations. It is said to allow people to accept and enjoy the moment, even if their goals seem far off. Used for its magical powers predating the Egyptians, bloodstone is considered both protective and enabling.

- **Carnelian**—This stone traditionally has been used to promote harmony and love within families, as well as to repel anger, envy, and distrust. It is said to remove sorrow and apathy, encouraging a happier and more caring environment.

- **Citrine**—This stone was used in the past to improve financial well-being, increase wealth, and encourage initiative in the workplace. It is said to free you from fears that might be holding you back and open up paths of enterprise.

- **Fluorite**—Known as a powerful stone to heal the mind, this stone increases concentration and aids in decision making. It also enhances creativity.

- **Jet**—Actually black amber, jet has been attributed with all the properties of amber, as well as the ability to ward off spirits. It is said to absorb negative energy. Long used as jewelry for the grieving at funerals, jet is a traditional stone of mourning and can be burned, emitting fumes that drive away evil spirits.

- **Lapis lazuli**—Revered for its properties by the ancients, lapis is said to have mystical properties that connect one to higher planes within the universe. It is considered useful in tapping into divine power.

- **Moonstone**—Long considered a stone for wishing and bringing about one's desires, it is said to be useful in transitions and new beginnings. Moonstone is reputed to be a stone of magic useful to psychics.

- **Opal**—This stone is helpful in tapping into your psychic powers and achieving contact with a higher spiritual plane. Opals also bring about realignment of one's energies and open avenues of creativity.

- **Rose quartz**—Associated with the heart, both emotional and physical, this is a gemstone of love on all levels.

- **Turquoise**—The spiritual nature of turquoise has long made it popular. Its beauty and traditional association with the skies and heavens makes it perfect for mystical quests on a spiritual plane. Turquoise has a peaceful energy that is bestowed upon the user.

Don't limit yourself to using gemstones only when reading fortunes. They can be used for healing, worn as jewelry for desired results, and carried in your pocket or purse for their soothing properties.

The Least You Need to Know

- Salt protects, purifies, and enhances.
- Candles release your intention up to the heavens.
- Use colors, scents, and music to set a mood.
- Gemstones have properties that send out vibrations.

Part 2

Interpreting Images

We all perceive things differently when we gaze at images. What you may regard as a tree, someone else may see as a fan. What you see as fireflies dancing in a bed of sea grass, I see as winged fairies blessing leaves with wands of light. The secret of interpreting images—from ashes to tea leaves—is trusting your own imagination.

Creating your own images and using different elements adds to the pursuit of accuracy and seriousness because you virtually produce them yourself. After these pictures materialize, you have the chance to unravel their meanings using your own ideas. This will give you clues to how linked you are to secret channels into which not everyone can tune their minds and spirits.

Chapter 5

Reading Tea Leaves and Coffee Grounds

In This Chapter

◆ Origins of tea-leaf and coffee-ground readings

◆ Preparing for the reading

◆ Methods of reading tea leaves and coffee grounds

◆ Interpretations of the shapes and images

◆ Sample readings

Tea-leaf readings can be stimulating—and not just because of the caffeine buzz (although that is a possibility). Learning to "read" tea leaves or coffee grounds is an art that is typically easy to master and has been in practice for ages. With a few simple items, you'll be discovering images in that cup in no time.

In addition, you may find the origins of this gypsy trade engaging. So hold on to your tambourine—and let's get shakin'!

How Did This Art Begin?

Many conceptions surround the origin of tea-leaf readings, or *tasseography*. Some say it originated in China, while others believe that gypsies invented the system. Others credit the Scottish or the Irish for this type of divination.

def•i•ni•tion

> **Tasseography** (or **tasseomancy**) is the art of reading tea leaves or coffee grounds to forecast the future. The term *tasse* (cup) comes from the French, which, in turn, comes from the Arabic root word *tassa* (cup).

The theory that I find the most interesting and reasonable pertains to bell ringing. Ancients from many cultures such as China, England, and other European and Eastern civilizations believed that ringing a bell would ward off evil spirits and negativity. The vibration and the sound itself were thought to keep entities and opposing forces from entering any area adorned with a bell. Therefore, bells were hung in certain areas of a dwelling, especially at the front door. They were also hung on chariots and worn on belts and shoes. This provided protection from attacks from enemies. Bells were also used as time-keepers in villages and warned people of coming danger.

Churches also adopted bells. To this day, religious and spiritual groups incorporate bells and chimes (chimes were thought to have the same influence as bells—both dispel negative energy and attract positive influences) into ceremonies and rituals. These tokens of protection and cautions have many diversified applications, which are all positive. They involve protection, warnings, time indicators, and good luck.

With such a wide range of positive vibrations, a philosophy emerged about yet another use for a bell: foretelling the future. People started reasoning that if a bell could keep away negativity, the inside, or the heart of the bell, might be able to predict someone's destiny. Therefore, the inner parts of bells were examined. Most bells were hung outside, of course, so leaves, dirt, and other debris were found inside the bell. When the bell was opened, these clumped pieces fell to the rim, the middle, and the very bottom, and seemed to form images.

The Chinese first recognized that a teacup looked like an inverted bell. They also noted that after tea had been consumed, little clumps of tea leaves were left in the tea cup.

These remaining tea leaves also formed shapes, images, numbers, and so on. Hence, it is said that this might have been the beginning of divination using a teacup. As word spread, this art was passed on to many cultures all over the world. In particular, the gypsies adapted it to their lifestyle and love of divination.

What about coffee grounds? The Arabs discovered the coffee bean in approximately 600 C.E. Coffee eventually swept through the continents and became very popular in Western Europe. It didn't take long before the people who were already using tea leaves for divination noticed that coffee grounds clustered in the same way as the tea leaves. With this revelation, the visionary inquirer had a choice of coffee or tea.

The Cup, the Coffee; the Tea, the Brewing

A little preparation goes a long way. Before beginning tea-leaf or coffee-ground readings, you go through a ritual of sorts. First you select a special cup. Next you purchase your coffee or tea. Finally, you brew your drink. As you go through this process, think strongly about what you hope to achieve.

As you boil coffee, will you ask questions about your job situation? As you brew your tea, will you contemplate what the leaves will generally predict about your life in the next 3 months? Stay focused on divination and what your questions and concerns are.

Selecting the Right Cup

The best type of cup to use is a shallow and wide porcelain teacup. The inside must be plain white. If you cannot locate a cup that has a white interior, a light color such as pink, yellow, or light blue will also work. The idea is that you must be able to see the tea leaves clearly within the cup. A mug will not work because it is too deep, so don't even think about it.

When drinking from china cups, some people have a feeling of elegance and become more relaxed and open to intuitive thoughts. Nevertheless, a china teacup is not necessary—even Stoneware will work. However, although you might consider using a plastic or Corell type of teacup, you should avoid these, if possible: the vibrations from them are not as strong as those from a more traditional type of cup.

The outside of the cup can be as elaborate as you like. Gold leaf, ribbons of color, and even figurines or scenes can embellish the cup, if you like. The important thing is that you stay away from patterns or designs on the inside of the cup. Inside designs will alter the shape of the tea leaves and also make it difficult for you to see into the cup.

Notions Through Time

Cook, Cook, drink your tea, But save some in the pot for me. We'll watch the tea leaves in our cup When our drink is all sipped up. Happiness or fortune great, What will our future be?

—R.Z. Berry, contributing writer, *Afternoon Tea at Pittock*

Be sure to get a teacup with a saucer, too. The saucer will be significant later and is definitely necessary. If you cannot find a matching saucer, you could mix and match, but I recommend going with a matching set: it just "feels good." The cup you choose should also have a handle. In some traditions, the handle is not used or necessary. However, for our purposes, it makes the reading much easier because it works as a beginning and ending point.

If you do not own a teacup and saucer like I've recommended, I suggest buying one. Since you're purchasing just one, the cost should be somewhere in the range of $5 to $12. But remember that you don't need to visit the local department store's fine china department. Consider searching at an antique store, a secondhand establishment, or your local thrift store. And don't forget about garage or estate sales.

> **Visionary Insights**
>
> If you're wondering if a chipped or cracked teacup and saucer are workable, the answer is no. Tools of divination should be in good condition. If something is broken, the power that you are trying to attract for a good reading will be, too.

A Cup of Prophecy

To read coffee grounds, your coffee must be prepared so that the grounds fall to the bottom of the cup. Therefore, instant coffee will not work because the coffee obviously dissolves completely.

Drip coffee makers "download" your java using modern technology and typically pre-ground coffee. Consequently, little to no coffee grounds will be found at the end of this mechanical process.

Choose whole-bean coffee and grind it yourself. Most large grocery stores have grinders that you can use at no additional cost. (The blend is totally up to you.) Turn the grinding gauge to "coarse." The bigger the grounds, the larger the images.

Follow these steps to make your cup of coffee:

1. Boil enough water in a pot for the amount of coffee you want to produce.

2. Measure your coffee. Approximately 1 teaspoon for every 6 ounces works nicely.

3. Boil the grounds in a pot on the stove for only a few minutes, depending on how much coffee you are preparing.

4. Pour the coffee into your cup—no need to filter it.

5. Your coffee grounds should settle to the bottom of the cup.

6. If you don't seem to have enough (or any) coffee grounds on the bottom of your cup, sprinkle some into the cup before you start to drink.

7. If you like, add cream and sugar to taste; it will not influence the reading.

8. Stir, stir, stir. Kick up some energy. This will churn the grounds, which is good. They will settle down on the bottom in seconds.

Selecting and Brewing Tea

You can choose from a variety of teas. Any tea is acceptable when it comes to tea-leaf readings: decaffeinated tea will not give you a weaker reading.

Many black teas, such as Keemun, are said to be superior. This tea is considered the finest of all the Chinese varieties, and is aromatic and smooth.

Darjeeling, green varieties, and Oolong teas are also excellent for prophecy because they are full bodied. Yet you can also keep it simple and buy something such as Lipton's or Earl Grey. There is only one rule here: the tea must be loose. No tea bags, no tea strainers, please. The tea found in tea bags is ground too fine.

For our purposes I provide the simplest method of brewing tea for one single cup:

1. Measure a little more than 1 cup of fresh, cold, nondistilled water. Spring water and filtered water are good choices.

2. Boil the water on the stove in a tea kettle or saucepan.

3. Place approximately 1 teaspoon of tea leaves in your teacup.

4. The moment the water begins to boil, pour the boiling water over your tea leaves.

5. Steep the tea for 3 to 5 minutes, according to taste.

6. Add a small amount of cream and sugar, if you like; it will not affect the reading.

> **Visionary Insights**
>
> One advantage of using tea leaves over coffee grounds is that the tea-leaf process isn't as messy. In addition, the tea leaves are bulkier, which makes them a bit easier to read.

Let's Read Tea Leaves and Coffee Grounds

The person who is giving the reading is always referred to as the "reader" or the "seer." The person who is receiving the reading is called the "sitter." The sitter should think about a specific question or focus on what generally is going to happen in the future while enjoying his or her tea or coffee, following these steps:

1. The tea or coffee should be consumed, leaving a few drops of liquid in the cup.

2. With the left hand, the sitter holds the cup by the handle. The rim should be up.

3. The sitter swishes the tea or coffee quickly in a circular motion, clockwise, three times. This distributes the leaves or grounds around the cup.

4. The sitter turns the cup upside down on the saucer, allowing the remaining liquid to drain naturally. Do not tap on the cup.

5. After the liquid is drained, the cup should be turned back over. At this point, the leaves or grounds should have clumped, forming the shapes that will be interpreted.

If you are reading for yourself, follow the same steps. It's important, however, to be honest with yourself about what you see. This is why people sometimes prefer not to read for themselves.

The Actual Reading

As the reader, take the cup and examine it. Relax and take a few deep breaths. At first, looking at all the images can be puzzling. You may not even spot anything that you think resembles any of the likenesses listed later in this chapter.

Translating symbols into meaningful images is highly subjective. Different mental states can also contribute to the outcome of the reading. Therefore, as you gaze into the cup, don't become tense. Just allow the patterns to tell you what or who they are. You'll hear that inner voice say, "I am a spider, I am a circle, I am a tree."

When you begin to read, start from the left going clockwise, starting at the handle while you turn the cup.

Past, Present, Future

A few different ideas have arisen about what area of the cup indicates the past, present, and future. I think the three-part method is the lest complicated and most accurate:

- ◆ **The rim**—Events in the present
- ◆ **The sides**—Events in the near future (up to three months)
- ◆ **The bottom**—Events in the far future (up to nine months)

Some methods believe that formations to the left of the handle are things of the past, and to the right of the handle circumstances of the future.

Interpretations of Shapes and Images

In reading tea leaves or coffee grounds, it's important to use your intuition. There is more here than merely looking up the meaning of a symbol in this book.

When determining what something looks like, usually your first thought is the correct one. You may see an image that can be several things. For instance, the letter *Y* could also look like a bird flying or a kite to some. This is why you need to go with your first interpretation. If there are others with you, their opinion truly doesn't count. You are the seer. If you are not sure, keep turning the cup and focusing. Eventually, you will come to a conclusion.

The number of images that form in the cup varies from many to few.

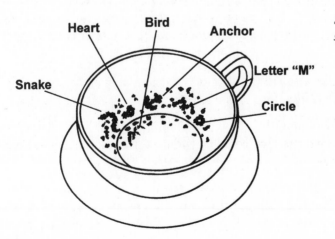

Some common tea-leaf symbols.

Heart Bird Anchor Letter "M" Snake Circle

General Shapes

Often the easiest symbols to translate are the symbol designs and geometric shapes. So if a circle or square pops out at you right away, focus on that image and proceed from there. Even if you need to pass over some of the other images at first, that's okay. You are learning, so don't push yourself to do everything 100 percent according to directions. You will eventually find your own way.

Here are the interpretations of basic shapes:

- **Circle**—Success and fulfillment
- **Square**—Challenge or stability
- **Triangle**—Good fortune and blessings
- **Straight line**—Journey or a new enterprise
- **Broken line**—Something that won't last, or a challenging trip
- **Wavy line**—Indecisive travel plans, change, or water

Dots around a symbol can indicate money. The character of the symbol determines the details.

Enlightening Extras

It is said that if a leaf clings to the very edge of the rim, someone has the sitter on his or her mind. If you want to know who it may be, look for a letter within the cup that will indicate a first or last name.

Letters

When you see letters, these can be significant. A letter next to an image of a man or woman, for example, could be the first or last letter of that person's name. When asking specific questions about a place, a letter can stand for a state or country, such as *C* for California or Canada.

Numbers and Numerology

Some people feel that a number is a number. For example, if you ask a question about a timeframe and a 2 appears, that could be two days, two months, or two years. The reader decides.

On the other hand, some believe that *numerology* plays a part in tea-leaf readings and that the number 2 does not stand for time, but for a psychic message. Here's an example. According to numerology, the number 2 means partnership, patience, harmony, and adaptability. You can certainly see the difference between the two. This is up to you to decide as the reader. There is a third idea of what numbers mean, listed next. When interpreting numbers, keep in mind that they have both positive and negative aspects, just like in astrology. It is the knowledge of these vibrations that may allow you to delve deeper into your true character and recognize your favorable and opposing traits. You decide what your intuition tells you is the best explanation for a specific reading.

Here are some traditional positive and negative interpretations of numbers:

1—Happy times are in the near future. *Positive:* Individual, active, original. *Negative:* Lazy, unstable, egotistical.

2—An event will soon bring you enjoyment. *Positive:* Charming, favors partnership, gentle. *Negative:* Dishonest, favors duality, two-faced.

3—Your wish will come true. *Positive:* Abundant, creative, humorous. *Negative:* Jealous, shallow, extravagant.

4—You will enjoy success regarding education. *Positive:* Loyal, stable, conservative. *Negative:* Vulgar, stern, boring.

5—A startling occurrence will shock you. *Positive:* Diverse, adventuresome, unattached. *Negative:* Oversexed, undependable, overindulgent.

6—You will be well liked and popular. *Positive:* Loving, artistic, balanced. *Negative:* Stubborn, dominant, skeptical.

7—Love is coming your way again. *Positive:* Scientific, intelligent, trustworthy. *Negative:* Selfish, meddlesome, stubborn.

8—Learning from experience is powerful. *Positive:* Successful, powerful, is a strong leader. *Negative:* Impatient, wastes energy, resentful.

9—Better times are ahead, with dreams fulfilled. *Positive:* Romantic, spiritual, generous. *Negative:* Overemotional, bitter, improper.

> **Enlightening Extras**
>
> **Numerology** is the ancient study and application of the meaning of numbers and how they can pertain and influence your life. Certain numbers have a special vibration that may affect your future.

> **Notions Through Time**
>
> Go down deep enough into anything, and you will find mathematics.
>
> —Dean Schlicter, math author

I don't go beyond explanations of numbers over 9 because the interpretations repeat themselves when using numerology. To decipher a two-digit number, you add them to produce a one-digit number. For example, the number 23, when added, is 5: 2 + 3 = 5. Therefore, the number 23 has the same interpretation as the number 5.

Interpretations of Symbols

The following interpretations of symbols are the most important part of tea-leaf reading. Although with time and practice you may develop your own impressions, these are the most common and proven interpretations by seasoned readers. Use your first guess and stick to it. Allow your intuitive self to take over. After a while you will learn to trust your initial thoughts.

- **Acorn**—Success is in store for you.
- **Anchor**—Your worries will soon be lifted.
- **Angel**—Expect good news, especially in love.
- **Apple**—Prosperity is coming through business.
- **Arrow**—Bad news is coming your way in matters of love.
- **Baby**—This indicates a series of minor but unfortunate events.
- **Bear**—Delays regarding travel will be annoying.
- **Bell**—You will receive good news. More than one bell indicates a wedding.
- **Bird**—You will receive joyous news. Birds flying means news will come quickly.
- **Boat**—A friend will pay you a visit.
- **Book (open)**—A new lover or new ideas are favorable.
- **Bottle**—Illness is coming your way but can be avoided.
- **Camel**—You will receive unexpected news regarding someone's past.
- **Candle**—Assistance from others will bring you joy.
- **Cat**—Beware of crafty enemies and quarrels.
- **Church**—A ceremony will take place.
- **Clover**—You will have good luck and fortune for a long time to come.
- **Cross**—You will make a sacrifice for someone you love.
- **Crown**—A wish will be granted.

- **Cup**—Success encompasses you.

- **Dagger**—Do not be too hasty. Use caution.

- **Dog**—You have many loyal friends.

- **Door**—This indicates a visitor from the "other side." Also means past knowledge.

- **Dragon**—Changes will happen suddenly for you.

- **Drum**—This indicates a trip due to a new work situation.

- **Ear**—You will hear something you did not expect.

- **Envelope**—You will receive news that will make you smile.

- **Eye**—If you are having difficulties, you will overcome them.

- **Fan**—Some type of flirtation is going on in your life.

- **Flag**—Beware of danger or quarreling.

- **Flower**—You will have much interest in a marriage.

- **Foot**—You need to take a stand and make a decision.

- **Fork**—Someone you think is a friend, isn't.

- **Gate**—It's time to move forward. You will not meet with trouble.

- **Gondola**—This indicates a love affair near the water or at sea.

- **Grasshopper**—News will come to you of someone in the armed forces.

- **Gun**—Conflict is coming into your life.

- **Hammer**—You will have to do work you don't like.

- **Harp**—This indicates a serious love affair.

- **Hat**—You will be presented with a gift or a raise in salary.

- **Heart**—This is a good omen of happiness and pleasure.

- **Horseshoe**—You will be the epitome of the word *lucky*.

- **Hourglass**—Stop procrastinating and make a decision.

- **House**—You will have security. Things are in good order.

- **Iceberg**—Be cautious with whom you share opinions.

- **Indian**—News from far away is in the offing.

- **Insect**—Your problems are smaller than you think.

- **Jewels**—You will receive a gift or give one to someone else.

- **Jug**—You will enjoy good health for some time to come.

- **Key**—You will change jobs or careers.

- **Kite**—Dreams will come true.

- **Knife**—This indicates separation from friends or a loved one.

- **Ladder**—Your lifestyle will be elevated for the better.

- **Lamp**—Financial gain is coming your way.

- **Leaf**—A new and better life will befall you.

- **Lightning bolt**—You will encounter negative energy from others.

- **Lock**—There is a great strain on you.

- **Monkey**—Beware of scandal. Don't embarrass yourself.

- **Moon (crescent)**—Fortune and prosperity are on the rise.

- **Mountain**—You will enjoy achievement, but with numerous difficulties.

- **Mushroom**—You will encounter minor business obstacles.

- **Necklace**—Many admirers will come your way.

- **Needle**—You will be admired for an achievement.

- **Net**—Someone may try to trap you at something.

- **Oar**—You have troubles at home, but things will be amicably resolved.

- **Octopus**—Others may be keeping things from you—danger.

- **Owl**—You will hear good news if this is near the cup's rim. If not—scandal.

- **Palm tree**—You will take a trip to a tropical area.

- **Person**—Someone will unexpectedly come to visit.

- **Pig**—Be careful of being greedy, or of someone else's greed.

- **Pipe**—You are thinking of a man. Other symbols nearby will tell you what he's thinking. Letters nearby could indicate a name.

- **Plane**—A journey awaits you.

- **Question mark**—Morals and motives are questionable.

- **Rabbit**—There will be a need for bravery.

- **Rat**—Someone is dishonest, a possible enemy.

- **Rose**—New friendships and popularity are in store.

- **Shark**—Possible bankruptcy may occur.

- **Shoe**—Your energy level will elevate. You will experience new ventures.

- **Snake**—This is a bad omen. Be careful to avoid trouble.

- **Spider**—You will receive gifts or compensation for a job well done.

- **Star**—All things are good—happiness, health, finances, love.

- **Teapot**—Many friends will visit you.

- **Telephone**—Don't forget to do or tell someone something.

- **Thimble**—Changes will happen in the home.

- **Tree**—This indicates recovery from mental or physical ill health.

- **Turtle**—Criticism proves helpful.

- **Umbrella**—This indicates annoying people, places, and things.

- **Unicorn**—This points to a marriage or relationship no one knows about.

- **Vase**—A friend is in need of your help.

- **Vehicles**—This indicates travel or a move.

- **Volcano**—Someone is overemotional—it could be you!

- **Wheel**—Something will be completed or fulfilled.

- **Wings**—Messages will be arriving soon.

- **Witch**—Bizarre circumstances will arise—something peculiar.

Sample Readings

When you have determined what objects you see in the cup, try to make a story out of it. Whether you are doing a general reading or answering a specific question, it is fairly simple to put together a scene.

> **Notions Through Time**
>
> Trust your own instinct. Your mistakes might as well be your own instead of someone else's.
>
> —Billy Wilder, film director

This is where you need to use your intuition. Simply put, say what your gut feeling is telling you. Another reader could interpret the same formations totally differently. Don't be concerned with what someone else would do.

Following are four examples of how I personally might interpret the exact same symbols in different circumstances.

The symbols in the cup are ...

- **Anchor**—Your worries will soon be lifted.

- **Birds flying**—News will come quickly.

- **Flag**—Beware of danger or quarreling.

- **Needle**—You will be admired for an achievement.

- **Number Seven**—Love is coming your way again, or the number 7 literally.

1. **General reading, interpretation 1:** Within seven days, you will be admired for staying out of an argument. As a result, present negativity in your life will be removed quickly. By walking away, you will have avoided a dangerous situation.

2. **General reading, interpretation 2:** I feel there is a strong indication that you will argue with someone, but the quarrel will end quickly. You will both feel a sense of relief that the air has been cleared. People will agree with you that you were right to end the confrontation before it got worse. The number seven appears in the cup. This tells me it could take place around seven o'clock in the morning or the evening. The other possibility is that the conflict could be resolved in seven minutes.

3. **Specific question: "Will I find a boyfriend soon?"**

Answer 1: Someone is going to come into your life quickly. Unfortunately, you may find that he has qualities you do not care for, and you may break off the relationship. Others will admire you for your judgment and foresight.

Answer 2: In approximately seven days, news will come that a fellow you know has broken up with his girlfriend. This is due to a quarrel or disagreement. Be careful that you don't get romantically involved too fast. You may be overanxious and wanting to feel that your loneliness has ended. He will admire you for your caution about relationships. However, I sense much negativity around this whole situation. Other people out there may be more suited for you. If you give him a pass, someone will move into your life soon.

You can understand how these scenarios can be altered. As I mentioned earlier, for this reason, many people cannot read for themselves. It is very easy to see what we want to see!

The Least You Need to Know

- The Chinese most likely laid the foundation for the art of reading tea leaves.

- Coffee grounds were used by those who already were using tea leaves, especially in Western Europe, when it was noticed that the grounds formed similar shapes like tea leaves.

- Choose a teacup that is shallow, wide, and light in color on the inside.

- The sitter must drink the tea or coffee for an accurate reading.

- Always trust your first hunch when reading tea leaves or coffee grounds.

Chapter 6

Ice Rendering

In This Chapter

- Use nature for a cold reading
- Seeing images in snow
- Reading ice cubes and icicles
- Watermarks—the stains of the future

Winter is a great time for divination. You can do more with snow than just shoveling it and making snowmen: you can perform a reading with drips and drops from chimney tops.

In this chapter, I talk about frosty images that ice rendering can create, and how you can interpret those impressions to determine future events. So let's begin before it all melts away.

Baby, It's Cold Outside

If you have ever lived in a cold climate with frost, ice, and snow, you realize that the winds of winter can hold you captive indoors, in a place that provides comfort and warmth—leaving little for you to do but watch a fire, sit in front of your kitchen stove watching your socks dry, or hugging your fuzzy cat like she's never been hugged before.

Winter is an excellent time of year to reflect on what has happened in your life over the last 12 months. It is also a magnificent time to do a fortune-telling reading to obtain a glimpse of what the new year may bring. Think of all the questions you may want answered about the upcoming year.

Will you finally get out of debt? Will you meet a romantic new partner? How will your career progress? If you are going to do a winter reading, why not use what nature has provided in the way of tools of divination for that season? When you use elements of a seasonal cycle, the reading is always more powerful because you are joining with what the native Americans call Father Earth and Mother Sky to yield results.

Frosty, the Fortune Teller

If you determine that you want to try to conduct an ice rendering, you are carrying on a belief of little-known origin. In fact, there isn't any origin I can find. But I do know, on a personal level, that I have been doing this for years as it was taught to me by my grandmother, herself a gifted seer.

I won't fudge on the roots of this form of divining, but I will defend it. It has worked for me many times, and maybe it will work for you. If it doesn't, then this chapter is just cold knowledge, and probably all you will come up with is a chill.

What You'll Need

These are the only things you need for ice rendering:

- Snow, icicles, or ice cubes

- A piece or several pieces of cardboard of any color, approximately 6 × 6 inches or larger (white cardboard will work in a pinch but will be harder to read, so avoid it if possible)

- A pen or fine-line felt-tip marker

For now, we'll use snow (I talk about using icicles or ice cubes a little later in the chapter). First, gather firm snow that is well packed and not fresh. To use fresh snow is not acceptable because it will melt too quickly. And please stay away from the yellow sort, thank you. Just a couple of handfuls will do. Put the snow in your bowl.

Bring your snow bowl into an interior area. This process will require concentration, and the cold weather may freeze your senses, leaving your reading a bit frigid.

The Cold and Simple Facts

Put a piece of cardboard of any color on a table or platform in front of you. Set down your bowl. Bare-handed or wearing gloves, grab a little snow from the bowl. Do not think about anything specific. Scatter a tiny bit of snow on top of the cardboard. Do not saturate the entire cardboard. When the snow melts but before the cardboard dries, blots will form, like the old *inkblot test*.

Once you see these watermarks and they have dried for about a minute or two, outline them with a pen before they dry completely.

Next, look at the designs and define what images you see. Turn the cardboard many times until you see an image that virtually jumps out at you. Another option is to use pieces of paper and cover different parts of the cardboard watermarks to see if you find different images that way. Look at the images, and put together an interpretation that makes sense to you.

def•i•ni•tion

An **inkblot test** is a psychological test in which a subject examines a series of inkblots using his or her own interpretations.

What does it look like to you? Remember, this is about you. Don't worry about what someone else would most likely see. For example, a friend of mine and I were just doing this. My watermark showed a woman typing with two angels above her head. My friend saw a woman with two children going away. Another friend saw a big dog with two bowls of food in front of it.

If you are with someone else, it is fun to see how that person sees your future, as opposed to your personal interpretations. Always go with your version, but note the other person's in addition. There is a possibility that he or she picked up something about you that you missed.

This is an entertaining event to experience with a group of people. One person can make the watermarks, thinking of general things while he or she is doing it. Then that person can stand in front of the group (or everyone can stand around the table together), and the group can analyze individually what they see. What wild ideas some people will come up with!

You can also have a few pieces of cardboard available and do more than one reading at a time. But I don't recommend more than four or you may get confused. And yes, you can use the same snow. Sprinkle some snow on each piece of cardboard while asking your particular question—one question per piece of cardboard. Just don't forget which cardboard went with which question.

The Big Meltdown

When working with icicles and ice cubes, there is a slight variation. Some people find this method more fun; others think all that snow sloshing can't be beat. Try them all, if possible, and see which one you can best relate to.

Icicles

If you are fortunate enough to have access to icicles, this may be a more interesting process. The icicles could be from a window sill, a tree, a fence, or any icy place. Hopefully, this is on your own property so you are not too far from your home. You don't want your fortune to melt away before you walk through the door.

Gather one or two icicles, put them in a bowl, and bring them back into your inside location. Holding the larger end of the icicle, allow the pointed end to drip onto the cardboard. You can move the icicle in any direction while it's dripping, if you like. As I said, do not saturate the cardboard. Less is better. When you feel that enough images are formed, outline them with a pen and intuitively read them in the same fashion as with snow.

> **Notions Through Time**
>
> Adversity draws men together and produces beauty and harmony in life's relationships, just as the cold of winter produces ice-flowers on the window panes, which vanish with the warmth.
>
> —Soren Kierkegaard, Danish philosopher

Ice Cubes

If you live in a warm climate, reading snow and icicles is probably out. However, there is still hope. You have ice cubes! Once you have your ice cubes, grab one or two in your hand and let them drip onto the cardboard, the same as with icicles. Follow the standard procedure discussed previously. Try to keep the area around the cardboard dry so the cardboard doesn't accidentally pick up more water.

Reading the Watermarks

After you outline your watermarks with a pen, you can read the images wet or wait for them to dry. Once they dry, the images will remain due to the conformations made by the pen. This is why it is important to outline them before they dry. Now relax and study the images you have created.

At first glance, what do you see? Remember it, but don't make a final decision. Is it a big submarine, a cloud of smoke, a person holding a wand? The possibilities are endless, and we all see something different. There are no exact interpretations for watermarks; only your personal impressions are the key to your future.

In other forms of fortune telling, usually your first impression is the wisest choice. In watermark interpretations, however, the more you ponder what the figures resemble, the more accurate you will be. This requires a little more concentration, but it is an interesting and entertaining experience.

You may not want to throw away your cardboard pieces of art. Save them, if you like, and look at them from time to time. Put them on your bulletin board or frame them. I have a few that are so unusual that I kept them.

The Least You Need to Know

- Use snow, icicles, or ice cubes to create watermarks.
- Outline your watermarks with a pen before they disappear.
- There are no standard definitions of the images.
- This is especially entertaining to do with a group.

Chapter 7

Spondanomancy

In This Chapter

- The art of reading ashes
- The winds tell all
- Reading letters in the ashes
- Casting a spell before reading ashes

If you like performing ceremonies at night and walking in circles, and if you aren't afraid of getting ashes all over yourself, this is the chapter for you. Granted, it is a little on the bizarre side, but it's all in good fun. Can you really draw letters in ashes at night and the next morning get answers to questions? You'll never know unless you try.

Whether conducting this time-honored type of divination alone or in a group, the experience in itself is memorable. The moon and the weather play an important part in this technique and must be taken into account. There is more planning with this process, not to mention the cleanup. But hopefully this will add a little stimulation to the mix of fortune-telling methods presented in the book.

The Ashes of Time

Spondanomancy, or *spodomancy*, as it's sometimes written, basically means writing in ashes. Some may define it simply as divining by examining ashes.

All these words get very confusing and can make your memory go up in smoke. Therefore, personally, I just say "reading ashes." It works for me. Use any term you like, but there might be value in remembering the word "spodomancy." This information may help you win a game of Trivial Pursuit!

Little is known about the origins of this form of divination. Some research claims that this type of prophecy was cultivated in Germany at the beginning of the nineteenth century, while others believe it was practiced during the Middle Ages, a period in Western Europe from approximately the fifth to the fifteenth centuries.

def•i•ni•tion

Spondanomancy, or **spodo-mancy**, is the art of divination by examining ashes.

Although reading ashes was still prevalent in Germany as recently as the nineteenth century, today this form of divination has little popularity. In this day and age, our fortune-telling methods focus on cleaner forms of divination. All that soot can make fortune telling a mess.

Method One—Blowing in the Wind

This is an outdoor form of divination only. I suppose you could do it inside, if you are willing to destroy your house, leave your windows open all night, and let ashes from a fireplace fly around. But I do not recommend that. So outside it is!

The first thing you need to do is consider a way to create ashes. And no, smoking a carton of cigarettes and saving the ashes won't work. You need ashes from wood. And no, we don't burn down the nearest forest preserve or your neighbor's wooden chair that his Uncle Angus made 20 years ago.

You really need branches or real logs. The fake starter logs you can buy for $1.99 each at the grocery store won't be as powerful. Yes, your intention is the most important thing when it comes to fortune telling, but this is old-time fortune telling at its best, so try to do it in the traditional manner. If you have no other choice, use the starter logs along with some paper. But at another time, promise to try the more natural method.

Let's Make Ashes

The first thing you need to do is plan a way to burn wood. The best place to do this is with a campfire in a safe and legal location. Some people use chimineas, which are small ceramic or clay firepots that can be purchased at garden stores and home-supply outlets. In addition to chimineas, there are many types of safe wood-burning receptacles you can use outside.

You can also take ashes from your inside fireplace once they have completely cooled (wait a day or so, if you need to). You will need approximately enough ashes to spread on a square area about 12 × 12 inches. There are no rules here; this is just the minimum.

If you use ashes from a campfire, they also should be cooled, and you should shovel them into a fireproof container. Same with the other firepots that you use.

> **Visionary Insights**
>
> When you are gathering ashes from an inside fireplace, use a shovel to put them in a fireproof bucket, can, or other fireproof device to take them outside.

Safety Warnings

When using anything involving fire, you must use common sense and caution. Follow these safety precautions:

- If you are under 18, don't do this without the supervision and permission of an adult who is your parent or guardian.

- If you don't know whether you can build a campfire in a certain area, ask your local fire marshal for the legal rules of fire burning.

- Do not burn pressure-treated wood because it emits a toxic gas. (Hint: If it's green, don't burn it.)

- Have a fire extinguisher, water, or a shovel near the fire, in case you need to extinguish it immediately.

- Watch out for pets and children when burning wood.

- Never leave the fire unattended.

- If you are using a firepot of some type, do not touch the outside of the container, which will get very hot.

♦ Check out campfire safety tips and how to make a safe campfire on the Internet or at the library, or ask your local forest preserve ranger.

After your ashes are accumulated, you can set them aside for days in a container outside away from the wind, or you can use them whenever they are cold. If you have a fireplace that hasn't been cleaned for a while, that's a way to clean the fireplace and get your future told all in one step.

Be sure to note what the weather will be like the day you choose to do your reading. You don't want a rainy or snowy day or you may end up with wet ashes that stick to the ground in a big mass of black sludge. A very windy day is not beneficial either, because a gust of wind will sweep away your ashes before you have a chance to set them down. Therefore, the weather is important, and for this method you must really plan ahead.

Notions Through Time

The trouble with weather forecasting is that it's right too often for us to ignore it and wrong too often for us to rely on it.

—Patrick Young, aeronautical pioneer

With ashes in order, you're ready to get started. All you need is a stick or something long you can use to write in the ashes.

How to Do a Reading

The best time to conduct this event is the night of a full or waxing moon. A new moon will also do, but the new moon doesn't really have the vibration of the waxing or full moon. The energy of the full moon is powerful and the mood is exhilarating. Also, since this is done outside, the view of a full moon adds intrigue. And for the practical, it's much better lighting!

1. In the evening, take the cooled ashes you have saved from your campfire, fireplace, or firepot, and spread them thickly outside in a small safe area where they will not be disturbed.

2. Using your finger or a stick, write your single question or concern in the ashes as best you can. This should be a sentence of at least four words. For example: "Does he love me?" Do not ask more than one question.

3. Leave the area and forget about it till the next morning. If you are concerned that you will not remember your question, write it down on paper and take it back in with you.

4. During the night, the winds will blow the ashes, leaving only a few letters from the question you asked readable. The next morning, you should find the magical letters left. These letters are considered the Oracles in which to divine your answer.

5. Look closely at the remaining ashes and decipher what letters are left. If you find that your letters have changed to letters you never wrote, use them as an Oracle. Destiny has determined the answer to your question by removing certain letters.

6. Write the letter or letters on a piece of paper, and take it inside to figure it out later if that is easier for you. Sometimes a letter like a *Y* or *N* can stand for "yes" or "no." Be imaginative while examining your soot!

> **Visionary Insights**
>
> I know what you're thinking: "What happens if the winds blow all the ashes away and nothing is left?" Well, yes, I see your dilemma. Interestingly enough, there is usually some type of letter or letters left. Of course, if it rains, that may be a different story. But sometime even in the rain, your ash Oracles will appear. If your ashes are all gone, try again at a later time that same week.

Clean up the ashes that remain and ponder your answer for a while. Never leave a mess, even if it is in your own home area. A clean environment is always best for you mentally, physically, and spiritually. Have respect for people, animals, places, and things.

Method Two—Letters in the Ashes

Hold on to your smoke. This is where you get dirty! The term that relates to this method of reading ashes is *gyromancy*. There are different interpretations of the word, but the common denominator is that gyromancy is a form of divination that is achieved by a person or a group of people walking or dancing in a circle. The person or group prints the alphabet on the ground in a large circle. Someone dances or spins until he or she gets dizzy and stumbles upon a letter. This goes on until an entire message is recorded or suggested via a few letters.

In this case we are using a group of three or more people. We will be practicing a moderate and safe form of gyromancy that does not involve getting dizzy, falling, or losing your equilibrium. This should be conducted outside in a safe and private area. The time of night is not as important as the phase of the moon, which should be full or waxing, as mentioned earlier.

1. Someone must be appointed facilitator. This person leads the group through the process. Whether your group will dance or walk should be determined in advance. Some people walking and others dancing will confuse things. Consider a swaying type of walk as a happy medium.

   This method is used for general future predictions. It could be about one person, all of them, the weather, the economy, or anything that makes sense. The facilitator should be the ultimate "reader," but everyone should speak their opinion, and the result should be a group effort.

2. Find a location that is private. Do not make a spectacle of yourself in public.

3. Use the same method of gathering ashes as described earlier in the chapter.

4. A large circle of ashes must be formed by the facilitator. Then, he or she writes the alphabet in the ashes, using a stick. The leader can appoint someone to help in this process. This is actually best done by using the ashes from a cold campfire that has been extinguished long ago. Draw the circle around the ashes with a stick and write the letters inside.

5. The leader tells the group to begin moving. Do not hold hands; everyone needs to be free. Turn, whirl, swirl—do your own thing while moving in a circle. This should continue for a few minutes.

6. When the facilitator feels that everyone has enough movement to bring up the energy, everyone takes a step toward the ashes without paying attention to where they are standing. (You might blot out a letter, but by looking at the remaining letters on either side, you will be able to determine which letters you stepped upon.)

   (Note: The original method was to fall down into the ashes, but I don't think you have to go that far. Stepping into the cold ashes works just as well.)

> **Notions Through Time**
>
> There is a bit of insanity in dancing that does everybody a great deal of good.
> —Edwin Denby, American poet and dance critic

7. Everyone looks down and determines what letter (or sometimes letters) of the alphabet they stepped on.

8. The group writes down the letters and determines their predictions as a group. This can be taken inside at this point, or you can remain outside.

As I mentioned in Chapter 4, it is always good to set the mood. Music is particularly good for this technique. I suggest Native American flute or drumming music, chanting sounds, or anything with a good rhythm.

Cinder Ceremonies

While you're kicking up some ash, you might want to consider a ceremony before you begin either method.

If you are going to do a ceremony, the night of the full moon is the best. If you can't wait for a full moon, conduct your event when the moon is waxing, which is the time after a new or crescent moon, when the moon appears to be getting larger before it reaches a full moon.

Perform a little *spell*, whether alone or with a group, for a positive result. For instance, if you are alone, you may want to cast a spell for good health, general well-being, and prosperity. If you are with a group, you might cast your spell for happiness for all, or success for all present, or world peace.

For the general well-being of the group, you may want to recite this request or chant to the universe. Say it three times: "Together we join in this place in this year, for balance, health, and peace we are here." End by saying "And so it is" or a similar closing statement.

def•i•ni•tion

A **spell** is a method of manifesting something you want into your life by using spoken, written, or chanted words. This is not about negative, evil things; it is an appeal to a higher power.

If you are not at ease doing something that is labeled a "spell," simply don't include it. End of story. You need to be comfortable in all things you do. I try to add a little bit of everything for all of the different mind-sets when it comes to fortune telling. What is right for you might not be comfortable for someone else.

The night of your ash reading, before you spread your ashes, set the scene with the enhancements I talked about in Chapter 4.

Decide what you want to ask for while casting your spell. Keep it general. Don't include people's names. Do you want to find romance, good health, or money, or do you just need a spiritual message? Once you know what you will be asking, stand in the area in which you will be performing your ash divination, and point the first and second fingers of your right hand to the moon. Holding out your hand with your fingers pointed, draw a circle around yourself in the air in a clockwise fashion. You will have to turn around as you do this. Do this three times. Next, picture a cloud of white light around you, which is your protection from negativity. Relax, think of your desire, and say:

Here and now,
not the past,
now I say, this spell is cast.

Visionary Insights

Never wish someone harm or ill intentions. And do not attempt to cast a spell to make someone do something that person does not want to do. That includes wanting someone to call you, love you, leave a job so you can have it, and so on.

Release your imaginary circle that you cast around you by visualizing it floating up to the heavens. That's it.

Now you can see why this type of divination is not practiced anymore: it's messy. You have to be very cautious, and you might wonder if it's worth the effort. Reading ashes can be entertaining and interesting, but if it doesn't light your fire, give it a pass. There are plenty of other types of divination.

The Least You Need to Know

♦ Spondanomancy, or reading ashes, is a little-used type of divination.

♦ You can do this method alone or in a group.

♦ Be cautious when working with anything pertaining to fire.

♦ Casting a spell, either alone or in a group, before you read ashes may give you a more positive result.

Chapter 8

Divining by Sand and Smoke

In This Chapter

- What you need to do sand divination
- Meditation to improve focus
- Steps for doing a reading
- Pipe dream: visions in the smoke

Divining by sand or smoke is a mode of fortune-telling in which your intuition is coupled with a few simple symbols created by the sand or smoke. This chapter taps into your connection to nature. You can also ask questions about your past, present, or future to get a clear outcome.

Some people think that telling your fortune by sand or smoke is the practice of sorcerers. That's simply not true. Most likely you will never be accused of being a "sand witch."

Circles in the Sand

Divining by sand has it roots in the Eastern world. Yet this is one of the most unspecific forms of divination. Emphasis on the historical background is so ambiguous that I would rather get right to the grain of things and tell you what you need to do a sand reading.

The equipment you need is very simple:

◆ A tray of any kind

◆ Approximately three cups of sand, which can be purchased at a hardware or garden store

◆ A long pencil or a stick (I like to use a stick—it's more natural)

◆ Something you can use as a blindfold

Enlightening Extras

Years ago, I would have suggested taking sand from a local beach if you were near the water. However, today with erosion … just buy a bag and help save our beaches. A local hardware store, home center, or garden shop should carry it.

Some of us simply like to do things in a big way. So if you think "big," why not? Build an entire sandbox of divination. You can find free instructions for building simple sandboxes on the Internet or at your local library. Hardware stores often have easy "how-to" pamphlets on such things as well. If you decide to reconsider the large wooden sandbox because of the effort it requires, just don't look down at your cat. The kitty litter box is not an option!

If you don't want to deal with building a large sandbox, but you want something big you can put outside, use a big plastic storage box. You can find them in all sizes at any discount store. Dig a hole, put it in the ground, and pour sand into it. Ta-da!—a tool of divination.

When you have your tray or plastic sandbox, or the mega-sandbox that adorns your backyard (even if you don't have any children), you are ready to go. All you have to find is that long pencil or stick. If you are using a big sandbox, you will obviously need a stick or thin dowel rod, which is simply a long, round piece of wood. The sizes can vary. For example, the length can be 36 inches and the diameter a quarter inch. It's like a long pointer without a point. (Dowel rods are available in hardware stores and home centers.)

Sand or Smoke: It's All Concentration and Intuition

As I've said throughout this book, the base of all psychic readings and impressions is concentration. The better focused you are, the more accurate your insights will be. That is why the most important element of psychic impressions is to learn to pay attention to what you are feeling. When picking up impressions, you must lose sight of logic. This is purely a *right-brained* activity. Only when you are interpreting (not before) should your logic be added.

Meditation Technique Before Divining

To pick up supersensory impressions, you must be in an altered state of consciousness, obtaining intense levels of concentration, yet focusing on relaxation. This is a very important factor when conducting a sand or smoke reading. Meditation helps you achieve this relaxed yet focused state. Schedule your meditation at a time when you can devote your full attention to the process. This may be at the very beginning of the day before you are distracted by your daily responsibilities. It would be helpful if you had a private space set aside for your meditation, away from the diversions of the household, which would allow you to avoid distractions and give your complete attention to your practice. If this is not possible, just be sure to choose a quiet place where no one will interrupt your concentration.

def•i•ni•tion

To think in a **right-brained** manner is to use the part of your brain that dominates emotions, intuition, and creativeness. There is neither logic nor analysis in this type of thought process. Artistic people are usually right-brained. To be **left-brained** is the opposite—dominated by logic and analytical thought with lots of verbal communication. For instance, lawyers are ordinarily left-brainers.

Let's begin with a simple breathing meditation:

1. Sit in a quiet place in a comfortable position. If you sit in a chair, keep your back straight so that your mind does not become sluggish. Sit with your eyes partially closed, and concentrate on your breathing.

2. Breathe naturally through your nostrils and become aware of the sensation of your breath as it enters and leaves the nostrils. The sensation is your object of meditation; try to concentrate on it to the exclusion of everything else.

   At first, your mind will be very busy, and you may think that the meditation is making your mind busier, but in reality, you are just becoming more aware of how busy your mind really is. You may be tempted to follow some of your thoughts, but remain focused on the sensation of your breath. If you discover that your mind has wandered, immediately return it to the breath.

3. As you breathe out, imagine that you are breathing away all disturbing thoughts and distractions in the form of black smoke that disappears into space. As you breathe in, imagine that you are breathing in all that is good in the form of white light that enters your body. Maintain this visualization with each inhalation and exhalation until your mind becomes peaceful and alert. As you concentrate on your breathing in this way, negative thoughts and distractions will

disappear because you are not capable of concentrating on more than one object at a time.

At the conclusion of this meditation, your mind is like a clean white slate that you can fill with virtuous motivation.

If you practice patiently in this way, gradually your distracting thoughts will subside and you will experience a sense of inner peace and relaxation. When the constant flow of your distracting thoughts is calmed through concentrating on the breath, your mind becomes clear and refreshed. Even though breathing meditation is only a preliminary stage of meditation, it can be quite powerful. You can see by this practice that you can achieve some inner peace just by controlling the mind, without having to depend on external conditions. When your distracting thoughts subside and your mind becomes still, a deep happiness and contentment rise from within.

> **Visionary Insights**
>
> Try doing your meditation right in front of your tray of sand or sandbox so you do not have to leave the area. If that's not possible, when you go to the area where you will be divining, take a few deep breaths to get yourself back into the mode.

Time to Get Moving

Now that your outer awareness has become inner concentration, you should be in an excellent state of mind for this technique of divining by sand or for the following smoke-reading process. If possible, go right from your meditation into the reading process.

How to Do a Sand-Sational Reading

There are no demanding rules here when it comes to divining by sand. Yet this can be such a rewarding occurrence.

Make sure you have your equipment in place:

- Sand
- Pencil or stick
- Blindfold

Your tray should have a minimum of 2 or 3 inches of sand. If you are using a tub or sandbox, you no doubt will already have at least that amount.

If you live near a beach or sandy place, you can go there to do the divining. However, people who see you may think you're strange, to say the least. Drawing attention to yourself will affect the accuracy of a reading. But hey, if you can find a secluded area, give it a whirl. Just remember to bring a pencil or stick.

If you like, set the mood by putting on some music and lighting incense or candles (see Chapter 4). Then follow these steps:

1. Seat yourself in front of your tray or in your sandy area.

2. Blindfold yourself or have someone else do it. (The reason for the blindfold is to keep out distractions so you can completely focus. That's another reason you don't want to go to the beach to do this reading.)

3. Hold your stick or pencil in your writing hand.

4. If you're using a tray, your wrist should rest on the rim. If not using a tray, rest your stick in the sand holding on to the end.

5. Ask a question to yourself silently, or focus your thoughts on a matter for which you want answers.

6. Wait until you feel you are led to start moving your pencil. This could take a few minutes, so be patient.

7. Holding your pencil loosely, let it move upon the sand freely. Do not try to write or guide it in any fashion. Continue to focus your thoughts on the subject of your interest.

8. When your hand stops moving, remove your blindfold. Look at the sand. You will see shapes and possibly numbers or letters.

Sand Marks and More

While looking at the sand, do your best to be honest and come up with your own answers. There are no mistakes here.

If you asked a yes-or-no question, see if you find a *Y* or an *N*. Can you see the initials of a person's name? Do you see an image that might give you guidance? Perhaps you were concerned about money, and you now see dollar signs in the sand.

This may sound easy and not very involved, but the actual sand writing is where your intuition plays its largest part.

Be imaginative. Did you ask whether you will get a new job, and the first thing you spot is what looks like a computer? Maybe you will be working with computers.

In this case, the interpretations of your sand marks are left to your intuition, as opposed to a list of signs and symbols you can review.

That being said, seven sand marks seem to appear commonly among those who divine by sand. Therefore, the general consensus is that these particular marks may be considered to have established meanings:

- **One short, deep line**—An unexpected visitor, caller, or message

- **One long, deep line**— A journey

- **A small circle** —A partnership

- **A large circle**—Trouble or a mishap

- **A cross**—Obstacles to surmount

- **An *x***—A love affair (the clearer the *x*, the stronger the chance of having the affair)

- **A triangle**—Success in business or work

Do not conduct your sand divining for more than 5 minutes.

If it is taking you longer to pick up messages, wait for another day or you will frustrate yourself and compromise your accuracy. "If it don't flow, it don't go."

If your hand simply will not move, wait until another time or day, and try again. It could take many days and many attempts before you get in sync with the intuitive part of your brain that moves your hand.

The Sands of Time

Consider your sandbox or tray from left to right as a one-year period, with the very left being the present and moving on from there. This will allow you to understand when something may happen. For instance, if your marks fall in the middle of the tray, that represents about six months. The first quarter of the tray would represent three months, and so on.

When you are finished, smooth out the sand in the tray by shaking it. If you have a large container or sandbox, use the edge of a piece of something flat and square, such as a piece of cardboard. It is important to remove your images because these have your personal energy on them and shouldn't be left exposed for all to see.

Where There's Smoke, There Are Visions

For hundreds of years, Native Americans invoked visions to see into the future. They used many different types of techniques to induce these impressions. Whether they were shamans, warriors, or chiefs, they all had something in common. They wanted to know their destiny. They looked for visions in sweat lodges, they smoked peace pipes, and they danced until dawn without food or sleep so they could induce a trance state. Another common method Native Americans employed was "seeing" into smoke for a glimpse of their future.

def•i•ni•tion

Shamans are members of tribal societies who act as mediums between the real world and the world beyond the physical. They practice magic of sorts for divination, healing, and occurrences in nature. **Sweat lodges** are a type of sauna used as a ceremonial tool. Sometimes these are teepees or dome-shaped structures made of branches and blankets. Hot stones might be put on the ground to heat the lodge, or sometimes fires are used.

This technique of seeing visions in smoke is easy to do and quite exciting. With practice, anyone can learn this method that not only predicts future events, but fills you with wisdom. And I'm not blowing smoke up your pipe, either.

When Smoke Gets in Your Eyes, You Can "See" Better

You have a few choices of how to create the smoke you will be reading. The obvious and most dramatic is a campfire. If you're at a campground, that works well, but if not, you have to scale down. A fireplace also works well, but we don't all have fireplaces. Therefore, get yourself a big, inexpensive, white or off-white candle. White or off-white is important because it doesn't have the interference of other vibrations or influences that the other candle colors do. White or off-white candles are pure in one sense, as in the color, but burn in a dark smoky manner. Perhaps it is a balance of the positive and the negative. And yes, it must be inexpensive, as in low quality. You want a low-quality white candle because it doesn't burn clean like the more expensive grade. A low-quality candle will produce more black smoke, and that's what we're looking for. So if your friend gave you a high-quality candle for your birthday, save it for something else.

> **Notions Through Time**
>
> I believe that there is a subtle magnetism in Nature, which, if we unconsciously yield to it, will direct us aright.
>
> —Henry David Thoreau, U.S. naturalist and writer

The shape of the candle doesn't matter. If you can't find a large candle, use three or more smaller ones.

Let's Get Smokin'

Before we get started, keep in mind that you must always use safety when dealing with fire of any kind. That means never leaving a burning candle or campfire unattended, and safely extinguishing it when you are done.

You will need the following:

- Chair
- Inexpensive white candle
- Matches or lighter
- Tape-recording device
- Something to snuff out the candle—a cup or snuffer

Follow these steps:

1. Locate a quiet, safe place where you will be undisturbed.

2. Place a straight-backed chair near a table or desk. It is important that your feet be able to touch the floor from this chair. If you are outside you can sit on the ground in any comfortable position as long as you make contact with the ground, which gives you that connection to nature. You can also sit in a chair, or on a log or rock, if you feel more comfortable.

3. Turn on your tape recorder or recording device.

4. Light your candle (unless you are outside with a campfire already safely burning).

5. Sit in the chair with your feet flat on the ground or touching the ground and your hands on your legs, with your palms facing up.

6. Close your eyes and ask your higher power or guide to protect you from negativity.

7. Take a few deep breaths and visualize white light descending from the top of your head to the floor. As it runs down your body, feel yourself relaxing.

8. Open your eyes and see the smoke rise above the candle or campfire. Continue to gaze, but do not follow the smoke up to the ceiling or sky or move your head about. Keep your head steady and focused in one spot that is comfortable.

9. Keep your mind as clear as possible. In time, you will see people, places, and things take shape in the smoke.

10. Describe aloud what you are seeing so that your recorder can pick it up.

11. As the images fade, you will know it is time to stop.

12. Thank your higher power or spiritual guides for their presence.

You may not see images right away, but keep practicing. With time and effort, your labor will be worth the wait.

Extinguish your candle and listen to your recording. You may want to make notes in your journal for future reference.

The Least You Need to Know

♦ Meditation techniques help in sand divining and smoke visions.

♦ When writing in the sand, hold your pen or stick loosely, and don't force it to move.

♦ Your intuition is more important in these techniques than definitions of symbols.

♦ Use an inexpensive white candle for smoke impressions.

Chapter 9

Candle Wax Divination

In This Chapter

- ◆ Candles really do light the way
- ◆ What candles work best
- ◆ A new moon candle ritual
- ◆ Two ways to divine without getting burned

Nothing beats the warm glow of candles in a room for creating a romantic atmosphere. But there is a time and place for everything, and the candles we will be working with create something even more stimulating: they create a way of fortune telling by reading the melted wax. Throw in a little new moon ritual, and *poof*—you have answers and messages that may dazzle you!

You can let the candle burn down and see what sticks to the surface, or you can use a bowl of water. I'll tell you about both methods in this chapter.

Lighting the Fires of Time

Before electricity, the use of candles was the main means of shining light into dark places. Therefore, it would make sense that as the candles dripped and the wax melted, our ancients found that the wax formed designs. This form of divination was especially prevalent in Europe during the Middle Ages.

def•i•ni•tion

Magick is sometimes spelled with a *k* to differentiate it as something done by magickal practitioners and others who practice supernatural methods, as opposed to magicians who perform "stage magic" or who are "illusionists." However, for simplicity, I use the spelling magic throughout this book.

Naturally, in those times, almost everything seemed to be used as a form of fortune telling, and this was no exception. But this one is particularly good because it's fun and interesting. Perhaps you will agree if you choose to experiment with it.

Candle magic (sometimes spelled *magick*) was also practiced. Candle magic deals with spinning spells to get what you want. Note that there is a difference between *candle divination* and *candle magic*. In candle divination, which we will be doing in this chapter, you are reading future events or fortune telling. You are not attempting to change your future or alter events that you would like to happen, as you would with a spell.

Burning Hot for the Optimum Reading

Fire is considered an element of mystic metamorphosis or change. Therefore, using fire and wax to divine the future is a very powerful experience. It shifts your consciousness into an altered state, allowing you to analyze psychic impressions.

Color Your Wax

For candle wax divination, the best candles to use are either black or purple. Far from being considered negative, a black candle generates psychic insights. A purple candle represents wisdom, intuition, and success. Also, because of their dark colors, it's easier to "read" the wax.

Black candles are not as difficult to find as you may think. Companies sell them scented as licorice, and you can also find them on the Internet or in candle stores.

They are very common around Halloween, and some people buy them on sale the day afterward and use them for the rest of the year.

If you are asking a specific question, you may prefer to use a specific candle color, such as green for money. This is your choice. Refer to the color interpretation chart in Chapter 4. However, as a quick reference, here are the most popular colors and their meanings:

- **Blue**—Health and truth
- **Green**—Prosperity and money
- **Pink**—Love and friendship
- **Red**—Passion and sexuality

It is still the easiest to use a purple or black candle because this way you are covered on many topics.

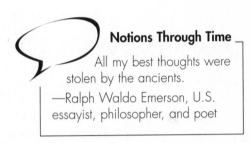

Notions Through Time

All my best thoughts were stolen by the ancients.
—Ralph Waldo Emerson, U.S. essayist, philosopher, and poet

You Need a Nice Shape

When reading wax drippings, it is important to use a candle that drips. Stay clear of dripless or paraffin candles. The drippier the candle, the better.

The best shape to use is a taper or narrow dinner candle. The reasons for this are presented later in the chapter. Do not use extra-long candles because they will have to burn all the way down according to one method, and that could take too long. Therefore, use a short or medium length.

That Smells Good

If you like fragrances, there is no reason not to use a scented candle. This should be a pleasant experience, so do whatever it takes to feel good (as long as it's legal, of course).

If you buy an unscented candle, you can dab a few drops of a scented oil on the candle to give it a little kick. Please do this before you light it.

You can also include incense with this form of divination, as suggested in Chapter 4, if you want to set the mood.

New Moon Candle Ritual

If you like rituals, you can include this one before proceeding with your candle-wax fortune-telling process. While it's not necessary to do this ritual before practicing candle divination, doing so may boost your powers of perception by helping to open your third eye, the source of your intuition.

The day or night you are doing your wax reading, face east (you can stand or sit either inside or outside) with your lit candle in hand. Remember, the direction east corresponds to starting anything anew.

Visualize a protective white light around yourself.

Say these words:

> *New Moon bring my future bright,*
> *a powerful reading for me tonight.*

(Say this even if you do it during the day—it doesn't matter.)

Now take three deep breaths through your nose, and exhale through you mouth.

Visualize your white light lifting, and begin your candle wax divination.

> **Enlightening Extras**
>
> A good time to conduct your candle wax divination is the day or night of a new moon or when the moon is waxing. This is a time of new beginnings. A full moon works well but can be too overwhelming if you have never done this because the energy is profound. (See Chapter 2 for more on the moon phases.)

Two Methods of Reading Wax

When you feel that you have chosen the candle that will work for you and have selected your day, it is time to begin.

A Mess Can Be Good

This process is a bit on the untidy side, but it is still engaging and provides a good reading.

Here's what you need:

- Candle
- Candle holder (plain and inexpensive)

- Tin pan or throw-away plate

- Lighter or matches

Place your candle in a simple holder. Put a tin pan or something disposable and non-flammable under the candle that can sit on a table. Place the candle in the middle of the pan or plate, and light the candle. As you light the candle, think of your question or keep in mind that you want general information and are looking for messages, not answers.

Allow the candle to drip for a long time, or down completely. I am talking up to 30 minutes—not 3 days to a week! The wax will finally drop onto the tin pan or plate, forming shapes. While you are waiting for the candle to burn down, carry on as you normally would during the course of the day. However, stay in the general area or room where the candle is located so you can keep an eye on the flame. Safety is always the most important thing.

If the candle has not completely burned down, you can extinguish it when intuition tells you that enough wax has fallen. Keep the candle in place: lifting it may disturb the wax that has already fallen. You will see that the melted wax has made shapes and forms. Look at these forms, and try to determine what you think the shapes mean to you. Write down your thoughts; later, as the days move on, see how accurate you were. You will be surprised.

For example, if you see a heart and you were asking a question about love, it is a good sign. If that heart looks like it is broken, though, you could be headed for heartbreak hotel. If you see what looks like dollar signs, it could be money coming your way. An airplane could mean a trip.

It may be helpful to review the tea-leaf interpretations in Chapter 5 for insights.

Once you feel that you have picked up messages or had questions answered, clean the area and reflect on the images in the wax. Some people leave the candle sitting out for a few days and keep going back to the melted wax to see if they can find any new visions the next day. This requires room and understanding from those living with us. Once you extinguish the candle, do not reuse the candle for another session; the energy has already been depleted.

Visionary Insights

Always practice safety when working with candles and fire. Make sure the burning candle is well away from children and pets, and never leave a burning candle unattended.

Who Says Water and Fire Don't Mix?

Another form of reading wax is to drip the wax into water. This is fun.

Here's what you need:

- Candle

- Bowl (the bowl should be plain, with no print on the inside; it doesn't matter if the outside has a design)

- Lighter or matches

Stand or sit at a table, a kitchen sink, or somewhere with a solid platform. Fill your bowl halfway to the top with cool water. Light your candle and ask your question or think about a general message. Once the wax starts to accumulate on the top of the candle, let the excess wax drip into the bowl of water. The wax will float on top, forming an image. If you are asking questions, you can ask and drip, and ask and drip. If you are doing a general reading, do not examine the water wax until you feel you have used enough wax. You do not have to let the entire candle burn down. Also, be careful that you do not allow the hot candle wax to drip on your hands. Drip it into the water before it starts to run.

As the wax floats in the bowl, you will pick up images as mentioned earlier. Feel free to use the tea-leaf interpretations here as well (see Chapter 5). It's fascinating how these images can pertain to the questions asked or the messages that appear; I don't think it's just a coincidence how this wax is patterned.

Notions Through Time

Coincidence is God's way of remaining anonymous.
—Albert Einstein, U.S. physicist

As I was writing these words, I took a break and did a candle divination asking if I would get a "go ahead" from a party about a writing endeavor that's important to me in the future. I got an answer of "yes," which logically I was 99 percent sure was wrong, because the possibilities were slim to none that I could get this break. But sure enough, it transpired within 30 minutes, and I got a wonderful, positive response. I was extremely glad I was wrong. The point is, you should not be too quick to judge. Give it awhile and see what happens. Your answer may not always take place within a few minutes, but be open-minded and do not put out negative arrows of disbelief.

One other observation to make while dripping your wax in the bowl is that it can sometimes cast shadows on the bottom of the bowl, depending on the lighting around you. If you see the mystifying shadows and they are clearer than the wax or you are led to read them instead, please try! It's amazing what can be found in the shadows.

The Least You Need to Know

- ◆ Because fire is considered an element of change, candle divination can be a very powerful way to divine the future.

- ◆ Medium or short tapers in a purple or black color are best for divination. Don't use dripless or paraffin candles.

- ◆ Performing a new moon ritual before candle divination may help boost your powers of intuition.

- ◆ You can use two methods to read wax; both can yield some amazing images.

Part  3

Fortune Telling with Games

Are these just parlor games or "real" fortune telling? Well, that depends on how skeptical you are. If you are closed-minded, then they are only games of amusement. (And actually, what's so wrong with fun and games?) However, if you are adventuresome and are open to all things the universe has to offer, then they are a means of foretelling your destiny. Either way, they should be entertaining. And for some of us wild and psychic thinkers, they also can spell out our future!

A Ouija board and a deck of cards can go a long way on the night of a full moon. At least they are more dependable than some men I know, and you don't have to shave your legs first.

Ouija Boards: The Directions You Won't Find in the Box

In This Chapter

◆ A fun game or a controversial form of divination?

◆ How to make your own Ouija board

◆ When and where to use the Ouija board

◆ Teaming up or going it alone

◆ Everything you always wanted to ask

◆ Tips for using the Ouija board

Ouija boards … a mysterious portal to the other side or just a game that relies on people's nervous systems? Are you really receiving messages from those who have crossed over? Or was this just another idea from a toy-maker to generate sales? Let's explore the answers to these questions.

Are you worried about the tales you've heard and the movies you've seen featuring Ouija boards? Well, fear not, my thrill seeker. The devil himself will not be squeezing you into the board. Neither will lightning strike you (at least, if there's no thunderstorm brewing). Relax as you learn the secrets of how to use this form of divination by yourself or with someone else. The Ouija board's mystic history, exotic appearance, and arcane abilities make it one of the most fascinating of all the forms of divination.

Portal to the Unknown?

A *Ouija board* is said to answer questions and give messages. Some believe the messages come from the deceased or from beings not of this world. You'll have to see for yourself, once you master the simple techniques, whether you feel you are making contact with the beyond.

Two people typically use a Ouija board. To begin, each person gently sets his or her fingertips on the *planchette*. A question is posed, and the planchette moves across the board, stopping on a series of numbers or letters, or the words *yes*, *no*, or *good-bye*.

def•i•ni•tion

A **Ouija board** is the trademarked name for the William Fuld/Parker Brothers board. The general name for this oracle is a "talking board." However, because of its popularity, the trademark "Ouija board" became commonly used to describe any talking or spirit board. A **planchette** is a heart-shaped pointer that is used to point to the letters or words on the Ouija board. Placing the fingers gently on top of the planchette enables it to move across the board, spelling out messages.

The word Ouija is actually pronounced "Wee-Ja." However, over time the name somehow became incorrectly pronounced as "Wee-Gee." William Fuld, an inventor and toymaker, brought new life to the game in 1892 when he was granted a patent, after the original one that had been granted to its inventor, Elijah J. Bond, expired.

Fuld claimed that the word Ouija was a combination of the French word *oui* for "yes" and the German word *ja* for "yes." A board made by the William Fuld Company has the pronunciation on the box as "We-Ja." In 1966, when Parker Brothers acquired ownership of William Fuld, Inc., it offered the option: The box said "Whether you call it Wee-Gee … or Wee-Ja … the Ouija board spells fun!"

Some say whatever way you pronounce it, the concept of the Ouija board spells controversy. The age-old question is, what makes the pointer move? Are you unconsciously moving it yourself, is your partner moving it, or are there really disembodied entities moving it? And even if you are unconsciously moving the planchette, is something out there still leading you to certain letters and sentences?

If you have an old Ouija board in the attic or basement, hold on to it. Parker Brothers stopped manufacturing the boards in the early part of 1999. Its replacement is a glow-in-the-dark version. If you do not own a Ouija board, you may want to buy one of these new ones, or you can purchase a used one, find an artisan who makes them, or make one of your own (as discussed in the next section).

Visionary Insights

Auction sites on the Internet are a great way of finding old Ouija boards. Don't forget about garage sales, thrift shops, and consignment stores. Think about becoming a collector if you really take a liking to them. Each one has its own unique energy, offering a little something different.

Making Your Own Board

To create your own Ouija board, use a large piece of cardboard or poster board, approximately 14 inches wide by 10 inches high. Also find a cup or wine glass to use as your pointer or planchette.

Using a felt-tipped marker of any color, write the alphabet in two rows on the middle of the cardboard. From left to right, the top row should be the letters "a" through "m." The bottom row should be the letters "n" through "z."

Under the bottom row of letters, write the following numbers:

     1 2 3 4 5 6 7 8 9 0

(That's a "0" after the "9," not a "10.")

Under the row of letters, in the center, write the word "good bye." On the top left corner of the cardboard, write the word "yes." On the top right corner, write the word "no."

Place the wine glass or cup upside down on the cardboard to serve as your planchette, and rest your fingers on top of it. You are ready to begin!

When and Where to Ouija

You'll need to gather the following supplies to play with your Ouija board:

♦ Ouija board, bought or homemade. Make sure it is dust-free.

♦ Table, counter, or desk. Traditionally, you can use your lap to place the board on as well.

- Paper and pen or pencil.

- Two chairs.

- A third person who acts as the note taker, or a tape recorder or camcorder.

You can set the environment with music, candles, and any other of the elements discussed in Chapter 4. What's important is that you feel that you are setting the appropriate mood and that you are able to concentrate undistracted on the messages that come through.

Night Fright

When you are just starting out with the Ouija board, you might not want to do it at night. Some say that because the world slows down at night, the veil between the two worlds—the world of the living and the world of the dead—grows thinner. Although this can result in some powerful Ouija board sessions, you might not be ready just yet for that kind of encounter. Some people find it frightening. Better to start during the daytime, when you can get used to the way the Ouija board works and acts.

Other Times

When you have some experience, you can use your board any time. As I mentioned in Chapter 2, full moons are powerful times for any divination. Some people won't use Ouija boards on the days or nights of solar or lunar eclipses; some say negative entities have easier access to the physical plane at the time of eclipses because it is a gateway for things to enter our domain more easily. This can also be said for thunderstorms. However, I feel that if you protect yourself with white light techniques, as recommended in Chapter 1, and you are strong of mind, you may want to try it and see what happens. Fortune telling is supposed to be fun, so experiment a bit.

Visionary Insights

Halloween, also known in the Celtic tradition as Samhain (pronounced "Sowen"), is a great time to use the Ouija board. According to ancient lore from all over the world, this is the time of year when the veil between the worlds is thinnest and when communing with the dead is not only possible, but desirable. In Mexico, *Dios de los Muertos*, or "The Day of the Dead," is celebrated with dancing skeletons and much merriment! So get in the spirit, so to speak, by pulling out your Ouija board, and see if anyone from the Great Beyond has something to say!

A Safe Place

The best place to use your board, as with any divination tool, is in an environment where you feel safe and won't be disturbed. Many people bring their Ouija boards to cemeteries, but some warn not to use this mystical seer in a cemetery because you may attract negative entities that could harm you. A better reason to stay away from cemeteries is out of respect for families who may be visiting. For safety reasons alone, if you're going at night, use good judgment.

Whether you are inside or outside should not make a difference when using a Ouija board. Try facing west, where the sun sets, when using this oracle; west represents endings and, therefore, death. Consider that our loved ones travel to the west when crossing over to the other side. Hence, this becomes their doorway.

Haunted places can seem like ideal spots for a session, but the question of whether to use a Ouija board there is debatable. Locations where there is known to be legitimate paranormal activity may make your indicator move like the wind! The results can be fascinating. However, make sure you are dealing with "beings of the light" (the nice ones). You will know by the way you feel during the session whether they are friendly. Also, if you start to see language that is not dignified, stop the session.

Naturally, you should not trespass on anyone's property to conduct such an experiment. However, if you are staying at a bed and breakfast or hotel that is said to have ghosts, you may want to bring along your board or create a makeshift board. As always, if this makes you uncomfortable or strikes great fear in you, just don't try it.

If you bring a Ouija board into someone's home and that person asks you to remove it, do it without asking questions. Do not try to debate or defend it, because this can be a sore spot with some people. Give them the respect they deserve with a smile on your face, and be understanding.

The Traditional Way to Use the Ouija Board

The Ouija board is perhaps more conducive to pairing up with other interested parties than any other form of divination. The traditional directions of the Ouija board say that the best results are achieved when two people of the opposite sex participate. You may want to experiment with someone who is open to this experience. Opposite genders may give your session more balance, but two females or two males can also create a strong force.

If you are going to work with a partner, make it a person who is like-minded. Having to convince someone to help you is wasting your time and energy. It's like starting a trip with extra baggage. It is fine for the other person to be skeptical, as long as he or she does not joke or make light of your intention. If you can't find someone to undertake this process with you, opt for doing it alone.

Getting Ready

When you find a suitable partner, do a bit of planning. You may ask a third person to join you and act as a note taker who will write down the letters on which your pointer stops. This way, you don't have to break the flow of energy by lifting your hand from the planchette to write things down. If you do not have a person who can act as secretary, you may use a tape recorder. You can speak the letters or numbers into the tape recorder and write them down later. If you have neither a note taker nor a tape recorder, try to remember the letters the best you can, or ask the spirit you are working with to wait while you break away and write down the information. Spirits are generally pretty patient (but not always!).

> **Visionary Insights** ___
>
> Standard directions suggest placing the Ouija board on your laps, but excellent results can be achieved when two people sit across a table from each other. Sometimes balancing the board on your knees causes a certain amount of stress because it is not stable. Experiment—what is right for one is not always right for all.

Light your incense, then your candles, or make whatever preparations you feel are appropriate. Then sit down. You and your partner should be seated facing each other. If you have a note taker, he or she should be standing or seated near you with a good view of the board. Your helper should not be in a position that makes you uncomfortable, such as standing behind you. If you are using a tape recorder, now is the time to turn it on.

As a form of psychic protection, you and your partner should visualize a cloud or circle of white light around yourselves, the table or board, and any other participants such as a note taker. This is a protective method of keeping negative entities out of your space. It should extend at least 6 feet out all around. You and your partner will see this differently in your mind's eye but it does not matter.

Both you and your partner should place the fingertips of both hands gently on the planchette or pointer. (If you have long nails, you can gently just touch your nails on the board. You do not have to have your fingers directly touching the planchette. The energy from your fingers moves through your nails.) Intentionally move the pointer in a circle a few times to get the feel of the board and stir up a little energy.

Both of you must be very serious and ask only one question at a time. Do not carry on a conversation or laugh. Rolling eyes and making faces may be tempting, but try to refrain. The note taker should be as quiet as possible.

Asking Questions

Preface your session by inviting the spirit to communicate with you, and asking the spirit to please try to spell as well as possible and speak in English. Only one person should ask questions at a time. When you get an answer, if the other participant wants to ask a question, that's fine. Both parties can ask and speak during one session. Here are a few questions you can start with:

1. **Is there a spirit present?** Allow several minutes to get an answer. The note taker should write down the question and any answers that are received. Be aware that you may not receive a "yes" or "no" answer. It may be something like "here" or "now."

2. **What is your name?** If the name you receive is confusing, write it down anyway. It could be initials or something that sounds like the letters. If the spelling is gibberish, you may refer to the spirit by just the first letter. For example, if the planchette spells out Qtzhm, call him or her "Q." Sometimes the guides do not want to give a name, so do not insist.

3. **Are you male?** *or* **Are you female?** Again, you may not get an actual "yes" or "no" answer. The answer you draw could be just the letters "Y" or "N." It may also be "m" for male or "f" for female. I have even seen answers such as "note" meaning no and "aye" meaning yes.

At this point, you are ready to ask your personal questions. You and your partner can take turns asking questions, if you like. Keep in mind that dead people don't necessarily know anything more about things like the future than they did when they were alive. Also, realize that spirits lie, just like people do. Just because you're a spirit doesn't make you a saint.

Keep your questions as simple as possible. For example:

- What are the initials of my future husband?

- Will I pass that course?

- In what room will I find car keys?

More difficult questions will confuse the spirit talking to you and should not be asked until you have more experience and your focus is very, very good. For example:

- What is my purpose in life?

- If Tony gets a divorce, will he want to date me, or will he be looking for a tall blonde?

- What are the names of the first-, second-, and third-place winning dogs that will come in today at the eighth race at the dog track?

I have had interesting sessions with the Ouija by asking about the afterlife. After all, that's one thing dead people do know about. For example, when it seems certain that a spirit is communicating through the Ouija board, I might ask, "What should we do to prepare for death?" or, "What words would you use to describe the afterlife?" I don't want to give you the chills, but I've received some pretty interesting answers!

One time while consulting the Ouija board with a friend of mine, we asked that the spirit talking to us give us a sign so we knew we were in contact. Within 30 seconds, a picture of my friend's deceased aunt fell off the fireplace mantel to the floor! Her cat saw the picture on the floor and ran out of the room. To this day if we bring out the Ouija board, the cat will not stay in the room. Was it the fact that the picture fell and scared the cat, and it now associates being frightened with a Ouija board? Or did the cat sense a presence?

You might want to ask about specific people you know who have died. Sometimes a spirit is willing to be a go-between and relay messages from another spirit. If someone dear to you has died, consider trying to communicate with that person directly or through another spirit. If you do make contact, I'm sure I don't have to tell you what questions to ask. You'll have plenty.

When you feel you have completed your session, thank the spirits, place your planchette on *good-bye*, and release your circle of light or whatever protective energy you have put around yourself for the session. To do this, simply visualize the cloud or circle of light lifting and floating to the ceiling, moving through the ceiling, and out into the atmosphere or outer space. Put your board away in a safe place. Now is the time to sit with your note taker or tape recorder and decipher what it all means.

Three or More Participants

If you have more than two people, follow the same directions as for the two-person method. Have each person place only two fingers on the message pointer. Do not use more than four people. Four is a number that will work, but be prepared to feel a bit crowded. You are better off with three actively working the planchette and the fourth person acting as the note taker.

Try to avoid getting involved in confrontations about who is moving the pointer. Everyone does influence it, to a certain extent, but that doesn't mean they're doing it on purpose. Do not shift the positive energy into one of confrontation. If you feel someone is particularly heavy-handed, ask him or her nicely to remove their hands for a few seconds and place them back on the planchette gently. Do not make anyone feel guilty.

The Solitary Method

You may have heard that if you use a Ouija board alone, bad spirits will overtake and possess you. Too much Hollywood! If you use protection techniques as suggested earlier in this chapter and in Chapter 1, you can use any board successfully by yourself without any negative reaction.

Follow the same directions as you would with two people. If you do not have a recorder to record your answers, you can use a one-handed technique. If you are right-handed, place the fingertips of your left hand on the planchette and have your right hand ready to go with a pen to write down the communication on a piece of paper. If you are left-handed, do the opposite. This works well if you get used to it. If you are not comfortable with this technique, ask your spirit to be patient while you pause to write. Before starting, visualize your protective white light around you, the board, the table, and finally the entire room. You are more vulnerable when alone. When you are finished, place your planchette on *good-bye*, release your circle up into the cosmos, and close the board.

On one occasion when I was single and attempting to work the Ouija board by myself, I asked the board if a certain gentleman was going to contact me. It said "yes." I continued to ask "when?" and the board said "here" but spelled it "herre," which is not unusual. Suddenly the doorbell rang. It was the gentleman I had just been inquiring about. He said he was in the neighborhood and had a "feeling" it would be okay to simply drop by. Coincidence?

> **Enlightening Extras**
>
> Some Ouija boards do not use the greeting words of hello or good-bye, but may use greetings, welcome, or open. For closure, they may use end, finish, or close.

Ouija Wisdom

There is much Ouija folklore and many warnings that have no credence, but some precautions make good sense. Here are some tips for using the Ouija board:

◆ When buying a used board, it's important to clear it before you use it. There are many ways to clear things of old energy from other users. Try one of these methods:

1. Put your Ouija on a platform of any type: table, chair, desk, and so on. Make a sweeping motion, with one of your arms outstretched as if you were sweeping air. Visualize all the energy of any past owners or anything that has attached itself to the board leaving to the west. Repeat it as many times as you like, until you "know" the board is clear. You can turn the board over and do it to the back surface as well, if you like.

2. Buy a smudge stick of white sage and smudge the board. Native American, health-food, and metaphysical stores usually carry these. To smudge, light the stick and blow out the flame. It will begin to smolder. Make circular motions over the board (not touching it), and know that it is being cleared of any negativity and vibrations. When you intuitively feel that the board is cleared, extinguish the smudge stick. Some people clear their boards before and after every use. That's certainly an excellent idea but is not necessary.

◆ Do not use the board when you are depressed, angry, high, or intoxicated. Although this is true in general for any divination, it is especially important when using the Ouija because you are directly inviting spirits to come into your space. Under inebriated or altered conditions, you are in a weakened state of mind and are leaving yourself wide open to dysfunctional entities that can penetrate your protective aura.

◆ At the beginning of your session, if the planchette moves gently in a deliberate configuration, someone may be trying to give you his or her trademark. In other words, certain shapes such as a "figure eight" or a wavy line can be a spirit's identification. Every time you feel that particular shape, you know it is the same spirit.

◆ If you are worried that you are moving the pointer yourself to create words, you may want to try closing your eyes. When the pointer stops, open your eyes, note the letter, and continue on. If the pointer is moving too quickly, though, this won't be practical.

♦ Understand that spirits are not always good spellers. You must make a certain amount of effort to interpret the words: for example, "wkr" may be the word *work*. A naughty spirit once spelled out "ruez" during one of my Ouija sessions. Translated, the spirit was asking, "Are you easy?" Sometimes it's a good idea to say each letter aloud.

♦ If a spirit starts spelling out any type of profanity or you are receiving messages of an intimate nature, ask the spirit to leave or ask other guides to escort the spirit out for you, and then continue. If you are deeply offended or concerned, you can just stop the session completely.

♦ While you are in the middle of a Ouija consultation, a new spirit may suddenly come through. If you get the feeling a new one has taken over, merely ask if there is a new spirit present. Ask its name and whatever else you would like to know.

♦ If you do not understand what the spirit is trying to communicate, feel free to ask the question again, or ask the same question in a different way.

♦ If you ask for a "sign" of whether someone is present, you may be disappointed. This board does not give signs; it facilitates communication.

♦ If the planchette starts going around in circles or making crazy designs quickly, stop the use and wait until another day. You may have an entity that has become angry for some reason.

♦ If your indicator finds its way to the word *good-bye*, that means the spirit is leaving. Do not ask it to stay longer. It is finished. You may continue by asking if another spirit is present. If not, end the session.

♦ If you are trying to contact a dead loved one, be careful. If a spirit wants to contact you, it will. Trying to pressure someone from the other side may not be a good idea. We do not really know what it takes for them to return to this realm. Stick with the spirits who are willing to talk.

♦ Do not give up if you do not get the results you are looking for. Try, try again. Everything takes practice.

♦ Keep your Ouija board in a safe place and out of sight. Having it open to others can allow it to absorb their energy like a sponge.

♦ Always use caution and safety with everything you do pertaining to a Ouija board experience. Use common sense, and think of the board as a means for interesting insights and as a type of paranormal investigation and research. Do not live your life according to the words of this talking oracle.

◆ If you want to get rid of a Ouija board, you can sell it or give it away. Some people feel you should never burn a board or throw it in the trash. But if you clear your board, give it a quick blessing, and place it in a bag, you can no doubt burn it or throw it out without fear. The board is not going to pop out of the trashcan and come looking for you! The clearing and the blessing negate any remaining energy.

These tips are the results of previous exploration. The way you use your Ouija board still comes down to you and your personal beliefs. Always do what is best for you.

The Least You Need to Know

◆ Be patient with the spirits because they are not always clear and do not always spell correctly.

◆ Do not try to push the pointer with pressure—just lightly rest your fingers on it.

◆ Use your instincts about whatever spirits you are communicating with. If it doesn't feel comfortable, end the session.

◆ Don't live your life according to what the Ouija board tells you. Spirits often don't know much more than living people!

Chapter 11

Cartomancy

In This Chapter

- ◆ The future is in the cards
- ◆ The meanings behind the cards
- ◆ Reading cards in sequence
- ◆ Sample card spreads and interpretations
- ◆ Reading cards using the cross method

Regular playing cards were developed for amusement and divination. The divination eventually came to be known as cartomancy.

The 32-card method I present in this chapter is one of the simplest and most accurate forms of cartomancy. It allows you to get started in minutes. Different spreads are used for different types of questions and time frames, as you'll also discover here. You can learn how to accomplish these spreads and understand the definitions quickly. Before you know it, as a card reader, you will be more than able to make the cut.

Cards as a Form of Divination

Several cultures today can claim to have invented playing cards. But as with most traditions that have been handed down from our ancients, it's difficult to pinpoint who really started both the games of playing cards and using cards as a form of divination. Was it the ancient Celtic races, the Gypsies in Russia, the Italians, the Germans, the Egyptians, or the French? All of these groups, plus many others, are potential inventors. Because no concrete proof points to one of them, though, we can only speculate.

Many people think that playing cards developed from *Tarot cards*, but it's the other way around. Some believe Tarot cards originated in Italy, but others argue that their origin was Egyptian. Tarot cards are very common and complicated. The information about Tarot is extremely abundant and beyond the scope of this book; if you're interested in learning more, you might want to check out *The Complete Idiot's Guide to Tarot Spreads Illustrated* (see Appendix B).

Cartomancy is making a comeback, so we'll focus on that here.

def•i•ni•tion

Tarot cards are a deck of 78 cards with varied pictures and symbolic images. They are used as a form of divination and as a tool for spiritual guidance. **Cartomancy** is the art of reading regular playing cards.

On a Personal Note ...

Reading regular playing cards is by far one of my favorite forms of fortune telling and my passion. When I was not even as tall as our kitchen table, I remember my grandmother reading cards in downtown Chicago. As she read, her clients would sip tea, and, in due course, she would read their tea leaves when they were finished—kind of a two-for-one reading.

My mother, grandfather, and sister all did readings. We were just one big, happy card-reading family. I cannot remember a time as a child when a deck of 32 cards wasn't sitting on the table or desk; it was a normal daily event at our house.

I highly recommend taking some time to learn this art. It is not only good for predicting the future, but it's also good for your nerves: when you're tense or anxious about something, the cards can give you something to do. I must have worn out a few decks asking if that guy I just met was going to call. Then if he didn't call, I could ask the cards if I would meet someone else. See what I mean? There was always hope. Sure beats the heck out of downing a pint of butter pecan ice cream or driving an hour to pass his house in hopes he might be walking the dog.

To this day, I carry cards in my purse, and I have a deck in front of me at my computer at all times.

Using Thirty-Two Cards

A regular deck of playing cards has 52 cards, which may have originally represented the 52 weeks of the year. For our purposes, we will use only 32 cards, so take out the cards numbered 2 through 6 and the Jokers.

There are a couple of different ideas as to why 32 cards are used. Some fortune tellers or gypsies use 28 of the cards to denote a 28-day lunar cycle (even though a true lunar cycle technically is 29 ½ days). The other four cards are added for information about the seasons, destiny, thoughts, and purpose, which I won't address in this beginner's look.

On the other hand, some say 32 cards are used for the sake of simplicity. The removal of 20 cards to simplify a card "reading" does seem sensible. Therefore, the lower numbers that are deemed less powerful are removed, with the exclusion of the ace.

Choosing a Deck of Cards

When looking for a deck of cards, any deck will do. The cards can be used or new; it's even okay if they smell like smoke because you bought them on an auction site from a family of smokers. Naturally, some card readers out there will disagree with me, and they are entitled to do so. But this is my professional opinion, and I'm sticking to it. The only reason one would go through the trouble of buying a simple deck of cards on an auction site or at an antique store is if that person likes or collects antique decks or old souvenir-type cards. I personally collect such cards because it's fun. Regardless, the readings with such cards are not different than with new ones. Some people just feel their "dated deck" is their special "fortune-telling deck."

Whether you buy a new deck of playing cards or use someone else's, you should clear them before the reading. To do this, simply face west (where the sun sets ... the place you send negative or stale vibrations). With the swish of your hand across the cards, move that energy out into the west. This can be done indoors or out.

Sometimes people are concerned about the design on the back of the cards. It doesn't matter one way or the other. You can select a plain design or one with lots of interesting detail. It's the front of the card that matters.

Before doing any reading, you may want to shuffle and look at your cards to get a feel for them. This is not necessary, but it's a way for you to feel more comfortable when you start your future reading.

Meanings of the Cards

Throughout this chapter, I will refer to *dark (negative)* and *light (positive) cards*, as well as *face cards*. It's a good idea to start to pay attention to these groups of cards, because this will become important later.

Let's look at the individual meanings of each card. You don't need to memorize the meanings, but try your best to become familiar with them. After a while, you will know their meanings by heart and won't even know how you did it.

Hearts

Hearts represent emotion, love, friendship, and all things personal.

Interpretations of hearts:

- ◆ **Ace**—Pertains to the home. The card or cards surrounding it denote the nature of the home situation.

- ◆ **King**—A young to middle-aged man with a fairly light complexion.

- ◆ **Queen**—A young adult female with light hair and light eyes. Usually kind and affectionate.

def•i•ni•tion

Dark (negative) cards are the black spades and the clubs. These cards are considered to have a more negative nature. **Light (positive) cards** are the red hearts and the diamonds, which are considered lighter in nature. **Face cards** are the court cards, which are the kings, queens, and jacks. Regardless of the suit, face cards are not considered positive or negative.

- ◆ **Jack**—A young man or woman under 18 or a child with light hair and light eyes. If next to the king of hearts, it represents the thoughts of the person you see as the king of hearts.

- ◆ **Ten**—Good luck, happiness, and maybe even a commitment proposal—at the least, moonlight kisses!

- ◆ **Nine**—Best card in the deck! This is your "wish card." If you are asking a question and this card comes up, you will get your wish. If a dark card is next to it, pay attention to the meaning of that card because it could indicate a delay.

- **Eight**—Romance, emotional commitment, forgiveness, love.

- **Seven**—A surprise. If it's next to a face card, that will tell you the source of the surprise.

Diamonds

Diamonds represent money, papers, and fortune.

Interpretations of diamonds:

- **Ace**—A letter or message. Nowadays, it could be an e-mail. If a face card is next to it, the message will come from that person. If a positive or light card is next to it, it will be a good message. If there is a dark card next to it, it will be indifferent.

Enlightening Extras
Because you interpret face cards as people, pay attention to the way you view them at the present. If a lady has blond hair but you know she dyes it, you should still look at her as blond.

- **King**—An older man with gray hair, or a middle-aged man with a light complexion and blue or green eyes.

- **Queen**—A light-haired lady over 30 with blond, white, or red hair, typically with blue or green eyes.

- **Jack**—A young man or woman under 18 who has a very light complexion and light eyes. If this card is next to the king of diamonds, it represents the thoughts of the person you associate with the king of diamonds.

- **Ten**—Big bucks! Lots of money and profit.

- **Nine**—A surprise. The cards surrounding it will tell you what kind of surprise it will be.

- **Eight**—Inheritance, something given in the form of money, or something of value—something beyond a normal paycheck.

- **Seven**—Success, or a gift that will surprise you. This also is a very important card: it can negate the negativity of the nine of spades, which is the most negative card in the deck. If you are asking a "yes" or "no" question, the nine of spades, which will be explained in a moment, is considered the answer "no." It is a card of disappointment. However, if you get the nine of spades pertaining to a question and the seven of diamonds falls above, below, or next to it, it cancels the negativity and means there is still a chance for a positive outcome.

Clubs

Clubs represent business endeavors, work, and wisdom.

Interpretations of clubs:

- ◆ **Ace**—Gifts or something given. It also can represent jealousy of a person or situation.

- ◆ **King**—A man with a medium to dark complexion, most likely over 18 to middle-aged.

- ◆ **Queen**—A young female adult with brunette hair and blue or brown eyes.

- ◆ **Jack**—A young man or woman under 18 with a medium complexion and brown or blue eyes. If this card is next to the king of clubs, it represents the thoughts of the person you associate with the king of clubs.

- ◆ **Ten**—Journey or change. It can also mean a business situation that is a bit chaotic.

- ◆ **Nine**—Luck "for sure." This card needs to be read with the cards around it for clarity.

- ◆ **Eight**—Uncertainty, stress, or anxiety in any area of life depending on the cards next to it, but especially in business dealings.

- ◆ **Seven**—Messages and possible delays in plans. This could mean someone coming to your door.

Spades

Spades represent mostly the disagreeable things in life.

Interpretations of spades:

- ◆ **Ace**—Trouble, or death if upside down. However, this is not always a physical death; it could be the death of a situation or emotion. If the card is right side up, it could mean a passionate love affair. This is the only card for which I use an upside down (reversed) meaning.

- ◆ **King**—A middle-aged or older man with a dark complexion.

- ◆ **Queen**—A female over 30 with dark hair and dark eyes. It can also indicate a lady who is fair but is older and gray-haired.

- **Jack**—A young man or woman with a dark complexion. It can also mean the thoughts of a man you see as the king of spades.

- **Ten**—Hospital, court, school, or building; also, facts to be revealed.

- **Nine**—Disappointment. If I had to pick the worst card in the deck, this would be it. The only way to balance the negativity is if the seven of diamonds is above it, below it, or on either side of it.

- **Eight**—Trouble and things looking doubtful. However, this can also mean a situation that will take place at night.

- **Seven**—Health. This could be good or bad health, depending on the cards surrounding it. Also, it can denote that disappointment is coming your way.

> **Visionary Insights**
>
> My grandmother used to say that if the ace of spades comes up upside down, you should turn it right side up immediately. If you do it fast enough, you might prevent a negative situation from happening. To this day, I turn that card in a New York minute. Why take chances?

Cards in Sequence

When "like" cards of the same denomination fall together in a card spread so that the corners touch in any manner, the meanings can take on a whole new dimension.

When you create a card spread, pay attention to cards of the same number, such as three sevens, that have corners touching.

Additionally, whenever you have three cards together that have the same number, you should consider their color. If you find you have two black cards against a red, it is negative. The seven of diamonds (red), the seven of hearts (red), and the seven of spades (black) will produce a positive outcome. On the other hand, the seven of clubs (black), the seven of spades (black), and the seven of hearts (red) will be negative. This applies to pairs as well: red cards are always more positive and pleasant than black cards.

The meanings of the cards that have the same denomination are as follows:

- **Two aces**—Your wish. If you are asking a specific question, you will get your wish. **Three aces**—Problems moving away from you. **Four aces**—A change in your life.

◆ **Two kings**—An officer, lawyer, or accountant. This could also mean older brothers. **Three kings**—Good news coming your way soon. **Four kings**—Bright situations and circumstances.

◆ **Two queens**—A new friendship. This could also mean sisters. **Three queens**—Trouble, gossip, arguments. **Four queens**—Company coming to call; a lot of people on the way.

◆ **Two jacks**—A new romantic partner. This could also be young brothers. **Three jacks**—Someone from your past returning to you. **Four jacks**—Relatives or close friends from far away are returning, or you will hear news of them.

◆ **Two tens**—Change of places or time in your life. **Three tens**—Time to make new friends, and new opportunity for fresh starts. **Four tens**—Lots of money knocking at your door.

◆ **Two nines**—Business changes ahead—be prepared. **Three nines**—You need to make a decision or one will be made for you. **Four nines**—New projects, ideas, and notions. Start something you like to do.

◆ **Two eights**—A trip to another state or region. If these are two red cards, the trip will be pleasant and fruitful. If they're two black cards, the trip may have delays and disappointments. If they're one black and one red, the trip will be so-so, with good and bad elements. **Three eights**—A struggle regarding work, love, or moving. **Four eights**—A major change of many matters in your life.

◆ **Two sevens**—No doubt. This means that there is no doubt that something is going to happen or not happen depending on the question asked. Two light sevens are positive and two dark sevens are negative. If you have one of each the outcome is undetermined. For example, if you ask if you are going to get a job and you get two light sevens in the mix, it means that yes, you will. **Three sevens**—A surprise. Whether the surprise is good depends on how many red cards you have to black. **Four sevens**—Schemes, conflict, and cunning. Be careful with whom you associate.

Card Spreads

As I mentioned earlier in the chapter, before you do an actual reading, you must take out 20 specific cards from the deck. Remove all the two, three, four, five, and six cards, and the Jokers, and set them aside. That will leave you with 32 cards.

One-Month Spread

This method offers you insights in a week-to-week time frame. All 32 cards are laid out at once and then read, following these steps:

1. Shuffle your cards. As you shuffle, think of your intention or question. If you are looking for a general reading, think or ask, "What will my future hold?" If you have a specific question, think of that one question. You can also think of both.

2. When you are done shuffling, do not cut the cards. Cutting the cards "cuts" their energy, and you want them to flow. I know this is one of those ideas that has contrasting opinions. But I frankly don't believe in cutting cards.

3. Starting from the top of the deck, place the cards, one by one, face up from left to right in four rows of eight. The top row represents the present week of the month; the second row, the second week; the third row, the third week; and the fourth row, the fourth week. Even though the first row represents the first week, that does not mean that each card represents a specific day. It does not. The week should be read as a whole.

4. When your cards are laid out in front of you, begin to read. First glance at the 32-card layout in general. Are there any cards in groups or sequences? If so, interpret those according to the previous meanings.

5. Now read row by row. The first row is the first week you are presently experiencing, and so on.

Sample Reading for First Week of a One-Month Spread

Here is a real reading I just did for myself. I asked about how my month would go. Here is the reading for the first week:

◆ First card: ace of hearts—Pertains to the home. The card or cards surrounding it will denote the nature of the home situation.

◆ Second card: jack of hearts—A young man or woman under 18 or a child with light hair and light eyes.

◆ Third card: eight of clubs—Uncertainty, stress, or anxiety in any area of life, depending on the cards next to it, but especially in business dealings.

◆ Fourth card: seven of diamonds—Success, or a gift that will surprise you.

◆ Fifth card: queen of spades—A female over 30 with dark hair and dark eyes. It can also indicate a lady who is fair but is older and gray-haired.

◆ Sixth card: jack of clubs—A young man or woman under 18 with a dark complexion. It can also mean the thoughts of a man you see as the king of clubs.

◆ Seventh card: nine of spades—Disappointment.

◆ Eighth card: ten of clubs—Journey or change. This can also mean a business situation that is a bit chaotic.

Here is my interpretation of these cards: I (Queen of Spades, a woman who has dark hair and dark eyes—no gray, though) will struggle in a work situation (eight of clubs) around the home (ace of hearts). This involves a young man or woman with light hair and eyes (jack of hearts), and another younger person who is darker (jack of clubs). Because of this struggle (ten of clubs), a journey or trip might be canceled (nine of spades), but it will work out for the best (seven of diamonds).

Enlightening Extras

The day after I interpreted this reading, I learned its application in my life: I had planned to go out of town that day but ended up having to cancel. The reason: our home construction workers arrived a day early. They were two younger guys, one blond and one dark. There were also obstacles we had to deal with, but all was successful.

Now try your own reading. Take one week at a time, and then form an entire story out of the month. Write it down, if you like, or record your reading with a tape recorder. It is important to keep a log of your readings so you can determine how accurate you are.

One-Question Card Spread

If you have only one question it's very easy:

1. Shuffle the 32 cards and spread them out face down from left to right.

2. Select 7 cards. Keep them face down laying 4 on the top row and 3 beneath.

3. Turn them over. From this you should decipher your answer.

For example, I asked my cards if a brunette girlfriend of mine would hear by the weekend from a gentleman she wanted to date. He had said he would call her.

Here is the layout I threw:

- ◆ **Eight of hearts**—Romance, emotional commitment, forgiveness, and love.

- ◆ **Nine of spades**—Disappointment. The only way to balance the negativity of this card is if the seven of diamonds is above it, below it, or on either side of it.

- ◆ **King of clubs**—A man with a medium to dark complexion, most likely over 18 to middle-aged.

- ◆ **Jack of clubs**—A young man or woman with a medium complexion and brown or blue eyes. If this card is next to the king of clubs, as happened in this reading, it represents the thoughts of the person you associate with the king of clubs.

- ◆ **Queen of diamonds**—A light-haired lady over 30 with blond, white, or red hair, typically with blue or green eyes.

- ◆ **Queen of clubs**—A young female adult who has brunette hair and blue or brown eyes.

- ◆ **Ace of spades** (reversed)—Trouble, or death if upside down. However, this is not always a physical death—it could be the death of a situation or emotion.

The result: He is thinking of love, but not with her. She is a brunette, and he has a blonde on his mind. He will not call her this weekend. She needs to move on. He is in love with someone else. My friend is "dead" in his mind: the queen of clubs faces the ace of spades, reversed.

Sorry, call me a tough reader, but I tell it like I see it! These are the cards I selected, and so it is. Bear in mind, that when you pick cards, if the cards aren't what you had hoped for, you can't change them. You don't get to reshuffle or do the reading over. It has to "stand" as is.

If you want to get a real idea of how I am interpreting these cards, re-create my example reading. Pull out these exact cards and line them up the way I wrote. You can visually see what I am seeing. Then read my explanation. Hopefully, it will help you understand a little bit better. Hey, you might see it differently, and that's okay, too.

What Are You Thinking?

This next reading is very powerful and should be used sparingly. If you do this layout over and over again in the same day you will not get any true answers because the energy will be too scattered. Often people reshuffle the cards and try again until they see what they want to see. This is not a good practice.

In this layout, you can determine what someone is thinking about in the present, where he or she is going in the future, and any concerns that person has about the past. This can be an individual who is not present with you at the time. Naturally, you can do this for yourself as well. I find people will do this reading to see what is on the mind and heart of someone they are romantically interested in without the other party knowing. (Spying? Maybe.)

In the following spread, you place the cards in the shape of a cross. The first card is placed in the center; this is what will determine what is on your heart. If you are reading for someone else, it is what is on that person's heart. If the person you are reading for wants to know about someone else, it concerns that person he or she is querying about. The second card moves you up to the top of the cross; the third card draws you down to the bottom; the fourth card goes to the left; and the fifth card is at the right.

Enlightening Extras

If you are reading for someone else, it is best for you to shuffle and select the cards. I have found that the reading is more precise if I select the cards instead of having the inquirer do it. Bear in mind that this is about that person and not you, so with that thought you can easily select the cards for that person because your intuition should be greater than his or hers and you will get better results. Also, you have been handling the cards, and you have developed a connection with them and should continue the process without the other person's energy interfering. The person for whom you are reading may be curious, nervous, excited, or not really concentrating.

Here's how to do it:

1. Sort through your 32 cards and pick out the face card—king, queen, or jack— whose physical description best describes the person you are interested in. And, of course, it can be you!

2. Put that card face up in front of you. This is called the subject card.

3. Shuffle the rest of the cards.

4. Hold the stack of cards in your hands.

5. Keeping it face down, put the first card on top of the subject card. This is what is on that person's heart.

6. Put the second card face down above the subject card. This is what is on that person's mind.

7. The next card gets placed below the subject card. This is what he or she does not care for in his or her life—something that is annoying and a source of irritation. It can be a person, situation, place, or a feeling.

8. Place the following card to the left of the subject card. This is what is passing or has already passed. Note that it does not matter whether the subject card is "looking" or facing in this direction—it is still the past.

9. The next card gets placed to the right of the subject card. (This is what's in the person's future.) Note that it does not matter whether the subject card is "looking" or facing in this direction—it is still the future.

10. Continue spreading the cards in this manner, putting them on top of each other until they are all gone and have formed five little piles.

11. Look at the cards in the pile with the subject card. This is what that person has on his or her heart.

12. Look at the cards in the pile above the subject card. This is what that person has on his or her mind.

13. Look at the cards in the pile to the left of the subject card. This is what is currently passing or has already passed in the subject's life.

14. Look at the cards in the pile to the right of the subject card. This is what is in the future of that person.

15. Look at the cards in the pile at the bottom of the subject card. This is what that person dislikes.

This cross method should be very helpful when you want to know someone else's thoughts or views.

> **Enlightening Extras**
>
> Symbolically, crosses mean different things to different people. They can mean protection, contemplation, the four directions, or the sun and the heavens. A cross can also have religious or spiritual connotations, as if asking for guidance from your higher power.

Below is a sample cross reading of a group of cards that would be considered on the heart of the person who we are divining about. For example, if you were reading about your boyfriend it would be how he feels. As before, re-create the placement of the cards to give yourself an idea of what they mean.

We will use my friend again and the man she was interested in dating. The cards are about what is on his heart or in his emotional thoughts, not hers.

After I place all of the cards, on his heart (the card on top of the subject card) there are actually six cards. All the other categories will have only five cards, but the extra card always ends up here, on the heart.

The following cards give us insights as to how this man emotionally feels about people, places, and things. It can give you insights as to whom he loves and cares for, as well as his passion for projects, events, and knowledge. Is this an invasion of privacy? Is all fair in love and cards? That's for you to decide.

- **King of diamonds**—An older man who is gray, or a middle-aged man who is very light with blue or green eyes.

- **Eight of diamonds**—Inheritance, something given in the form of money, or something of value—something beyond a normal paycheck.

- **Eight of hearts**—Romance, emotional commitment, forgiveness and love.

  Note that **two eights** next to each other mean a trip to another state or region. If they're two red cards, as here, the trip will be pleasant and fruitful. If they're two black cards, the trip may have delays and disappointments. If there is one black and one red card, the trip will be a combination of both elements.

- **Ten of spades**—Hospital, court, school, or building.

- **King of spades**—A middle-aged or older man with a very dark complexion.

- **Eight of clubs**—Uncertainty, stress, or anxiety in any area of life depending on the cards next to it, especially in business dealings.

Here's the interpretation of what is on his heart:

Well, right off, no women, but that doesn't mean there isn't one for which he has a feeling. This could mean that right now other things are more important to him. Yet, maybe the gal I saw earlier wasn't the love of his life I thought she was. This is where you must use your intuition. Maybe I was seeing lust earlier but not real love.

This group of cards would indicate that he might have a sick father or male friend whom he cares for. Also, the fact that we have two eights next to each other (both red) means a trip, but a pleasant journey. Therefore, he might feel that he needs to visit a sick relative. That person will also be visited by another male who is a family member or friend. The good news is that the sick person will be okay. So for the moment, this is what is most important on his heart.

The Least You Need to Know

♦ For many generations people have been divining using a regular deck of playing cards. They are a less complicated system of reading yet provide detailed and extensive results.

♦ Thirty-two cards are used that have individual meanings, including descriptions of people and emotions. Past, present, and future insights are also unveiled in this technique.

♦ You can read for yourself or someone else, using a variety of spreads or card layouts.

♦ It is very possible to obtain an understanding of someone you are interested in, without them being present.

Chapter 12

Dominoes and Dice: Not Just Games!

In This Chapter

- The not-so-shaky history of dice
- Let 'em roll—method one
- Throw again—method two
- Interpreting what the numbers mean
- Divining with dominoes
- There's a whole lotta dots goin' on

Dice readings date back before many other forms of divination. Some people have practiced fortune telling with dice for centuries.

Let's find out what all the mystery is about. It will be easy to start rollin' with the two methods cited in this chapter. And the meanings of the numbers just tumble off the pages.

Roll Those Bones

Astragalomancy is the term that was originally given to reading "knucklebones," a term that is derived from the Greeks. This type of divination involved the throwing of small bones, usually from sheep. In modern times, we sometimes still use this terminology, although it is not commonly heard. (With a name like that, I can see why.) The bones were six-sided and inscribed with symbols. Romans, Greeks, and Egyptians are all said to have used these bones as a way of fortune telling.

Supposedly, it is from this bone-throwing technique that dice eventually evolved. In fact, the Egyptians lay claim to the invention of what we would know as modern dice in 1400 B.C.E.

Dice have been found in Egyptian tombs and uncovered in archeological excavations. The outcome of casting dice or bones was believed to be a message from the gods because they controlled how the dice would fall. The use of dice today is still called "rolling the bones."

> **Notions Through Time**
>
> Whose game was empires and whose stakes were thrones,
> Whose table earth, whose dice were human bones.
> —Lord Byron, from *Age of Bronze*

Fortuna, the daughter of Zeus, a Roman goddess, was believed to determine the outcome of the dice. Gamblers today still refer to her as Lady Luck. Ancient cultures also used such things as stone, flat sticks, seashells, and nutshells as tools of divination, marking them with symbols said to have meanings. All of these things gave way to the dice we have today.

Dice throwing for fortune-telling reasons is not as popular a method of divination as it once was. Only a few seem to continue to practice this fashion of prophecy. Personally, I would like to see a comeback of this rolling way of making predictions.

Roll Into Method One

This method of dice divination is fast and easy. The first thing you need to do is to purchase dice that all match. You will need three. If you already have a set, do not add a new one to form your group of three: it is important that one is not more worn than the other two (or vice versa). This way the energy is balanced.

The color of the dice and the material of which they are made are not necessarily important. However, dice made of ivory or bone are claimed to be more open to picking up vibrations from life force energy.

Natural materials such as stone and wood run second to ivory and bone. As I type, I have my black plastic dice that I won while playing blackjack on a cruise ship. They seem just as good as the antique bone dice on my shelf. It's your call, though: if you are a "dice-sensitive" person, you may sense a variance. Whatever you do, don't accidentally buy *trick dice*, or your fortune will get very boring!

The only other items you will need to get started are a cup, a box, or some type of container you can use as a dice shaker. Naturally, you will need a flat surface on which to toss your dice.

def•i•ni•tion

Trick dice are usually weighted on one side to always throw a 7 or 11. They are also referred to as "loaded" dice. They are often used in magic tricks. Additionally, when playing a dice game, throwing a 7 or 11 typically makes you a winner.

If you like, set the scene with music, candles or incense, and refreshments, to make this an awesome experience. Be lighthearted about throwing dice. It's always good to concentrate, but with dice, your level of concentration does not have to be as intense as with other forms of fortune telling.

Take a few moments to clear the dice of any negative energy. The best way to do this is to give them a quick wash under cold water and visualize anything negative going down the drain. Just be careful not to drop the dice down the garbage disposal!

Shaking Things Up

Dice divination is one of the easiest forms of fortune telling you can perform. You should have answers to all your questions in no time. Follow these steps:

1. Place your three dice in the cup, box, or container.

2. Shake them as long as you feel is necessary. While shaking the dice, think of a specific question.

3. If you are asking a precise question, one throw should be enough.

4. After you have thrown your dice, add the numbers on the faces of the dice together.

5. Look up the corresponding number in the "What the Numbers Mean" section later in this chapter.

This should give you insights to your answer. Dice prophecies are said to come into fruition within nine days.

A General Reading

When you ask for a general reading, you will need to throw your dice three times in a row. This will allow you to create a storyline about your future. In this case, think to yourself that you want to "see" whatever the dice have to say.

After you have asked your question, add the numbers after each throw and write them down. Look up the corresponding numbers in the "What the Numbers Mean" section later in this chapter.

Don't be tempted to keep throwing until you get answers you want. Be honest! When consulting the dice, don't conduct more than three sessions a day. That's plenty of information to toss around—any more can become too confusing.

Roll Into Method Two

This method takes a little more preparation but is loads of fun, especially if you are throwing a party. In addition to your dice and a cup or other dice shaker, you will need a piece of cardboard or posterboard about 12 inches by 12 inches minimum. Then follow these steps:

> **Visionary Insights**
>
> Many dice tricks are amusing and entertaining. One book you might like is *The Complete Idiot's Guide to Magic Tricks* by Tom Ogden (Alpha Books, 1998).

1. Draw a circle about 7 inches in diameter on the cardboard.

2. Shake the dice as described previously and throw them within the circle as best you can. Any dice that fall outside of the circle do not count. Add only the numbers on the faces of the dice that fall within the circle.

Try dice divination in groups as well, letting each person ask a question in turn. You can also all ask the same question and give each person an attempt to answer. Write down everyone's answers, and within nine days see who was the most accurate.

What the Numbers Mean

After you have added the numbers on the faces of the dice, as indicated in the previous methods, use the following key to see what the future has in store:

 ◆ Three—You'll experience an enjoyable surprise.

 ◆ Four—You'll encounter disappointment and frustration.

- Five—A new friend or lover is coming into your life.

- Six—You'll possibly suffer the loss of something or problems in your business or school.

- Seven—Gossip or scandal will surround you.

- Eight—Blame will come to you when you are innocent.

- Nine—A relationship (maybe a wedding or lover partnership) will begin or start over.

- Ten—Something new is coming to you in the way of work or love. This could mean the literal birth of a child or enterprise.

- Eleven—You will say good-bye to a loved one.

- Twelve—A message of good news awaits you soon.

- Thirteen—Unpleasant news is coming.

- Fourteen—Romance will open its gates—walk in carefully.

- Fifteen—Use caution, and don't be tempted to do or say something that is not your business.

- Sixteen—A journey is ahead for you. It should be safe and enjoyable.

- Seventeen—Situations involving water surround you. This is a positive sign involving things of an emotional nature.

- Eighteen—A wish may come true, so be ready for it soon. This will be something you have been hoping for.

In addition to these meanings, the dice provide some extra messages by the way they fall or don't fall on the table or outside the circle:

- If you throw the dice twice in succession and the same number appears, in addition to the previous meanings, it means you will receive news from far away.

- If the dice fly off the table as you throw them, you may be involved in an argument. Of course, if one of the dice hits someone, that could be the cause of the argument right there. So throw with care!

- If one die lands on top of another and doesn't tumble down, this indicates that you will receive a gift.

When reading these meanings, put together the results so you create a complete message for yourself. Do not look at the throws individually. For instance, if one group of numbers tells you that a surprise is coming your way and another group speaks of a trip, put the meanings together: perhaps you will be surprised about taking a trip or being invited to go on a trip. Intuition is always the key.

Dominoes Have a History, Too

Dominoes are typically a set of 28 small rectangular white tiles with a line in the center dividing the tile's face into two squares. Traditionally dominoes were made of ivory, bone, wood, or stone; nowadays, we find dominoes of plastic and other materials.

Dominoes are supposedly the offspring of dice. Each square is marked with black dots, or "pips," or is left blank. The dots are grouped in the same manner as dice. The back of each domino was traditionally left plain, although today the backs may have designs or symbols. The number in a set can also vary. For simplicity's sake, stick with the traditional 28-tile set.

Dominoes originated in India approximately in 1120 C.E. However, in China in the twelfth century B.C.E., dominoes were widely used as a form of fortune telling. At that time, the spots were black and red, and the tiles numbered 32 pieces. Earlier types of Chinese dominoes are different from the American and European types. The Chinese styles are longer, and certain tiles are duplicated. *Mah jong* is said to have evolved from a game played with Chinese dominoes.

def•i•ni•tion

Mah jong is a four-player game the Chinese produced using tiles that resemble domino pieces. The players often used this game as a form of gambling. Different designs adorn these tiles. As the game is played, the pieces are drawn and discarded, as in a card game. Eventually, one player wins with a particular hand of combinations.

As with all original designs, things get altered to suit different cultures and different belief systems. Dominoes are no exception. Explorers from France and Italy who visited China returned to their homelands sporting these tools for divination or games. When dominoes reached the shores of England around the eighteenth century, the dominoes shed their colored dots and gained white ones on black tiles. The game's popularity spread widely.

It has been theorized that the name *domino* possibly arose from the fact that, in Europe, people in the social arena wore black-and-white masquerade costumes called "the domino."

Finding a Set

Dominoes are easily purchased at game stores, discount establishments, Internet sites, and sometimes even large grocery stores. You can opt for a traditional set or look for something that is more colorful. When it comes to divination the dominoes' design will not alter the accuracy. Look for a set that suits your personality and that you find appealing.

A set of "no frills" wooden dominoes will cost about $4. The prices vary from there depending on material and embellishments. Most sets, even the inexpensive types, come in a vinyl case, tin, or wooden box for safekeeping. Do keep them in their container after use. If for some reason your set does not have a container, store the dominoes in a soft cloth drawstring bag or a small container. All forms of mystical tools should be treated with respect and care.

After you purchase your set, clear any negative energy from them by passing either hand over the entire set with a sweeping motion, moving the air above them toward the west.

What Do the Dots Mean for You?

Different systems of reading dominoes are used for fortune telling. One way is not necessarily better than another; there are just different choices. You should be the judge of which is the best—don't be drawn to what the majority feels is the favorite.

To conduct a domino reading, all you will need other than your set of dominoes is a table or platform on which to work with them. If you feel you would like some type of enhancement, consider soothing music, incense, and candles as discussed in Chapter 4. You can also include a friend if you like.

Before you begin, decide where you will be doing your reading. An inside location is usually easier because of lighting, electrical outlets for music, and other practical considerations. However, an outside location is interesting and can lend itself well to this type of fortune telling. The important thing is that you make your decisions and get organized in advance so you don't find yourself searching for items at the last minute.

> **Visionary Insights**
>
> The good thing about dominoes is that they usually don't blow away when you're outside—unless, of course, you live in hurricane country. And if that is the case, you should have consulted the dominoes before you went outside to see what the weather was bringing!

Now that you have your thoughts and dominoes in order, it's time to select a system you would like to use.

The Western System

This system, probably developed by Western cultures, does not use all the dominoes. You can do this method by yourself or with one other person.

Start by removing the dominoes with any blanks on them. You will not be using these. By this I mean the blanks on the face of the dominoes. Some of the divided dominoes are split where one side has dots and the other divided side does not. There are also dominoes that are entirely blank displaying no dots at all on either side of the divided tile. Both types are not used in this method and should be set aside.

Once you've set aside the dominoes with blanks, spread the remaining dominoes on the table face down (dot side down) in front of you. Shuffle them by moving them around with your hands. You do not throw the dominoes like dice. If you're working with another person, you can both mix up the dominoes together. Four hands are better than two! Merely swish them around and around until you feel they are well mixed. While mixing the dominoes *do not* think about any questions—especially if you are working with someone else, because doing so will commingle your two energies.

Once the dominoes are shuffled, think about a specific question or a general message you would like about your future. While contemplating your question, using any hand, one by one pick a total of three dominos. Set them down in front of you from left to right. Select one, turn it over, and place it on the left. Select the next, turn it over, and place it to the right of the first. Select the last tile, turn it over, and place it to the right of the middle.

If you are working with a friend, take turns picking one domino at a time until you each have a total of three face up in front of you. For example: you pick a tile for your question then your friend picks a tile and then it's your turn again, and so on. You will both end up with three dominoes. Your individual set of three should answer the question you ask or give you a general idea of your near future, meaning the next few weeks.

Once you have your three tiles set in front of you, it is time to make an interpretation.

Interpretations for the Western System

The divided faces or two halves of the dominoes are read individually. For example, if a two-four is drawn, meaning if you have two dots on one side of the domino and four dots are on the other side, you read the meaning of the number two and then the meaning of the number four, and draw your conclusion. A two means friends and social events and a four means money and finances, so the message you may decipher is that you will celebrate with your friends over a money situation, or you will loan a friend money, or perhaps you will spend money on a party. Use your intuition: the first thought that comes into your mind is usually correct. After you translate the first of the three dominoes, move on to the next domino and put together another thought, and so on. Once you have the meanings of all three dominoes, you can tie together a story, answer, or understanding for yourself.

Interpret the tiles according to the following definitions:

- Ones—Travel or a journey
- Twos—Family, friends, and social activities
- Threes—Love, romance, sexual fulfillment
- Fours—Money matters of all natures
- Fives—Work, career, and education

Doubles Are Special

The "double" dominoes take on special meanings. They all refer to new beginnings and possibilities:

- **Double one**—A trip to a place you've never visited
- **Double two**—New acquaintances and lots of fun
- **Double three**—A serious love affair coming soon
- **Double four**—Unexpected money in a shocking but good way

> **Enlightening Extras**
>
> A couple dominoes are negative. A four-two combination means disappointments may occur. A three-one combination indicates negative news, although only temporary. However, look at these dominoes as only warnings to be cautious; they are not definite outcomes.

◆ **Double five**—A change of careers or classes at school

◆ **Double six**—A wedding, engagement, or anniversary

The Eastern System

For this method, you use the entire set of dominoes. You can do this on your own or with up to seven other people, each taking turns picking from the same pile.

Shuffle your dominoes face down as in the previous method. Because you can use up to seven individuals you may want to select only one or two people to shuffle the dominoes. After the tiles are shuffled, you or each person can then think of a question. If you are working with a group, have each person take turns choosing one tile at a time until you each have three tiles. In other words, no one takes all three tiles at once. One picks a single tile, and then the next person chooses. This continues until everyone has three tiles in front of them.

Interpretations for the Eastern System

Unlike the Western system, you do not read each half of the domino separately, but you read the domino as a whole piece.

Now interpret the meanings:

◆ **Blank/blank**—Trouble is brewing. This could be in any area of your life: love, business, school, and so on.

◆ **One/blank**—A caller who travels by or over water. Good health emotionally and physically. Be frugal at this time.

◆ **One/one**—A decision is awaiting you. Consult with a family or friend for insights if you are not sure.

◆ **Two/blank**—A successful trip is before you. You are a good communicator, and it will be to your advantage. Be careful that you do not get your heart broken or your purse stolen.

◆ **Two/one**—Chaos in love and your home life. Try to listen to what other people are saying.

◆ **Two/two**—Don't ignore health issues if you are not feeling well. Your communication with friends and business associates will go well.

- **Three/blank**—Jealousy or envy encompasses you. Problems at home need to be dealt with for peace.

- **Three/one**—Surprises, surprises, surprises! Good news in the offing. But beware of an affair with someone else's lover.

- **Three/two**—You need to relax and take a vacation. Don't tell lies, or you will be exposed and feel embarrassed.

- **Three/three**—Money coming into your life is great. However, your love life needs to be looked at carefully. If it needs fixing, fix it!

- **Four/blank**—Twins may influence your life. A change in your life and how you think are also stirring around you.

- **Four/one**—You have bills you thought were paid that are not. Children may annoy you in the near future. Be patient.

- **Four/two**—Someone will flirt with you in front of a partner. Be careful and don't flirt back. Problems at home are coming from every corner. Know that this will pass, and stay calm.

- **Four/three**—Children or young people under 15 will disappoint you. Watch your driving so you don't get a traffic ticket.

- **Four/four**—Creative people will be doing well. Regardless, if you are more of a business type, your energy will be scattered for the next week or so. Think clearly.

- **Five/blank**—Be a friend to someone with a problem. Be a good listener. Don't rush a relationship. Get to know people.

- **Five/one**—You may meet someone who is a "player" or charmer, who is not sincere. Run the other way! Save yourself from being used in a relationship.

- **Five/two**—The birth of a child. New ventures of a creative nature are in your stars—or, should I say, dominoes?

- **Five/three**—Things will start to balance out in your life. Money, friends, happiness. There are no extremes either way, just stabilized energy. That's good.

- **Five/four**—Someone may think you are taking advantage of him or her financially. Try to earn your own money and get out from under this person's control.

- **Five/five**—You may change residence. If you have any concerns, it will be wonderful. Do it scared, but do it!

- **Six/blank**—The ending of a situation, a transition. Gossip is also around the corner, and it can be aimed at you.

- **Six/one**—When you are middle-age or older, you will have good luck and a happy marriage, even if it isn't your first.

- **Six/two**—Gifts surround you. A possible marriage proposal from a qualified and loving person.

- **Six/three**—Good news regarding a vehicle or other forms of transportation. Stability in a relationship is present or will be soon.

- **Six/four**—Legal issues may creep up, so be careful of what you sign. You may marry early.

- **Six/five**—You will have to work on a relationship to make it work. The efforts may not be worth the outcome. Choose wisely in matters of the heart.

- **Six/six**—Good omens are around you for the next two weeks. Lots of luck and happiness. Enjoy it—you deserve to have fun.

Some people feel that the Eastern system is more complex than the Western system, but I actually find it easier. Try both methods to see what works best for you.

The Least You Need to Know

- The first dice, invented by the Egyptians, were most likely made of bones—hence the term "rolling the bones," which is still in use today.

- Consult with the dice only three times a day, at most. You can get into a dice-throwing frenzy trying to get the answers you want.

- You can use dice and dominoes as an ice-breaker for parties or group entertainment. Plus, the equipment is not costly.

- Although dominoes were fashioned after dice, the divination process is different yet equally as interesting.

- Two different systems can be used for reading dominoes. In the Western system you use only part of the set; in the Eastern system you use the whole set.

13

Knife Prophecies

In This Chapter

- ◆ Origins of knife prophecy
- ◆ All you need to read the knife
- ◆ Body, mind, and spirit prophecies
- ◆ Lifestyle prophecies
- ◆ Family and marriage/partnership prophecies

Unlike other methods of fortune telling in the book, this chapter offers a light-hearted approach to determining our fates. It can serve as a great way to "break the ice" in a larger group setting, or it can be adapted to small groups, possibly even individuals. There is really no set number as to how many people can participate. Just use common sense. Fifty people around a table simply won't work. I recommend no more than 8 to 10 people.

This method offers the intrigue of prophecy combined with the simplicity of a mere "twirl" of the knife! It is a remarkable way to combine the higher power of the cosmos with each individual's personal life force, to create unique opportunities to see the future.

In this chapter, you learn how to use the tools of knife prophecy, explore the significance of knife prophecies, and have the opportunity to choose from 90 preselected prophecies. Your guests merely sit and gain unique insights to their futures.

An Amusing Pastime

Knife prophecy is said to have originated in a couple of places, such as the Pacific Islands and Great Britain. No one is sure who the first person or group was who came up with the concept or its exact origin. Regardless, it was invented as a pastime for amusement and excitement; knives were easily available and the cost was almost nothing. With more serious forms of divination gaining popularity, knife prophecy eventually fell to the wayside and was rarely heard of. But the fun still exists.

Tools You Will Need

Very little preparation is necessary because most of the tools for this process can be found in any home, most of them in the ordinary kitchen or home office.

The main tool for this procedure is merely a table knife, such as a steak knife or any other sharp knife that has a weighted handle. You need to have the weight on the handle to allow the knife to spin more easily. You may choose to use a circle of white cardboard or a round platter on which you can place your knife so that it sits much like the hour hand of a clock.

In this chapter, I've provided ten sample prophecies for each of the nine categories: health, education, spiritual messages, job/career, money, social life, love/romance, family, and marriage/partnerships. Write these prophecies on slips of paper, one prophecy per slip. You may find it more interesting and challenging to have each participant write some prophecies as well. You are limited by the categories you agree to, so try to include a good variety of subjects. Consider the makeup of your group of participants before you determine which categories of prophecies to use. What may be fascinating to a teenager may not have any interest for an adult, so adapt your categories accordingly.

Now, keep the slips of paper with the prophecies of the same category together; they will go into containers, one container for each category. Use creativity in choosing the containers for the prophecies; they don't all have to be alike. For simplicity, you might choose nine cups or glasses, but you don't have to limit yourself to the obvious.

You might find it more interesting to select objects with a bit more ingenuity, such as an upside-down baseball cap, Mom and Dad's fiftieth-anniversary dish, Fido's dinner bowl, or bunny's lettuce dish. Depending on the makeup of your participants, there could be some significance to getting your prophecy from a doggy dish or a symbol of love such as the fiftieth-anniversary dish!

How to Proceed

Now that you have the tools necessary to participate in knife prophecies, you may begin. First, place the written prophecies in the containers of your choice, one category per container. For example, you may place five prophecies relating to love in one cup, five prophecies relating to career in another, and so on. Your goal is to create a variety of possible outcomes for each participant. Fate will take care of the rest! Put the containers in a circle, with the knife in the center, resting on its plate or circle.

Next, advise the participants to each take a turn spinning the knife, and note where the blade stops. The spinner should take a prophecy out of the container that the knife is pointing to.

It is suggested that women twirl with their right hands and men twirl with their left, always twirling counterclockwise. Because men are considered more "logical" than women, or left-brained, they should use their left hands. Because women seem to be more emotional, or right-brained, they should use their right hands to spin the knife. (Although this assumption may seem quite outdated by today's standards, understand that the practice of knife prophecy stems from our distant past, thus reflecting the mores of that time.) The participants continue taking turns selecting prophecies, as long as there are prophecies remaining in the containers.

> **Visionary Insights**
>
> If the blade stops between two containers, this indicates indecision or ambiguous feelings on the part of the spinner. The participant should spin a second time.

Body, Mind, and Spirit Prophecies

A direct correlation exists between the body, mind, and spirit, in that each is dependent upon the other. Without a strong, healthy body, one cannot focus on developing the mind through education and life experience. Only when we are comfortable with our physical and mental states can we reflect on our spiritual development. The following prophecies, therefore, fall into closely related categories.

Health

◆ Use preventative physical maintenance to negate possible ill health in the future.

◆ Doctors, prayers, and common sense can all fit into your life with great success.

◆ Health is more important than money. You have heard it time and time before, but it is still true. Remember it.

◆ Consider not only your physical health, but also your emotional health. You are a combination of both.

◆ You need to laugh more often than you do now. Laughing may be a release from stress. Watch a comedy on television now and then. Choose to laugh.

◆ You may find yourself accompanying someone to a medical facility. Don't be impatient about waiting. You are showing this person a kindness.

◆ Consider making some changes that will make you more attractive. This is not vanity, just something that will boost your self-esteem.

Enlightening Extras

When dealing with supernatural wisdom regarding health, always look to a health-care professional first. Bring in divine intervention and fortune-telling insights as an addition, never as an alternative.

◆ You have a friend who needs to take off a few pounds. Be supportive and help your friend any way you can.

◆ You have one really bad habit you need to relinquish. Hop to it—stop procrastinating!

◆ When you have the blues, watch a comedy or a read a funny book. Laughter is the best healer of all. Did you hear about the guy who walks into a bar with a monkey?

Education

◆ It is never too late to learn a new trade or add to your scope of knowledge.

◆ Something you never thought you would find of interest will be taught to you this year. You'll love it!

◆ You have artistic talent and should pursue it. It may be a hobby at first, but it could turn into a money-maker.

◆ You may find yourself dealing with animals of some type. This will bring you new knowledge.

- Don't underestimate your brain power. You have gifts you can't even imagine. Be open to all new ideas.

- There are different types of education. You would be surprised what you can master from books and the Internet. Not everything is done in a classroom.

- You and a friend will take a class together. The fun will be more pronounced than the learning.

- Someone you are close to will tell you something others have been trying to explain for years. Somehow, with this individual's insights, you will finally understand what the rest were trying to say.

- Education is expensive but is not always judged in dollars and cents. You will learn a lesson that comes at a cost, but it will be worth it in the long run.

- Remember the story of the little engine that said, "I think I can, I think I can …"? That should be your chant for the next few months. You can … and you will!

Spiritual Messages

- You have been neglecting your higher power. Take some time and get back to your old philosophies.

- To be religious and spiritual are two different things. However, you can be both.

- Bring more equilibrium into your life. You are focusing too much on one specific issue.

- Call upon Archangel Gabriel to help you develop your intuition and psychic abilities.

- Do not attempt to force your personal spiritual beliefs on someone else. We all have the right to believe what we choose.

- Next full moon, you will dream of a future event that will bring you great satisfaction.

- Animals tend to like you because they can feel your warm nature. You have been blessed with animal communication skills.

- It is said, "When you pray, you ask, and when you meditate, you listen." You need to start meditating.

- When you are missing a dead loved one, look to the west because this is their portal to the other side.

- Sometimes doing what is best for us ends up being what is best for other people. Sometimes it's okay to be a little selfish.

Lifestyle

The following prophecies address matters regarding your job or career choice, issues relating to your finances, and various aspects of your social life. Because all three are interrelated, you should be able to see a clear picture of your future by combining your selected prophecies.

Even if you decide not to venture into using knife prophecies, it is still interesting to read the insights and contemplate how they might be of value in your life.

Job/Career

- Step up to the plate for your next working challenge. You are starting to slack off a bit.

- Someone from your past will ask for help with a temporary position or task. Think about saying "yes." You won't be sorry.

- Change never really hurt anyone. It is fear of change that makes it difficult. Look at your career or job moves as a positive step on your life's journey.

- A new opening for a job placement might come knocking at your door. Be careful that you aren't drawn to it by the glitz and glamour; it may not be financially beneficial.

- Not everyone has the same opportunities for vocations as some. Do not judge people by what they do for a living.

- Some day in your life you will be challenged with the choice of two careers. Think carefully and ask advice.

- You're the artsy type. Things of a creative nature appeal to you.

- Several job changes will be in your future over the next year. That doesn't mean that's a negative—just a way to keep you active.

◆ Do you want a job or a career? You will need to make a decision about which direction you will travel.

◆ Someone you would never expect to talk to you about your future occupation will surprise you with promising ideas.

Visionary Insights

If a participant in a knife prophecy session is very resistant to one particular message that he or she gets, tell that person to pay attention to that message. Often we need to attend to that which we most resist.

Money

◆ Learn to stretch a dollar. You're spending too much lately.

◆ It's grand not to be a material person, but don't take it too far. Buy yourself a little something now and then.

◆ Someone with good intentions will ask you for a loan. Be warned—grant the loan only if you don't expect to get it back for nearly eight months.

◆ Money will always be available to you. You are making your financial situation out to be something it isn't.

◆ Gambling is fun for you but won't produce the results for which you hope. Beware of games of chance.

◆ Start saving now. By the next season, you will have unexpected expenses. If you are ahead of the game, you will have no problem.

◆ Spend a little extra on the next gift you buy for someone. It will be worth seeing the smile on that person's face.

◆ Although it's nice to feel that your security can come from someone else, you need to be self-sufficient.

◆ Praying is great when you are in need of funds. But it is better to pray after you find a way to produce profits.

◆ Dwell on your financial problems 20 percent of the time and the solution 80 percent of the time. This is something you have been lacking.

Notions Through Time

It's a kind of spiritual snobbery that makes people think they can be happy without money.

—Albert Camus, French writer

Social Life

◆ Travel is in the stars for you, my happy wanderer. You'll take three safe and fun trips in the next 6 months.

◆ You will be invited to attend a function or party of some type where they will serve cake. You may feel that the event will be unexciting and may say no to the invitation. Don't. You will have an amazing time.

◆ Start making some new friends. Your life will be changing in a positive fashion. A few fresh acquaintances can put a little spark in your life.

◆ You have exquisite taste and are very stylish. To some, this may be shallow. But taste and style are the attributes of a person who is creative and has a flair for the good life.

◆ The money may not be there, but the class is. You enjoy the arts and cultural events. Find happenings that are free or reasonably priced. If you seek, you will find.

◆ Take time to work on your body so it can fit your new spirit that will be emerging in the next three months.

◆ Decorate your home a little this coming month. Get rid of outdated decor and come up to the times.

◆ You're a person who loves nature but can feel equally at home in the city. Try to incorporate both aspects into your life.

◆ "Cream always rises to the top." You will someday be in the public eye! (In a good way.)

◆ You are a social climber, and there is nothing wrong with that. Your personality can get you far.

Matters of the Heart

We all are concerned about those we love or will love. In these prophecies, you will find insight into your future romantic life, strong emotional issues regarding your family, and an indication of what the cosmos has in store for you in long-term relationships or marriage. By interpreting your selected prophecies, a vision of your present and future love relationships will become clear.

Love/Romance

♦ There is more than one soul mate per person in the world. Don't get your mind set on the thought that if you miss one or lose one, there won't be another.

♦ The next party you attend will bring an introduction into your life of a future love. It may not exactly happen at the party. You might meet someone who knows someone.

Notions Through Time

The ultimate function of prophecy is not to tell the future, but to make it.

—Joel Barker, independent scholar and futurist

♦ You will endure a broken heart on some level in the next year. You can avoid it if you pay attention to what your lover is trying to project. The key is listening.

♦ A good friend will need an outlet for her confusion with a relationship. Do not go against her love interest because they will end up back together and you will be seen as the "bad guy."

♦ You will have two love interests at the same time. Can you handle it? If not, you'd better make a choice quickly.

♦ Your future relationship may seem too good to be true. In your case, it will continue to be, as long as you don't sabotage your connection.

♦ You will find someone who is like-minded on some things and the total opposite on others. All in all, it's a match.

♦ Dreaming about finding a mate is great, but go out and look. It may be conducive to your happiness if you meet someone in a natural environment.

♦ Be careful about appearing too needy when you're first introduced to someone. In other words, even if you feel you really have chemistry at first sight, play it cool.

♦ Do not force romance. If you aren't a poet or don't like long walks on the beach, be honest. If you find someone you really care about, even a trip to the grocery store can be romantic.

Family

♦ A relative from your past will suddenly appear in your life. You may not be too excited about the interaction. However, be kind; this person will be leaving shortly.

◆ Friends can be like family, and you are neglecting someone special. Send some love that person's way.

◆ We all need to talk and vent. But you are thinking too much about yourself right now. Ask about how others in your family are doing.

◆ Your parents aren't perfect, and neither are you. Whether they are alive or have passed, let go of any ill thoughts about any incidents you may be holding inside.

◆ Family events can be a tiresome affair. But rise above the situation and attend with a smile on your face.

◆ Family pets or pets belonging to friends need love, too. Do something special for a pet; that animal will be appreciative.

> **Visionary Insights**
>
> Prophecies always raise the question of whether the future is set. If we can see what it is to be, does that mean there is no chance to change it? Most wise ones say the future is only a possibility—or, given present circumstances, perhaps a probability. But, they say, it can always be changed.

◆ Even if you have a small family or no family at all, you are never alone. Nature and all its wonders are your family.

◆ Some families hug and some don't. Some share feelings and some don't. But it's never too late to start.

◆ Send a card to someone in your family you hardly ever talk to or see. What a hoot to think what that person will do after receiving it.

◆ There comes a time in life when we can't expect our families to be everything for us. Try a little harder to take some pressure off. The rewards are plentiful.

Marriage/Partnerships

◆ Watch some Internet dating sites. They don't accept you if you have been married three times or more. These are not for you.

◆ Your spouse or partner may surprise you with a gift you just don't care for. I am not encouraging lying, but what's a little fib to keep from hurting his or her feelings?

◆ You may feel the urge to pull away from your partner. Do it, but only for a few hours or days. We all need our space.

◆ If you are over 25 and are not married or in a long-term relationship, you will be within the next 2 years. Of course, you have the free will to say, "No, thank you."

◆ A person who is attached emotionally to someone else may look to you for a relationship outside his or her relationship. Be warned.

◆ If you are involved with someone who doesn't want to make a commitment after a long period of time, give yourself a time limit. Let him or her know what your time limit is, and then move forward if nothing happens.

◆ You will or have had more than one marriage or partnership in your lifetime. Don't be blue. Practice makes perfect!

◆ Your marriage may be questioned by others who see something you may not. Don't be so relaxed that you don't see future dilemmas.

◆ Don't assume that because other people you know may have partnerships with challenges, yours will also follow suit.

◆ Some partnerships are truly blessed, which is very rare. Yours is, or will be, one of them. Congratulations, you must have done something right.

What may seem like a silly game to some might become more significant with the passing of time. Tell everyone to hang on to their prophecies and plan to meet in six months or a year to revisit them. There's often an amazing correlation between the upcoming events and the prophecies each person chose.

The Least You Need to Know

◆ Like many other forms of divination, the origins of knife prophecy are shrouded in mystery.

◆ Doing knife prophecies is a real ice-breaker for a get-together or party.

◆ Using only topics that suit your specific group will make the prophecies more relevant.

◆ Unlike other forms of fortune telling, knife prophecy is more fun than serious.

◆ Even if you are not planning to play this mystic game, you may want to contemplate some of these "words of wisdom."

Chapter 14

Tablets of Fate

In This Chapter

- What are tablets of fate?
- A link to the Sphinx
- Making your own Sphinx card
- The meanings of the Venus, Sun, and Celestial numbers

The Egyptians reportedly originated tablets of fate by etching symbols on pieces of stones to be used as a form of fortune telling. During the seventeenth century, fortune tellers or seers traveled the streets of England and Scotland, quietly selling tablets of fate to seekers of the unknown. As this concept filtered into other continental areas, the tablets were converted into a paper version.

What were these pieces of papers all about? How can we get them today, since those days have long vanished into the tunnel of time? I don't see any soothsayers on my block with a stack of papers. Do you? The good news is that we can create our own.

What in the World Are Tablets of Fate?

Over time, these *tablets of fate* were made into chapbooks. Chapbooks were poor-quality printed matter that were sold by street venders and that usually addressed daily matters. Consequently, tablets of fate were inexpensive pamphlets or single pieces of paper that supposedly gave people the key to their future according to planetary influence. For our purposes, throughout this chapter I will refer to the tablets of fate also as cards.

def•i•ni•tion

Tablets of fate were pamphlets or papers peddled by seventeenth- and nineteenth-century street vendors that addressed daily matters according to daily planetary influences, such as daily horoscopes. Other tablets of fate were standard and did not change daily.

This ancient form of divination found a modern twist in the seventeenth century, but it disappeared for a while (must have been fated) before reappearing in the nineteenth century.

The tablets (square pieces of paper) each had 16 different numbers on them, with separate tablets for specific concerns linked to certain planets and their vibrations. The searcher asked a question, spun the tablet, and pointed to a number without looking. Then the searcher deciphered the number and answered the original question.

Buyers made their street purchases and ran home to see what the fates had in store for them that day. Those concerned with the daily planetary influences could purchase those types of tablets daily if they chose to. Those tablets were akin to daily horoscopes, as opposed to the other tablets sold that had firm information that assisted one in predicting the future. This type did not need to be purchased daily. These non-changing tablets are the types we deal with in this chapter.

Tablets of fate are an unusual form of fortune telling, and you don't hear much about them in this era. Regardless, it is remarkable that you can attain such correct answers with the spin of a paper.

In the following sections, I discuss the meanings of four of the many tablets of fate:

- ◆ Sphinx, which deals with granting permission
- ◆ Venus, which deals with questions about love
- ◆ Sun, which deals with issues of time and timing
- ◆ Celestial, which answers general questions

Get Permission from the Sphinx Before You Begin

Before you can even consult with the tablets of fate, you must gain permission from the *Sphinx* tablet. Without permission, you could create a very negative response. And it's not nice to fool the Sphinx!

Don't underestimate the power of the Sphinx: it has been credited with obscure powers and great wisdom from the gods. The mysterious powers of the Sphinx supposedly began when a young prince fell asleep between the paws of the Sphinx while on a hunting trip. The young prince, who later became King Thutmose (who ruled between 1417 and 1425 B.C.E.), stated that the Sphinx spoke to him during a dream and asked him to clear away the sand because it was choking him. If the prince did this for the Sphinx, he would reward him with a kingship and much good fortune. The Sphinx had been almost completely buried until this time.

def•i•ni•tion

The **Sphinx** is a renowned statue made of sandstone near Cairo, Egypt, that depicts the head of a king and the body of a lion. It is believed to have been constructed more than 4,500 years ago. Among the mysteries of the world, the figure of the Sphinx is considered mystical, and so is the location where it rests.

The clarity and powerful message of this dream stayed with the young prince until he did become king. He felt that he must respect the request of the Sphinx because his promises to the young boy had actually been fulfilled. After he cleared away the sand, the king also built a chapel next to it to worship this sun god. To this day, many prayers are said at this location by people requesting the help of the Sphinx to solve their problems in life. The belief in the Sphinx's mysterious powers has never waned.

The Sphinx Card

Before you conduct a reading from the tablets of fate, you must make a Sphinx card:

1. Find or cut a square piece of cardboard approximately 6 × 6 inches. Any size will work if you want to go larger. The important thing is that the cardboard must be square, not rectangular.

2. Using a pen or any color felt-tipped marker, draw 16 equal boxes, with 4 rows across and 4 rows down.

3. Write the following numbers, one number in each square:

   Top row from left to right: 6 13 16 8

Second row from left to right: 15 5 1 12

Third row from left to right: 3 10 9 4

Fourth row from left to right: 14 2 7 11

♦ On the back of the cardboard, write "Sphinx" as your personal reminder, or draw a picture of the Sphinx on the back. Whether you write or draw on the back of any of the number tablets is up to you. You simply need a way to distinguish one tablet from another.

Ta-da! You have now made your first tablet of fate.

Before you consult the Sphinx, I suggest that you make your other three cards—Venus, Sun, and Celestial, as described later in the chapter—so you are ready to go if the Sphinx card gives you permission.

Well, Sphinx, What Do Ya Say?

The following process is done to ask permission to continue the reading and should not be skipped.

1. Place your Sphinx card on a table in front of you with the numbers side up.

2. Close your eyes and spin the cardboard. If it won't spin, just keep turning it around and around slowly at least three times or more. Do not flip it over.

3. When you are led to stop, then stop; keeping your eyes closed, point your finger on the card. If you want to use the eraser part of a pencil or a pointer of some sort, that's fine.

4. Open your eyes and see where your finger or pointer has landed.

If it has landed directly on a number, read the meaning of that number in the next section. If it lands on a line, read the meaning that is closest to the number on which your finger points.

If you miss the card completely, try three more times. If after three times you keep missing the card, wait 24 hours and start again. Or maybe stop your use of caffeine for a few hours.

The Sphinx Number Meanings

After you spin the card, if the numbers are upside down or sideways as you view them, it's important to read the reversed meaning of the number. No cheating!

1 Upright—You can proceed today. Reversed—Today is not good.

2 Upright—Tomorrow is the day for you. Reversed—Yes, yes, try right now!

3 Upright—Try on Thursday (unless today is Thursday). Reversed—Any day will work except Thursday.

4 Upright—You are too restless for a reading, but if you must, go ahead. Reversed—Don't bother today. Let it go for now.

5 Upright—Sunday is the best day this week. Reversed—Sunday will not work.

6 Upright—What are you waiting for? Do it now! Reversed—Wait seven days and try then. (That includes today.)

7 Upright—Your answer is there for you anytime you want to proceed. Reversed—Not looking good today. Try again another day.

8 Upright—Tuesday is the best day for you. Reversed—Sometime next week is better.

9 Upright—Try the same weekday as you were born (not meaning your actual birthday). Reversed—Give it a try today, but calm yourself before asking questions.

10 Upright—Saturday will bring your best answers. Reversed—Not Saturday; not worth the effort.

11 Upright—No messages for you today. Reversed—A surprise is waiting for you. Go ahead and try.

12 Upright—If today is Monday, proceed. If not, wait until then. Reversed—Monday is not a good day for a reading this week or next.

13 Upright—Hop to it and move forward. Reversed—Follow your own intuition—either proceed or don't.

14 Upright—Friday will bring you the most accurate answers. Reversed—Start now and divine your future.

15 Upright—Wednesday is the way to go for the best outcome. Reversed—Not today. No way!

16 Upright—It's a go-ahead. Reversed—Shouldn't happen today ... sorry!

Other Tablets of Fate

The following tablets of fate are made almost exactly the same way as the Sphinx card, with the exception of the numbers. Just as you ask the Sphinx card whether it is okay for you to consult the tablets, ask your questions to the specific tablet of fate that refers to your special concern.

Notions Through Time

Fate laughs at probabilities.

—E.G. Bulwer-Lytton, English writer

Focus on your question while you are spinning the card. When you decide to stop, drop your finger or pointer on the card and read the meaning of the number you randomly selected.

Venus Numbers: All About Love

Remember to write "Venus" on the back of the card. Draw your 16 squares as with the Sphinx card, and fill in the square as follows:

Top row from left to right: 5 11 1 9

Second row from left to right: 14 7 4 12

Third row from left to right: 8 3 16 2

Fourth row from left to right: 6 15 10 13

This tablet should be used when asking questions about romance. Here, too, read the reversed meanings when necessary.

1 Upright—Love is yours. Reversed—You may disagree with someone you love or are infatuated with. Be patient.

2 Upright—The person you are concerned about is going to make you wait for your answers. Reversed—This individual can't be fooled by you. Best to be honest and not try to play games.

3 Upright—Think logically, but ultimately your heart will guide you on this issue. Reversed—Don't fall prey to people who flatter you. They are full of wind and only that. Nothing serious.

4 Upright—If you are definite about what you think you are up against, go ahead with a relationship. Reversed—You may not be as wise as you think when it comes to this issue. Listen to the advice of others. You don't want to hear the truth.

5 Upright—Relax and stop worrying you. Everything is fine. Reversed—Get to know someone before making a judgment call.

6 Upright—You are to blame here. Sorry, the other person is right and you are wrong! Reversed—You can work things out; romantic love is a part of the energy around you.

7 Upright—If you are unhappy, it is because you may have created the situation. It's not too late. Try to resolve it. You can! Reversed—Don't get caught up in personal appearances. Look below the surface; love and excitement await you.

8 Upright—Forget about jealous behavior and worry about more important things. Reversed—Someone you think is only a friend has fantasies about you.

9 Upright—If you are in a relationship, your partner is faithful. Reversed—Stop dreaming about love and start working on it.

10 Upright—You are weighing heavy on someone's mind. Sexual thoughts are abundant. Reversed—People who are players and charmers don't fit into your future. Don't get pulled in.

11 Upright—Rainy days are coming your way. But the sun will shine again. Reversed—Your love life might be like a roller-coaster ride for the next few weeks. Fasten your safety belt. You will ride it out and still be okay to discuss it.

12 Upright—Someone is going to change his or her way of thinking. Be a listener and judge what to do. Reversed—Take caution in matters of the heart, or yours could get broken. If it does, there is someone else for you.

13 Upright—Your answer is "yes." However, it is with someone else you may not have met. Reversed—The key word is *slowly*. You cannot rush a relationship; it must develop on its own.

14 Upright—Your mind is filled with doubt. The things you worry about most likely won't happen. Reversed—All lust and little true love.

15 Upright—You may have said something that will come back at you. You spoke too soon. Reversed—Stop the jealous behavior. Have more self-esteem. A jealous person is not attractive to anyone. This also could mean that someone else is flirting with your lover, but he or she is not flirting back. Relax.

16 Upright—You have or will have found your true love. Reversed—Get out before it's too late. We all have more than one soul mate. You will find yours with time.

Enlightening Extras

When working with the tablets of fate, don't just repeat the same questions. If you don't like the answer you get, wait for another week or so and ask again. Things may change. The Sphinx is too smart for you changing the structure of the sentence to pretend it is new. Here's an example of what *won't* work:

◆ Will David call me today and ask me for a date?

◆ Any news from David today about his plans this weekend?

◆ Will I be home this weekend or out with David?

These three cases are all the same question asked differently. Sorry, you can ask only one question about a given situation.

Sun Numbers: Timing Is Everything

Use this tablet when asking questions about time or timing. As before, draw your 16 squares and fill in the squares as follows:

Top row from left to right: 10 3 6 13

Second row from left to right: 8 15 1 5

Third row from left to right: 9 11 7 16

Fourth row from left to right: 2 14 12 4

The timing on these numbers will not exceed two years. Be sure to read the reversed meanings when necessary.

1 Upright—Six months should just about do it. Reversed—Within seven days from today.

2 Upright—Simply put, it most likely will never happen. Reversed—Probably about two weeks, maybe three.

3 Upright—This will happen by the next new or crescent moon you see. Reversed—How soon this will happen depends on decisions you make now. Think clearly about this.

4 Upright—Not going to happen until everyone becomes more stable. Reversed—You'll be too old to care by the time it happens. Look to something different and let this go.

5 Upright—Within a year. Might be worth waiting. Reversed—You will have to be patient. But rather than wait too long, look to something or someone different.

6 Upright—You will be shocked by how soon this will happen. Reversed—This will be slow and tedious. Might not be worth the wait.

Notions Through Time

The ultimate function of prophecy is not to tell the future, but to make it.

—Joel Barker, independent scholar and futurist

7 Upright—Before the end of this year. Reversed—Within the spring.

8 Upright—Absolutely yes and now. Reversed—This will take place during the middle of the month, the 13th through the 18th.

9 Upright—It should have happened already, but something delayed it. Reversed—Oh dear, this could take two years.

10 Upright—The more you push, the longer it will take. You are making things go slowly. Reversed—Not going to happen.

11 Upright—Can happen at any moment or within the next two days. Reversed—You may think days, but this will take months.

12 Upright—Will happen within a 30-day period. Reversed—The numbers 3 and 9 come into play here. See if that means something to you. If not, wait and see what happens on the third and the ninth of the month.

13 Upright—It will happen on your lucky day. Check your astrology chart to find out when that may be. Reversed—Faster than you can imagine.

14 Upright—Probably in less than a week. Reversed—Don't push things. You need all the time you can get, even if you don't realize it now.

15 Upright—Move forward. Things will take time. Reversed—There is a little chance, but doubtful if it will happen at all.

16 Upright—It could take a full year. Reversed—Won't be too much longer now. Keep your eyes on other things. It's in the near future; no longer than three weeks.

Celestial Numbers: Answers to General Questions

This tablet combines the different aspects of several planets and addresses all general questions. Create the tablet using these numbers:

Top row from left to right: 8 13 6 2

Second row from left to right: 14 3 10 1

Third row from left to right: 9 5 7 12

Fourth row from left to right: 16 4 11 15

Because you are asking questions about so many different topics, you must work a bit harder to translate the meanings. Use your intuitive self to help with the process. As before, read the reversed meanings when necessary.

1 Upright—New beginnings will make things possible for you. Reversed—A recent idea may not work out the way you hope.

2 Upright—A business partnership is a good idea. Team with someone else to achieve your goals. Reversed—A joint effort may not be right for you. You could end up doing all the work.

3 Upright—Money and new sources of income are in the stars for you at this time. Lean into it, not against it. Reversed—Beware of those who could deceive you. Use caution with new and old friends, sometimes even family members.

4 Upright—Things look a little boring or just so-so. This isn't necessarily negative—just a time when not much will transpire. Reversed—Someone may ask you for a loan of money or a vehicle. This person is honest, but you may not be repaid on time.

5 Upright—Many changes are coming your way. Could be a change or job or residence. Reversed—Just remember that old expression "The grass isn't always greener on the other side!"

6 Upright—Victory and success. No more needed to say. Reversed—If you are waiting for a legal decision, it could take long. Legal documents and a delay are encompassing you.

7 Upright—A trip or travel is in the offing. If you are asking a yes-or-no question, the answer is "yes." Reversed—Messages, such as phone calls, a caller, letters, or e-mails, will enter your life within the next couple of weeks. Some important news is coming.

8 Upright—You have the power; now use it to help yourself. Reversed—Struggles and frustration may rain upon you. Don't make too many decisions in the next eight days.

9 Upright—Your wish will be granted … poof! Reversed—Your wish will not be granted.

10 Upright—Weddings, anniversaries, and times of celebration are around the corner. Reversed—Delayed plans can leave you or others a bit blue. Cheer up. There are worse things in life.

11 Upright—Someone very special and wise will be introduced to you. A unique encounter. Reversed—Someone you thought was very intelligent isn't as bright as you assumed. That's still no reason not to be friends. A realization is knocking at your door.

12 Upright—Those dark clouds will pass, and the sun will be shining through regarding this matter. Reversed—You will have to work hard to get what you want. No "free rides" in this case.

13 Upright—This is a period of happiness, as opposed to wealth. Reversed—You will hear news of someone you know who is not well. Send blessings his or her way.

14 Upright—Animals are a blessing in your life; don't forget them, whether yours or someone else's. Reversed—Learn to handle your money better.

15 Upright—A change of educational goals or job is something to think about. Reversed—If you're looking for an answer, the answer is "yes" but not right away. Hang in there. It's worth the wait.

16 Upright—Whatever you are hoping for is not the best for you. Don't be disappointed if it doesn't happen. Reversed—You may be destined for a career in which you are on stage or in the limelight: audiences around you, and fame and fortune.

The Least You Need to Know

◆ Tablets of fate were sold in the streets by fortune tellers in the seventeenth and nineteenth centuries.

◆ You must consult the Sphinx to see if you have permission to read on that day.

◆ Venus is the tablet that deals with questions about love and romance.

◆ Sun is the tablet that addresses issues of time and timing.

◆ Celestial tablets cover all your general questions and concerns.

Part 4

Seeing into Your Future

"What you see is what you get." Sometimes you may want to get what you see, and other times you may not want to get what you see. The vast sea of information provided here will hopefully aid you in transcending to a level of intuitive thought you have never experienced. Face readings, bumps, and clouds with humps float through this section.

Whether you're intently examining a line in a palm or solemnly gazing into a crystal ball, the promise of real "sight" may be at hand. It is this vision that can project one through the portal of ordinary life to arrive at an entirely new vista. A place few people travel. A place where you may find the most valuable person … yourself.

Chapter 15

Reading Facial Features and Bumps

In This Chapter

- A method of divination with Eastern roots
- Do the eyes really have it? A study of facial features
- What head shape and bumps reveal
- The skull divided
- Don't dump those bumps ... they're meaningful

What are the technical names for the methods of being able to read someone's face and the bumps on people's heads? Whether this is of great importance or not, you will find them provided in this chapter. But let's think of it in a simpler format. This chapter is all about how to do prophetic readings using the information from someone's face and bumps on the head. After a while, you will be able to merely look at someone and get a feel for that person's general personality.

The how-tos for accomplishing these tasks are headed your way. Hopefully you won't encounter any bad bumps along this path. Oh, that was bad. I admit it.

Is It Scientific or Just Woo-Woo?

Physiognomy, or *personology*, is the term we use in the West for the art of reading faces. Face readings have a very long history in the East. The Chinese and other Asian cultures have conducted these types of readings for centuries. From reading faces, they could ascertain a fairly accurate read on the character and social status of a person, and could predict that person's future. These readings are based not on people's facial expressions, but on the actual face itself.

In Western cultures, starting with the Greeks, a more scientific slant was applied to the process. The key people who contributed to this philosophy were Johann Kaspar Lavater, a Swiss philosopher who in approximately 1775 was noted for his work on physiognomy; Edward Jones, a federal court judge whose first phase of research was from 1920 to 1940; and Robert Whiteside, who continued this research in the 1950s and who conducted a study proving that this theory had credible validation.

Even today, some business professionals are said to use this type of insight into someone's disposition for job interviews, for closing sales deals, and in major decision-making processes. These methods are practiced throughout the world but more so in the East, Europe, and the Western world.

> **Notions Through Time**
>
> A man's face as a rule says more, and more interesting things, than his mouth, for it is a compendium of everything his mouth will ever say, in that it is the monogram of all this man's thoughts and aspirations.
>
> —Arthur Schopenhauer, German philosopher

We read faces subconsciously, whether we believe in this skill or not. You've probably heard people say things like, "I never trusted him—he has beady eyes," or "She's a worrier—look at those lines between her eyebrows."

When it comes to actually foretelling the future by a face reading, we must look to the Chinese (who call it *Mian Xiang*) and Japanese, and follow their insights and methods, which are more esoteric than ours in the West. The Western philosophy looks at a person's character to determine what type of choices he or she may make in the future. The Eastern philosophy takes a more mystical view. This chapter takes a little from both approaches.

Studying the Face

The interesting thing about this study is that you can practice with people everywhere, even if you don't know them. The best person to start with is yourself.

Look at yourself in a mirror. Be strong. Do not be critical of your shortcomings. Use the following keys to conduct your own reading and readings for others.

There are different classifications of face types, but for our purposes, we use the basic three: heart-shaped or triangular, square or rectangular, and round:

Visionary Insights

If you have had facial plastic surgery, you cannot get an accurate reading from your "new look." You must remember what you looked like previously, even if you have to seek out an old photograph.

- ◆ **Triangular** (point down and wide part on top) or **heart-shaped** (a face with a larger forehead that narrows at the chin): Intelligent, occasionally temperamental, contemplative, good memory, always likes to learn new things.

- ◆ **Square** or **rectangular** (wide forehead and larger chin and jaws): Strong of body and of mind. Can be stubborn occasionally, always a leader, intelligent, logical, and usually on the go.

- ◆ **Round** (full cheeks and a round chin): Good-natured and loves family, friends, and the better things in life. Works hard and has natural intuitive abilities.

Sometimes our faces change, depending on weight. Therefore, judge what your face would be at your average weight.

Forehead

When looking at a forehead, combine the different types. For instance, is your forehead high and narrow or high and broad? Your forehead shows your way of reasoning.

- ◆ **High forehead**—Intellectual, problem solver, honest, and spiritual.

- ◆ **Low forehead**—Not too ambitious, simple-thinking, with little curiosity. Enjoys a plain and uncomplicated lifestyle.

- ◆ **Broad forehead**—Common sense, streetwise, business-oriented, and money-conscious.

Enlightening Extras

If you have "worry" lines, which are vertical lines between your eyes, it is said that you push yourself too hard and may be causing your own stress. If you have one line between your eyes, you need to share your burdens with others and find a way to ease the pressure.

♦ **Narrow forehead**—Shy, conservative in thinking, "narrow-minded," outdated in views.

Sometimes you will find that your general facial features do not fall into any category because they are in between extreme categories or are merely medium in size and shape. If that's the case, for that particular classification, think of yourself as balanced or neutral. In this position, being medium or in the middle is the best you can hope for, so choose a face type you mostly resemble.

Ears

Are the ears important? "I can't hear you." Of course they are. The ear size in proportion to the head size is what it's all about. Your ears show how you interact and relate to other people.

Before starting, look for a mole or birthmark on the inside of your ear. This means a long life and many talents!

♦ **Large ears**—Nonjudgmental, trustworthy, and a good listener.

♦ **Medium ears**—Fair, precise, thoughtful, and subtle.

♦ **Small ears**—Never lazy, shrewd, and nonconforming.

♦ **Flat ears**—Discreet, a little controlling, and cautious of others.

♦ **Protruding ears**—Stubbornness, walking to the sound of a different drummer, and commanding respect due to great intelligence.

Earlobes count, too. If you have large earlobes, you tend to be friendly. The larger the lobe, the friendlier you are. Those with smaller lobes are picky with whom they share friendships.

Ears that are pointed at the top can indicate a fun person with a lot of creativeness, yet these people lack dependability and aren't always as understanding of others who have problems or concerns.

Eyes

We have all heard that the eyes are "the windows of the soul." Well, it's basically true. Your eyes reveal your temperament, feelings, and demeanor.

When looking at the eyes, you must examine more than just the color of the eyes. Consider their size, their shape, and their relationship to the nose.

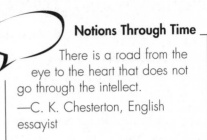

Notions Through Time

There is a road from the eye to the heart that does not go through the intellect.

—C. K. Chesterton, English essayist

- **Large eyes**—Enthusiastic, naïve, not very inventive or original. Protruding eyes indicate a nervous talker!

- **Medium eyes**—Practical and balanced. These are the best type of eyes one can have, as you do not work in extremes.

- **Small eyes**—Deep-thinking, calculating, suspicious, and perhaps temperamental. (I said "perhaps temperamental"—don't get all uptight.)

- **Eyes close together**—Not much patience, but can figure things out accurately about life.

- **Eyes far apart**—Faith and belief in others to a fault. Can be easily tricked! Also loving, giving, and, dare I say, "sweet"?

Also notice the brightness of the eyes. Sometimes when people are not feeling well, their eyes tend to get dull. However, when they are happy or in love, their eyes have a twinkle.

Eye Color

Eyes come in a large variety of colors, so when deciding what eye color you have, choose the one that is closest to yours.

- **Brown** or **black eyes**—Emotional, creative, intense, and affectionate. On the opposite end of the spectrum are lack of self-control, moodiness that shows, and a temper now and then. (Oh well, at least we're not boring.)

- **Green eyes**—Talented, energetic, sometimes emotionally up and down or jealous, and a tendency toward concealment. Intelligence is obvious, and a sense of enterprise is outstanding. (No slackers here.)

- **Blue eyes**—Though a good memory is lacking, an optimistic attitude and excellent concentration abilities shine through. Sometimes tend to hide their feelings. Self-control and vitality also are apparent. (That works!)

- **Hazel eyes** (green/brown or yellowish/brown)—A gentle spirit and tenderness of heart are the most prevailing. Passiveness and innocence abound. ("Make love, not war." I like that attitude.)

- **Pale blue** or **gray eyes**—Analytical, organized, and business-minded, with common sense. Attainment is usually found through planning and researching. (What, no passion or sex appeal? Okay, a few of you have it.)

Occasionally, as people age, eye color will change slightly, especially people with light eyes. If this happens, you need to read the eye color that the person has currently, not the color of his or her youth.

Eyebrows

The eyebrows typically go along with the eyes. But here are a few specific understandings of the brows. They tell us of your temperament.

If you have a mole or birthmark in between your eyebrows, you are an old soul and have great wisdom and knowledge. You were born wise and will always have that gift. Your advice will usually be welcome if done gently.

> **Visionary Insights**
>
> So you pluck your eyebrows or alter them in some manner? That's great, but the eyebrows I refer to here are those before the changes. "Can you even remember?" she says with the raise of an eyebrow.

- **Thick eyebrows**—Lovers and fighters. Intensity and emotions stir within, for positive and negative reactions.

- **Thin eyebrows**—Quiet type of personality, with inner calm. Not much talk—more deep-thinking or meditating. An "old soul."

- **Straight eyebrows**—An ability to draw people toward you, with a vibrant nature. Organized and fun-loving.

- **Arched eyebrows**—Imaginative, trusting—a people person.

- **Eyebrows curving downward**—Impulsive behavior and eager anticipation. Inability to think things through, and later being sorry for poor decisions.

- **Eyebrows curving upward**—Love of the game—any game, as long as it involves people. This can include mystery novels, movies, and attempts to solve a puzzle.

- **Bushy and unkempt**—Thought process unlike that of the average person. Chaotic, sometimes discourteous when young. But you "get it" once you're over 30. At that time, you wonder, "What was I thinking?"

- **Eyebrows that meet in the middle**—Worry, worry, worry. Stop it! It does no good, even though you do it by nature. Possibly prone to depression.

Further study will reveal that often you can judge what type of work a person is involved with via the eyebrows. Without a doubt, there are other areas of the face to examine, but this is a good indicator at a quick glance.

Nose

Your nose tells of your financial situation, your work ethics, and a little about your romantic nature. There are so many noses and so little time. Therefore, here are the most common nose types.

- **Large nose** or **Roman nose** (large nose with an arch)—You want it, you get it. Determination, bravery, assertiveness. Attractive to the opposite sex. Controls finances and enjoys future financial protection.

- **Small, short nose**—A social butterfly, but a workaholic. Seductive. Gets a job done, enjoys financial security.

- **Wide nose**—Offers moral support to others and is romantic. Sometimes, however, may be too much of a free spirit and does not take responsibility for obligations and work.

- **Narrow nose**—Classy, sophisticated, artistic, and in harmony with one's self. A survivor, and someone who spends money wisely. Everything, including love, has its time and place.

- **Crooked nose**—Not a relationship person, by nature.

- **Small ball at tip of nose**—Artistic endeavors; surrounded by creativity and imagination.

- **Large, bulb-shaped at tip of nose**—Money will always be a concern; likes to accumulate things.

The Chinese say that when your nose is shiny, you will be lucky in finances. Good time to gamble? Hmmm ....

Chin

Your chin denotes your level of individuality. So chin up. It can be average, pointed, broad, dimpled, or square, to name only a few.

- **Broad chin**—Strength in body, mind, and spirit. Devoted and having high principles.

- **Narrow chin**—Lack of energy and not much of an appetite for life. Never wanting to be the boss. A no-pressure kind of person.

- **Pointed chin**—Dissatisfied, weak, judges too quickly.

- **Square chin**—Headstrong, independent, someone you can count on in time of need.

- **Double chin**—Good-natured, lack of discipline, and sometimes shady if it serves him or her well. True happiness is achieved after middle age. Note that double chins develop with age and weight gain, which means that our disposition can also change with time and weight change. But even some younger slender people have the signs of a double chin.

- **Oval chin**—Enchanting, artistic nature, kind, and caring. Oh, come on ... you're nearly perfect.

- **Dimpled chin**—A player of the opposite sex. Artistic, enthusiastic, and self-serving.

When examining the chin, look at the jaw and determine whether it is in proportion to the upper part of the face. If the chin and jaw are larger than the forehead, that individual is pushy and insensitive. If the opposite is true, with the forehead larger than the chin and jaw, the person you are reading for is gullible and easily manipulated. A chin in proportion with the other areas of the face is the best; something that doesn't stand out one way or the other.

Mouth

Your mouth shows your personal expression. Like the eyes, the mouth is one of the most meaningful features of the face. It is related to communication skills.

- **Small mouth**—Egotistical, not very open-minded, generally not a friendly person. Good memory, though!

- **Large mouth**—Generous, open to new ideas, energetic; loves to talk.

- **Straight mouth**—Consistent, easygoing; everything in moderation.

- **Turned-up mouth**—Optimistic, great sense of humor, easy to be around.

- **Turned-down mouth**—Pessimistic, with a serious nature; can bring others emotionally "down."

When analyzing the mouth and lips, the interpretations should be combined for a true idea of someone's character according to these features.

Lips

Lips reveal your sensual side and physical aspect. That's not too hard to figure out.

- **Full, thick lips**—Sensual, sometimes egotistical, lacking in concentration. Success comes with difficulties.

- **Medium-thick lips**—Good taste in all things; first class, affectionate, a cuddler.

- **Protruding lips**—Common emotional roller-coaster rides. Aggressive and prone to arguing, yet sympathetic and understanding a moment later.

- **Thin lips**—Determined, reserved, tendency to be emotionally cool; doesn't discuss feelings easily. Trustworthy, and doesn't mind being alone.

Eastern wisdom tells us if only the top lip is thin, you will have financial problems. If only the bottom lip is thin, you may tend to break promises and are not dependable. Both things can be resolved with a little effort.

Face Time

When reading faces, remember to look at the whole picture (or should I say face). Then you can create your own reading.

For example, if you have a chin that shows negative characteristics but your forehead is strong, the forehead might balance out some of the negativity.

> **Visionary Insights**
>
> If you're interested in learning more about face reading, I recommend *The Chinese Art of Face Reading: Mian Xiang* by Henning Hai Lee Yang (Vega, 2002).

The Bumpy Roads of the Past

Phrenology, the art of reading the bumps and shape of the head to predict the character and inclinations of a person, was first devised by Dr. Franz Joseph Gall, a Viennese physician (1758–1828). So was he a soothsayer turned doctor or the other way around? The answer is, he had no inclinations toward fortune telling. This was a scientific speculation.

Dr. Gall devised a detailed theory that the brain was divided into separate parts, each of which represented certain characteristics. By drawing a map of the brain and numbering each section, he identified specific attributes: emotional, intellectual, and physical.

That said, let's still give credit to the fortune tellers and the seers who figured this out before Gall was even born. They simply didn't have a fancy word to call it. These diviners may not have measured and analyzed logically, but from years and generations of reading bumps, they discovered something unique. They thought they sincerely were gifted mystic readers. Why wouldn't they? They knew every time they found a location of a bumpy lump or a lumpy bump, they could predict something about that person's nature, therefore summarizing where that person was most likely going in life. Experimentation and repetition with the same results led them to their conclusions.

> ### Notions Through Time
> The important thing in science is not so much to obtain new facts as to discover new ways of thinking about them.
> —William Lawrence Bragg, physicist

Phrenology did catch on eventually and, at least for some, became an accepted predictor of human nature. As the practice got a "heads up" from certain European social groups, it spread and phrenology societies sprang up in the 1800s. It became a popular issue to both practice and debate. To say the least, it was great dinner conversation.

By practicing phrenology, whether for fun or science, you can explore the aspects of the human skull and test your own conceptions of what determines personality and character.

The Head Divided

To make this easier for the beginner, what I present here is a limited version of the areas of the head and how to read them. Much has been simplified, and only the most important areas are noted.

When you have had a chance to study the definitions and areas of the skull that are assigned to each attribute (explained in a moment), you are ready to start reading heads. Start with people you know. A bald person is great to practice on because the areas are easier to find. We all usually know someone who is bald or partially bald, whether it is due to aging or personal style. The hard part may be getting him to agree to sit while you surf his head!

Have the person turn his head so you see his profile. Next, visually examine the general shape of the head. Decide which areas are large, flat, or in between. After you have visually scoped out the head, get hands-on and touchy-feely, finding the raised areas and depressions unique to the subject's skull.

Areas of the skull.

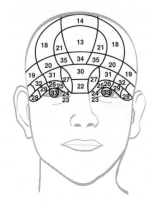

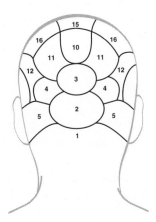

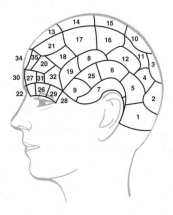

When judging a bump, take into account that too much of a characteristic can be an exaggeration of a quality, while smallness tips the scale on the other end. For example, in the area of combativeness (5), a depression or no bump can be considered insecurity and lack of courage. A medium bump signifies courage and the ability to act quickly and with determination. A large bump could tell of a foolhardy tendency toward risky and rash behavior.

Have a copy handy of our head diagram, and fill in each area as you read it with a number from 1 to 3: 1 being a small bump; 2, a medium bump; and 3, a large bump. The overall picture is important because certain strengths may balance out other weak areas.

When you are finished, make a total assessment from your diagram using the explanations that follow. By using these tools and with experience, you should become quite proficient at this form of fortune telling.

Don't Get Stumped by Bumps

On yourself or a friend, examine the head and look for a bump. Once you locate what feels like a bump compared to the "feel" of the rest of the head, use the previous chart to analyze your findings. For example, I have a large bump (on the scale, it's a 3!) located in the number 3 area of my head. I have had this from birth. The explanation tells me this is concentrativeness—one's inclination to be focused on the home (or details) or to be a wanderer (or visionary). A person with a high level of concentrativeness probably has the best-looking lawn on the street. Since I classify my bump as a 3, this is even more intense. And sure enough, this explanation could not be truer of my personality. Now give it a try on yourself or someone else and see what you can determine.

Feelings

This area (1 to 9 on the diagram) describes feelings and emotions.

   1 Amativeness—Sexuality and muscle movement. This area will be large in someone with great sex appeal and sensuality. In the extreme, you may find someone who is obsessed with sex or jogging.

   2 Philoprogenitiveness—Love, as in love for one's offspring. This is parental love, the thing that makes a mother fight to protect her child and a father argue with the umpire who declares his son is out of the game. In the extreme, you wind up with very spoiled kids.

3 Concentrativeness—One's inclination to be focused on the home (or details) or to be a wanderer (or visionary). A person with a high level of concentrativeness probably has the best-looking lawn on your street.

4 Adhesiveness—Attachments to love objects, such as pets, lovers, or friendships; loyalty. Too much in this area, and you may have a stalker on your hands.

5 Combativeness—Degrees of assertiveness, determination, and courage. Too little, and you have someone who is wimpy or just easy-going; too much, and you have the terminator.

6 Destructiveness/alimentiveness—A desire for annihilation, competitiveness in the extreme that goes a step beyond winning and must see the opponent vanquished. This can be good or bad, depending on whether the person is a bug exterminator or a dentist.

7 Secretiveness—One's tendency to be cunning, to guard one's thoughts and to be cerebral, internalizing one's plans. Good for a poker player or a CEO given to hostile takeovers. Bad for a party planner.

8 Acquisitiveness—Materialistic, enjoying things and acquiring them, given to collecting property and protecting it. Women who have a hundred pair of shoes qualify here, as do men who have to have the car or truck that all the other guys want.

9 Constructiveness—Mechanical skills and the ability to plan and build. Here is where you look at the head when you are hiring a contractor or mechanic.

Sentiments

Opinions, beliefs, and values lead these sections (10 to 21 on the diagram).

10 Self-esteem—The valuing of one's self. Coupled with other attributes, self-esteem can be a promoter of excellence or a tendency toward arrogance and cruelty to others.

11 Love of approbation—Love for attention and praise. This can range from the high achiever to the class clown. With other attributes taken into consideration, this area can indicate a narcissistic and egotistical personality.

12 Cautiousness—Sited as the source of fear, this attribute can indicate a person who is indecisive and overly careful, one given to thinking things through and careful planning, or someone so bold and rash that he or she literally "throws caution to the wind."

13 Benevolence—Cheerfulness, compassion, and concern for the welfare of others at one extreme, and a lack of consideration and ill nature on the other.

14 Veneration—Reverence, respect, religious feelings and spirituality. Too little here, and you have nothing to restrict other areas from going overboard and acting out. Too much here, and you may find the subject immobilized or obsessed with rules and religion.

15 Firmness—Determination and perseverance. You will see this aspect in the stance and speech of the individual, as well as his or her practices. Too much, and you have Hitler.

16 Conscientiousness—The knowledge of right and wrong, as well as obligation and justice. Someone who is strongly conscientious might be an extremist if he or she is not also given to benevolence and cautiousness.

17 Hope—This area can be as strong as living in a fantasy of one's own making, with happiness and love sprouting everywhere. But tempered with caution, hope can be more realistic.

18 Wonder—Delight and surprise, as well as appreciation for the magical moments and mysterious possibilities. In the extreme, childishness and fantasy can be a problem.

19 Ideality—The elevation of reality to a pure and almost mystical excellence. Wearing lucky socks to win a basketball game is one way in which the player takes the reality out of the game and provides himself with idealized powers of winning.

20 Wit or mirthfulness—From satire to pies in the face, this aspect is affected by other dominant traits. With benevolence, you have jolliness, while someone who is combative may prefer sarcasm and making others the butt of jokes.

21 Imitation—Prominent in creative and artistic people, this area enables them to pull information from what they see and use it again in paintings, screen writing, acting, and so on.

Intellectual Faculties

This is all the brainy stuff (22 to 35 on the diagram): those high-brow thoughts that we deal with scientifically, mathematically, creatively, and methodically.

22 Individuality—This area is said to assist in the perception of objects and things, leaning toward scientific facts and data. This may be considered the "geek factor" and is highly appreciated when playing trivia games.

23 Form—Another area highly developed in artists, this faculty helps in face recognition and the grasping of shapes and sizes. It gives a painter the ability to imitate what he sees and is also useful when picking someone out of a line-up.

24 Size—Another strength for judging things, this one has to do with size (how clever)! The general who can estimate the opponent's numbers and the rancher who can estimate the number of cattle in a field fall into this category. Very useful for guessing the number of beans in a jar.

25 Weight or resistance—Here we have physics; judging the effects of wind on a cannonball and adjusting accordingly is the attribute of this organ. Helpful in sports, the military, mechanics, and engineering, this one will get you into college.

26 Coloring—A strength in creative people, this area is about perception of colors: their shades and intensities as well as their complimentary qualities. Look for this in interior and fashion designers, as well as other creative types.

27 Locality—Location, location, location! Map makers, explorers, travelers, and astronomers are all able to scope out terrain, put two and two together to find things, and recognize familiar landmarks easily. If you need a GPS unit in your car to find your mother's house, you are definitely not in this group.

28 Number—Do the math, people! Here we have the number "geeks," the human calculators, the accountants and bankers of the world. If you can figure out what day your birthday will fall on in 10 years, this could be you.

29 Order—People with strength in this area bring order out of chaos, straighten objects on other people's desks, and make me very nervous when they come to my house. They are logical and thorough, and neat as a pin. Too much, and you have an obsessive-compulsive on your hands.

30 Eventuality—A large middle forehead indicates that the person has a large capacity for learning and remembering things. Quick-witted and fast-thinking, these people make good doctors, lawyers, philosophers, and professors. They are avid learners and have a tendency to wind up being know-it-alls.

31 Time—Timing is everything, as they say. In music especially, but also important for dancers and trapeze artists, this involves the ability to judge time, rhythm, and pace, as well as put things in chronological order. Archeologists and historians also fall into this group, even if they can't dance or play the violin.

32 Tune—Another area important to singers and musicians, this is the area that determines whether you can perceive pitch and sound, and to what degree. Complimented by the faculty of Time, a musical genius will have both to a high degree. Otherwise, you may just get a bird watcher who is very, very good at identifying bird songs.

33 Language—Writers and speakers who are eloquent and have a large and colorful vocabulary (not colorful in *that* way), as well as linguists and those who can pick up foreign languages in a heartbeat, all fall into this category. Also noticeable in people who love to hear their own voice and will talk your ear off if you let them.

34 Comparison—This area grants the person the ability to make analogies, to see similar patterns in dissimilar things, and to find common denominators that others may not see. Being able to speak figuratively and to teach lessons by giving examples are seen in people with this strength. Cooking, inventing, and riddle solving fall into this category.

35 Causality—This is the deductive power of reasoning, the ability to see cause and effect and to determine how one thing leads to another, so to speak. A good strength for detectives, investigators, and parents of more than one child.

Once you feel you are getting an aptitude for face and bump readings, attempt to put the readings of both together for more complete results. You may want to write down your results for each as you proceed, and then look back and draw a conclusion. The results should be interesting and informative.

The Least You Need to Know

♦ Face readings can be used for insights into a person's true character and how someone will make future choices.

♦ For a quick version of face readings, focus on the main areas such as the eyes, nose, and chin. These can reveal basic personality traits at a glance.

♦ To determine how to "read" the bumps on a head you must divide the head in your mind's eye into sections. From their locations you can make your determinations.

♦ Bumps on a head can determine what someone's qualities and inclinations are.

Chapter 16

Cloud Prophecies

In This Chapter

- The sky's the limit
- The different types of clouds
- Meet the nine Muses
- Something in the way they move
- Trusting your first impressions

Another form of tapping into your intuitive source is to look at nature. The great outdoors is a springboard to foretelling the future. Look to the mountains, the forest, and especially the clouds. Everywhere you turn in nature there is a way to open your intuitive side to foresight.

The gift of cloud prophesizing is truly a grant from a higher source in the universe. We can all learn to do it, but some will just have a more natural instinct for it. Some of you will recognize immediately that you have this perceptiveness and will experience an immediate high, while others may have to get their heads out of the clouds and try something different.

Cloud prophesizing requires concentration, but the formula is not complicated. The most difficult part of the task is to believe you actually have the ability to do this. Once you start to see a few small images that make sense to you, your self-confidence will grow—and so will your impressions.

Look Up to See Your Future

When we look to the sky and see the clouds drifting by, that in itself is a magical experience. It's pure nature. Yet it may seem as though those ribbons of mist know something we don't.

Do the angels live there? Do fairies jump from cloud to cloud? Do the gods and goddesses of ancient mythology relax there before coming to Earth? I'm not sure about that, but I do feel that these vaporous wonders can inspire our inner thoughts to make predications.

The technical word for cloud gazing is *nephomancy*. Supposedly this method of divination was widely used by the Druids, who were members of an ancient Celtic society. These pre-Christian priestly class people were believed to be magicians, according to the Romans. Little is known about the Druids, and what is known is often ambiguous.

That said, looking at clouds can spiral you up to a dreamlike state. Some clouds are forecasters of good news, while others herald overcast information. Undoubtedly, fast-moving thunderclouds are a forewarning of storms and inclement weather, so they may appear not as magical as the other beauties we see against a blue sky. Yet are they really any less enchanted? A prediction is a prediction.

As children we would look to the skies and simply say things such as, "Look. That cloud looks like an angel," or, "That one looks like a castle." Children still do that today and it's great that they are observant and seeing the figures, but we are going a step further. We are going to "read" what those angels and castles mean.

Types of Clouds

If you want to attune to the different clouds in the sky, you need to understand the different types of clouds that exist. Almost all of us had to learn the names of the different cloud formations in grade school. Yet those names can remain very faint. Fear not, I am here to refresh your shadowy memory.

> **Notions Through Time**
>
> Nature is a mutable cloud which is always and never the same.
>
> —Ralph Waldo Emerson, American poet

Meteorologists have created a classification system based on some fundamental cloud characteristics. These include the color, shape, density, altitude, and degree of cover of each cloud formation.

Cumulus

Cumulus cloud formations have flat bases. They are billowing clouds with a vertical doming, akin to a "cauliflower-like" appearance. They can look like cotton balls or scoops of vanilla ice cream. Cumulus clouds are seen most often during the summer months. The Latin *cumulous* means "heap."

Prophetic meaning: Cumulus clouds are usually associated with sensitivity and emotions: love, art, music, poetry, writing, and all that fluff and "woo woo" in life. (My personal favorite! What's wrong with "woo woo"? Some of us have to be the dreamers of the world.)

Stratus

Stratus clouds appear in a thin, sheetlike formation, covering large portions of the sky. They are frequently gray and thick, and appear in continuous layers with some rippling. The Latin means "covering" or "blanket." What a perfect description.

Prophetic meaning: Situations and goals that are not yet uncovered. New beginnings for projects, aims, lifestyles, and a change of attitude. Breaking bad habits and breaking free of things and people we don't need in our lives. "Lift the blanket," and there's a new world out there for you.

Cirrus

Cirrus clouds are very thin, white clouds with a wispy, feathery, or stringy appearance. They appear to be separated or detached. They are the highest of all clouds, sometimes appearing at 30,000 feet or more above the earth's surface. They are often formed by ice needles or crystals. *Cirrus* is Latin for "curl," which is more than appropriate because these clouds whirl and swirl against a canvas of powder blue with adolescence and excitement at their side.

Prophetic meaning: Business, health, realism, logic and all things of a practical nature. Wisdom from above directed to us below. "As it is above … it is below." Issues of a spiritual nature are also associated with these misty wonders.

Nimbus

Rain clouds are the common name for these pesky but often dramatic forms of nature. They are associated with steady precipitation and often occur in dark gray, thick, continuous layers. They can also appear as puffy, vertically rising rain clouds.

Prophetic meaning: Things of an opposing nature are the messages you will receive when looking at these formations. Don't assume that all the messages are negative; we still learn from contradictory things in life. And learning any lesson is of great value. It may not be something you want to know, but ultimately it is in your best interest. We all need a few dark clouds in our lives, or we wouldn't know what it is like to enjoy the "good" weather. There is always sunshine after a storm, so be patient.

Enlightening Extras

An interesting article was posted on hindustan.net by the editor of the Hindustan Network on Monday, October 10, 2005 at 9:53 EDT: "Cloud Reader Predicted Earthquake 5 Days Ago." The article stated that Shakeel Ahmad, a self-proclaimed cloud reader who makes cardboard boxes for a living, has a passion for reading clouds. He predicted the October 8, 2005, earthquake five days before it happened, but unfortunately his warnings were ignored. He also predicted that a second earthquake in India would come within weeks. Again, he was correct. Ahmad's theory regarding earthquake predictions is that the clouds form a particular mosaic pattern when an earthquake is coming.

Questioning the Heavens

To "read" the clouds, you have to start with a consciousness, not material things. No tools of divination are required. You are entirely on your own; your second sight or psychic abilities will lead you to your future. It's just you and the clouds, my friend. Just you and nature together as a team. No amount of money can buy that. You may be richer than you think.

The Nine Muses and Cloud Divination

According to Greek mythology, the Muses are the nine daughters of Zeus, who was considered the lord of all gods and ruler of Mount Olympus. He was also known for being the weather god and the one most associated with the thunderbolt. Mnemosyne, goddess of memory and words, gave birth to the Muses after lying with Zeus for nine continuous nights. Boy, that was fast—a kid a night!

The beautiful Muses presided over the arts and sciences, and culture. If you are considering endeavors related to the arts or science, consider a thought or query to the Muse (or Muses) who best suits your present or future venture as you stare into the sky.

If you have interests that relate to the following Muses, remember their names when you are starting your cloud readings. Begin with a brief dedication to the one, or several, you chose. I discuss those details later in the chapter.

Here's a closer look at the nine Muses and their attributes:

- **Calliope**—Meaning: Fair-Voiced. She is the oldest of the Muses. Calliope is associated with epic poetry and is illustrated with a writing tablet or book in her hand, sometimes surrounded in a golden hue.

- **Clio**—Meaning: The Proclaimer. This goddess is the muse of history. We see her usually seated with a scroll and several books about her. It is said that she introduced the Phoenician alphabet into the Greek culture.

- **Erato**—Meaning: The Lovely or Passionate. This daughter is associated with eroticism, love, poetry, and mimicry. She was the most famed of the nine muses. Artists portray her with a *lyre* (a small stringed instrument of the harp family), sometimes wearing a crown of roses.

- **Euterpe**—Meaning: The Giver of Pleasure or Rejoicing One. This fair maid is the muse of music. She is light-hearted and fun. The flute is the instrument with which she is associated. In addition, she is said to be the creator of the double flute.

- **Melpomene**—Meaning: The Songstress. The mask of tragedy that she sometimes holds and sometimes wears symbolizes this muse of tragedy. Her singing is joyful, yet she represents tribulation, perhaps "laughing on the outside, yet crying on the inside." In artists' depictions, you may see her with a sword, club, garland, or crown of cypress. Tragic actors wore boots called cothurnes, and so it is said of Melpomene.

- **Polyhymnia**—Meaning: She of Many Hymns. This lady is the youngest of the muses, and we observe her veiled and wearing long robes. Correspondingly, she's pictured looking contemplative, with a finger to her mouth as in deep thought. She is considered a beauty and very serious. Polyhymnia is the muse of sacred poetry, geometry, agricultural pursuits, dance, meditation, and mime. She brings praise to writers who have achieved infinite recognition.

- **Terpsichore**—Meaning: The Whirler. This muse represents dancing and choral song. In some beliefs, it is said that she gave birth to the sirens, creatures with the heads of females and the bodies of birds.

- **Thalia**—Meaning: The Flourishing. She is the muse of comedy and creative dramatic pursuits, such as acting. The Greeks felt that comedy was not just jokes and laughing, but anything that had a happy ending. Typically, she is seen with a mask of comedy, a staff, and a crown of ivy. Melpomene, the muse of tragedy, is her twin sister.

◆ **Urania**—Meaning: Heavenly. This muse is associated with astronomy, astrology, universal love, philosophy, and scientific pursuits. She is usually portrayed with a globe in her left hand and a baton or rod in her right, looking toward the heavens. We sometimes see her with a crown of stars upon her head.

Once you have ascended a step on your spiritual staircase, there is always another, and the process starts all over again. However, each riser takes you closer to spiritual wisdom. Don't underestimate these ladies of the heavens—they may be watching over you.

Visionary Insights

Whether you really believe in the Muses is not the issue. It's all about your intention and what thoughts can boost your intuition to get what you want. It's like praying in a church: you do not really pray to the statue, but to what the statue represents. So it is with the Muses. It is what the thought of them represents. It's merely easier on the mind. Our thoughts give us access to the universal life force, so consider the Muses as a springboard to your cloud interpretations.

A Cloudy Message

Now that you are familiar with the Muses and you know the basic prophetic meanings of the different cloud types, it's time to look up.

There is no time frame or even moon phases to refer to when divining by clouds. If you feel that the outside elements are calling you for a reading, go outside and look to the clouds. Do not overanalyze with thoughts such as, "This is a cloudy day, so the clouds outside will probably be rain clouds, or nimbus, so I will wait for another day." No, if you hear the call of the winds then follow the sound. Follow these steps:

1. On a day when there are clouds in the sky, go outside and distinguish what type of clouds you are looking at: cumulus (emotions), stratus (new opportunities), cirrus (practical concerns), or nimbus (lessons to be learned).

2. Once you make that determination, think about the cloud's prophetic meaning (refer to the details earlier in the chapter). This will tell you the type of questions you can ask about or the type of message you are meant to receive on that day.

3. If possible, relax in a chair or anything you can sit upon outside, or sit on the ground—any place outdoors that is safe and comfortable. This should *not* be done from a window or inside. You have to feel the real atmosphere around you.

4. Close your eyes or look away from the clouds. Ask a question or ponder that you would just like a general message. Bear in mind that the question or the general message will be directly associated with the type of cloud formation in the sky. If you have a connection to one of the nine Muses, think of that Muse's name (even if you can't pronounce it right), and ask in your own way that she makes herself present in this sitting. For example, you may want to know if your piano audition for the concert in the park this summer will result in a booking. You may say something like, "Euterpe [the muse of music], intervene and allow me to see a formation giving me an indication if I will succeed at my audition or not."

5. Inhale through your nose and exhale through your mouth. Do this three times.

6. Look up and gaze at the clouds. They may be moving quickly, remaining still, or gently stirring. Focus on them until you are in a hypnotic state or an altered state of consciousness. You will know that you are in this state because you will have a sense of being on a cloud "high." It is like daydreaming, or the feeling you get before you actually fall asleep but are still technically awake.

7. Once you are in this state of mind, think about your question or query, and intuitively go with your first thoughts regarding that matter. If you don't like what your first thoughts are, you must learn to accept this and not rethink your first impressions.

8. You may use a tape recorder and record your thoughts aloud so you don't forget them. But, if possible, try not to include mechanical devices; it's just more natural without them. Another thought is to record them in a notebook or journal (remember to date them for future recollection).

9. When you have your impressions and feel you have received the information you were looking for, or feel you are not getting any message that day, then stop. If you did not succeed, try again the next day. This could take a few minutes, or it could take 30 minutes or more. There is no time frame here; it is just you communing with nature. Therefore, make sure you have plenty of time so you are on no time schedule.

Although this may sound like an easy process, it takes extensive focusing. You don't just walk outside, ask a question, and look up. You really need to be quiet, relax, and wait till you receive your message. If it doesn't transpire the first time, try, try again. Don't give up.

The Least You Need to Know

♦ Clouds appear in four common categories, each with a different prophetic meaning.

♦ The nine Muses may aid you in advancing your intent.

♦ For cloud readings, your best tool of divination is your intuitive thoughts.

♦ Don't give up if you don't succeed—try again.

Chapter 17

Crystal Gazing and Scrying

In This Chapter

- ◆ We're always looking for answers

- ◆ I can see clearly now: clairvoyance

- ◆ Famous scryer Nostradamus

- ◆ Gazing into crystals and black mirrors

- ◆ Scrying takes patience and practice

You may have seen pictures of a gypsy woman with a turban, sitting at a table and chair gazing into a crystal ball. You most likely have heard those famous lines from *Snow White:* "Mirror, mirror on the wall, who's the fairest of them all?" And remember the Wicked Witch of the West showing Dorothy an image of her worried Auntie Em? What are these people really doing? They're scrying. That's what you will learn in this chapter—how to gaze at a reflective object and pick up images of the past, present, or future.

Clairvoyance is related to scrying, so we explore that skill a little as well. And you'll learn how to make your own reflective black mirror so you, too, can get "scry high"!

Answers Under Glass?

Since the dawn of humankind, men and women have searched for some sign of what lies ahead. Will we find someone to love? Will we have wealth and success? Will we live for a long, long time? As primitives, we sought signs in nature, such as the eclipse of the moon or the sun. We made human and animal sacrifices, reading entrails to seek patterns to events. And we sought the counsel of fortune tellers to help us face life's hurdles.

> **Notions Through Time**
>
> If I have the gift of prophecy and can fathom all mysteries and all knowledge, and if I have a faith that can move mountains, but have not love, I am nothing.
>
> —1 Corinthians 13

Methods varied, becoming more sophisticated with time. As early as medieval times, and perhaps before, people used scrying to see images of events that were not immediately apparent.

Scrying is an art. Some people can see visions or images immediately, and others must put more time and effort into this method. Scrying takes much concentration and practice, but it is well worth the results. Whether you have natural psychic abilities, you aren't sure, or you simply assume you don't have a psychic bone in your body, fear not! With training, you can still master this art.

Clairvoyance

Scrying is a form of *clairvoyance*. The word clairvoyance comes from the French, meaning "clear seeing" or "clear vision." Our physical sight can allow us to see only things that are material. When we use spiritual sight, or clairvoyance, we are allowed to see beyond the physical. For that reason, sometimes clairvoyance is referred to as our "second sight." The actual origin of clairvoyance is not known. When you see clairvoyantly, you see images, scenes, and events in your mind's eye.

def•i•ni•tion

Scrying is divination using a reflective surface such as a mirror, crystal, polished stone, or even water to see images about the past, present, and future. The word **clairvoyant** is made up of two French words: *clair*, meaning "clear," and *voyant*, meaning "seer." A person who is clairvoyant, therefore, is someone who sees clearly into the future.

Perhaps you have felt the presence of someone in a room with you when no one was actually there. Ghosts? Maybe, but most likely you were feeling someone in your life who was thinking of you at that moment or reaching to you from the past or future. Had you focused on a reflective object at that time, you may have "picked up" who it was and what that person was doing. These types of images or feelings could well mean you have natural clairvoyance but that it hasn't been developed.

So, where do these images come from? We have the innate ability to project images from our own consciousness onto a reflective object to see objectively with physical eyes. Some people unwillingly see images in regular mirrors, glass doors, or anything reflective. These are spontaneous and sometimes disturbing experiences; however, they are no different than someone gazing into a crystal ball.

To the newcomer to scrying, it is difficult to understand that by merely looking at a crystal ball, mirror, or anything contemplative, you can actually see images and shapes. Yet when you are daydreaming with your eyes wide open, your mind is totally elsewhere and you are not aware of exactly what you are looking at. We have all had daydreaming experiences. Scrying is something like that, but you induce it consciously for the purpose of seeing into your mind's eye.

Nostradamus' Gift

Nostradamus (1503–1566), a French astrologer, was considered a great prophet and psychic. In his book *Nostradamus' Visions of the Future* (The Aquarian Press, 1992), J. H. Brennan writes …

> As an astrologer, Nostradamus was only as good as his system … which, as Gauquelin has shown, cannot have been very good. Yet Nostradamus, even on the evidence of our limited investigation so far, managed to make extraordinary, accurate, and detailed predictions for a number of important people. Consequently, Nostradamus must have gone beyond the rote interpretations of his astrological findings. He must, in short, have used intuition and/or psychism focused through an astrological lens.

On the basis of results, it seems Nostradamus was possessed of a gift far beyond that of any other psychic in history. If he channeled that gift through astrology, it is interesting to ask whether the gift itself was a natural, inborn talent or something consciously developed. There is, in fact, substantial evidence to suggest the latter.

In 1560, Catherine de Medici summoned Nostradamus to the Château Chaumont where he had previously used astrology to foretell events for her. Again she ordered him to disclose future predictions. However, this time Nostradamus used no astrological guidance. Instead, he requested the use of a large room in which he would not be disturbed and there traced a magic circle on the floor, fortifying it with holy names of power and angelic seals. Before it, he set up a magic mirror, a black concave surface of polished steel. Nostradamus took Catherine by the hand and led her into the protection of the circle. Then he began an invocation to the angel Aneal, a member of the celestial hierarchy supposed to grant prophetic visions. The focus of attention was the black mirror, in which visions would appear. On other occasions, Nostradamus would use a piece of black obsidian to see his visions.

The description of these magical operations is taken from the work of John Hogue, an expert on Nostradamus, and it is only fair to say that not all historians would accept the story as valid. But for all that, there seems very little doubt that Nostradamus did believe in, study, and practice magic, and that his prophetic abilities were stimulated by the ritual practice of scrying.

Enlightening Extras

Here are only a few of Nostradamus's startling predictions that came to pass. Keep in mind he died in 1566!

- The French Revolution of 1789
- The rise and fall of the British Empire
- The atomic bombing of Hiroshima
- The first moon landing
- Terrorist attacks on New York

The Most Common Scrying Tools

Only a few differences exist between the two most common choices of scrying tools: crystals and black mirrors. Scrying can take place in many places, including pools of water, but these two appear repeatedly in the tradition. If you really enjoy this form of divination, you might try scrying in whatever seems most promising to you. I've known people who could scry simply by looking at a blank wall.

Crystals

Crystals, or round crystal balls or spheres, are the most common tools for scrying and the easiest to find. A clear quartz crystal is preferred to other types that have facets, smoky appearances, or different types of inclusions that can look like fuzz, lines, or cloudy images. A clear quartz crystal will have a reflective quality and electrical energy can promote psychic awareness.

Quartz crystals are found in our radios, transmitting and receiving radio waves. Quartz makes up the electronic chips that we have in our computers today. No quartz means no modern-day computers! This is a very effective stone.

Crystal Shopping

When purchasing a crystal, you don't have to purchase a quartz crystal ball. It can be any crystal in any shape, as long as it is large enough for you to be comfortable when you gaze into it. Bear in mind that some crystals have inclusions or imperfections, which can be distracting. Therefore, a crystal that has little to no imperfections is usually the best. In spite of that, when you get the feel for working with a crystal, even those tiny specks or flaws can sometimes be overlooked.

You may also find crystals with "veils." Veils are comparable to webs or murky wisps that look like vapor within the crystal. This is not necessarily considered a flaw; you may be drawn to it for many reasons.

It is said that you don't pick the crystal, the crystal picks you. If you hold a clear crystal or crystal ball in each hand and you feel more connected to one than the other, take the one that "feels good" and you will never go wrong. Therefore, if you can purchase a crystal in person at a New Age or gemstone store, that's great. Even if you don't see the stone in person, online purchases work well, too. A small crystal ball, sometimes called a crystal sphere, the size of a golf ball, costs approximately $30 to $40. Consider attending a gemstone show, if one comes to your area. I have traveled hours to shows just to find real bargains, and it was always worth it. Usually your local convention center can tell you what shows are coming to town, so call and ask. If you do find a crystal that is less expensive but has flaws, it is still workable, if you can look past the imperfections.

> **Visionary Insights**
>
> Some new-age type of establishments sell Lucite or acrylic translucent spheres. Although the energy may not be as strong as that of the quartz crystal, these spheres still work quite well and cost much less.

Clearing Your Crystal

When you purchase a crystal of any kind, you should clear it of the energy of others who have handled it before you. You might think of it like washing a vegetable that many at the produce store may have touched. There are many methods for clearing a crystal. The easiest is to hold it under a running faucet using cold water. While the water runs over the crystal, visualize the energy of others being removed from the crystal. There is no time limit here; stop when you feel it is cleared. You now have a cleansed stone. (In fact, you should clear all of your tools of divination in one form or the other. Clearing gemstones and other tools is addressed in Chapter 4.)

Charge Your Crystal

Next, you should charge your crystal for scrying purposes. This means to put a powerful energy into the stone that will aid you in crystal gazing. Wait for a full moon and set your crystal outside in a safe place, if possible. If you cannot place your crystal outside, than put it near a door or window overnight. I know you may be impatient, and waiting for a full moon to charge your crystal might be tiresome. Nevertheless, this is one of the most powerful ways to charge it.

If you absolutely do not want to wait, you can bury the crystal in the ground for 24 hours any day of the month, and you will receive the earth's energy. This method can also work nicely. You decide. Are you more of an earth person or a lunar type? Some people do both.

Black Mirrors

The difference between black mirrors and other methods of scrying is that some say black mirrors are clearer and less complicated. Yet others will say they can be a bit spooky. Nevertheless, give this form of divination a try because it is very accurate and will open up an entire new world of realization to the scryer. Black mirrors can definitely be windows to other dimensions. Unlike crystals, they offer an additional quality—communication with those from other realms: angels, dead loved ones, or *spirit guides.*

def•i•ni•tion

Spirit guides are people who have made the transition into the death realms or into a higher dimensional plane, and who have come back to us to help us on this plane. They appear during meditation or altered states of consciousness. Not all spirit guides are dead loved ones. Some are people we never met who feel they have something they can share with us while we are still on this planet. Animal spirit guides exist as well, especially in Native American beliefs. If you sense an animal that gives you comfort in times of need, and you see or sense this animal in your dreams or during meditation, you probably have an animal spirit guide. Don't confuse spirit guides with angels, who never had physical form.

Your crystal or black mirror should be kept in a soft bag or box, wrapped in cloth instead of being displayed. By keeping it protected and hidden, you keep its magical qualities from dissipating. The cloth color doesn't matter.

Finding a Black Mirror (or Creating Your Own)

You can purchase black mirrors from New Age gift stores or on the Internet. They usually start at about $6. A more expensive mirror is not necessarily better. Use your intuition—you'll find the right one. Clear and charge your store-bought mirror the same way you would clear and charge your crystal.

You can also create your own black mirror. Creating your very own mirror assigns it your personal energy and magic. Feeling a connection with the tools of your craft is important in making them work well with you. Here's how to do it.

Purchase an oval or round picture frame of a dark color no larger than 12 inches with good glass that has not been scratched. Remove the glass and place it on a piece of newspaper, somewhere outside where you can use spray paint. With a can of high-gloss black spray paint, apply the paint to the surface of one side of the glass evenly, making sure the paint does not run. If you can get an even coat on without having to apply a second coat, the mirror effect will appear more clearly. Let it dry completely.

The painted side should face away from you when you put it back in the frame. If you like, you can decorate the frame around your mirror with your favorite gemstones, shells, or beads, using a hot-glue gun or Super Glue. Also consider using pieces of old jewelry as a decorative border. The more you can personalize your mirror, the more of a connection you will have with it.

You don't have to clear or charge a homemade mirror because it's better not to wet it or bury it. But if you feel you must, pass your hand across it in a sweeping motion and visualize anyone else's energy moving away and out your door to the west.

In the Dark

The following information refers to crystal gazing as well as scrying into a black mirror. If you can do a little meditation or focusing beforehand you will be much more relaxed so I highly recommend it. You may do your scrying at anytime, day or night, when you need information, although evenings are the best for black mirrors because of the darkness. If you cannot conduct your mirror scrying at night, you must be in a darkened room or use a dark cloth around your head to block out most of the light. I suggest that you start by working inside in a very dark room because there is less interference of sound and motion. Outside is acceptable, but your skills must be highly developed to be successful.

Images will come and go. If you see something very negative or frightening, follow your instinct. If you want to stop the process, do so and try again some other time. If you feel it is a warning, you may want to continue. This is your individual choice.

On a lighter note, you may find yourself asking about your love life when you suddenly see a handsome stranger. Now this is a picture you don't want to see vanish because you would like to know the outcome and maybe even a name. Then, suddenly, for no apparent reason, the image will disappear. Images phase in and out, as in a dream. How many times have you awakened disappointed that you couldn't finish a dream? This is what you can expect from crystal or mirror gazing. Often just when you start to get a clear image ... poof, it's gone.

There is no standard reasoning for this. It is not that your concentration is not adequate, so don't push yourself. Trying too hard can be counterproductive.

Gaze Patiently

You will find that many types of fortune telling, such as reading cards or deciphering tea leaves, will deliver good results quickly. Scrying, however, requires patience and more practice than the other methods of divination. Everyone is able to achieve some expertise. But a few people really have an extraordinary gift for it, much like Nostradamus.

> **Enlightening Extras**
>
> Ancient scryers felt that the best time to do scrying was when the moon was on the increase, or waxing. They thought the impressions would be more plentiful and would appear more quickly.

Learning to scry is like learning an instrument. We can all learn to play the piano, for example, but a few special people seem to have more talent and a better ear for music than others. Only by experimentation with this magical tool will you be able to really know whether you are truly talented. Think of yourself as an artist. You don't just walk into a room and start painting. You need canvas, paints, lighting, brushes, and so on.

Plan Ahead

The art of scrying is developed over time, so think of your first experiments with it as a series of experiences, planned ahead of time in sessions. This will help you cultivate the necessary patience to put in the time it takes to get even the first glimmerings of results.

Here are some considerations for your first formal sessions:

◆ Choose the days, phases of the moon, places, and directions for at least your first two sessions in advance. Scrying must not be a hurried art, so take the time to consult your calendar and choose your times and places carefully.

◆ Set up in a quiet area with a table or desk. You may want to place your mirror or crystal on a black piece of cloth to further stop reflection. If the crystal came with a stand, use it! You do not want the sphere to roll off the table. Setting it on a dark, partially stuffed pillow will help, if there's no stand. If you are using a mirror and it can stand, make sure it does. If not, place the mirror flat and look down. You will have to experiment with what works best for you prior to your scrying day.

◆ If you are scrying at night, the room should not be totally blacked out, but should be dimly lit. You may choose to light a candle, if you like. However, keep the candle away from the crystal ball or mirror because it could reflect in the surface, which you do not want. A soft nightlight can also be used. If you have a dimmer switch for your lights, that is excellent. If possible, your back should be to the light, and a dark cloth should be over your head.

◆ If lighting incense or playing meditative instrumental music appeals to you for this session, have it chosen and in place in advance. Playing a radio is out of the question. You don't want a commercial about chicken wings to suddenly commence. Talk about something foul breaking your concentration!

> **Enlightening Extras**
>
> If you light a candle for scrying, the best candle color is white because it represents purity. Scent, sizes, and shape does not matter. If you can't find white, you can substitute off-white.

Session One

Finally, you are ready to conduct your first scrying session. Your first session should be only around 10 to 15 minutes in length. But rather than watching a clock, which would be a diversion, just estimate. Read through this whole procedure a few times before you begin: you will not be able to focus if you are reading these guidelines at the same time you are trying to evoke an image.

Place your crystal or mirror on the table and sit in front of it. There is no fixed rule about how close you need to put your crystal, but of course, you need to be able to see it. If you wear glasses, put them on.

Inhale deeply through your nose and exhale through your mouth. Do this three times to help relax.

At this learning session, you will not be asking any questions or looking for anything in particular. You should be looking for spontaneous images or symbols. Now stare into your crystal or mirror. See what comes into focus and what materializes where you are not directly focusing.

As you gaze, you will eventually and unconsciously find a natural and comfortable placement for your eyes and body. As you practice, you will find that you will automatically resume this posture and gaze. At first, however, feel free to maneuver about until you have reached a position that is stress-free and relaxing. This, in itself, is a large step toward eventual success.

As you gaze at the crystal or mirror, you will find that your mind tends to wander. You will suddenly start thinking about that test you have to take or those bills you have to pay. This is totally normal. You will think about not only important things, but also things of little importance. Don't be surprised if you start thinking about that awful sweater you bought 3 years ago and why you did it. What were you thinking?

If you find your mind straying, let it do so. Don't force yourself to concentrate. You will eventually learn how to control those thoughts by simply acknowledging them for a few seconds and letting them pass naturally. With time, those outside distractions will simply just not appear; you will be able to focus totally on the crystal.

> **Visionary Insights**
>
> While you are learning, you should do your scrying in the same place under the same conditions at the same time, if possible. This will help increase your concentration.

If your eyes begin to tire as you are scrying during this first session (and they will), close them for a few seconds or look at something else in the room. Tell yourself that at the next session you will have more stamina and more control of your senses.

You are slowly programming your mind to dispel thoughts in which you are not interested. This will be a breakthrough to being an accomplished seer. For now, just continue to gaze for 10 to 15 minutes and see if you get any type of impressions.

If you do not notice anything as you come to the end of your first session, keep relaxing but go to the next step. Focus on something specific that you will be doing in the future, such as going to an event. Think about how you got invited, who else is attending, where it will be held, and so on. See if you can envision in the crystal or mirror what will take place. Can you see people or symbols? Perhaps you will see a hazy tree or some other cryptic scene. Later make a note of it in your journal.

After you attend the event, see if you remember the significance of the tree or whatever else appeared to you. Was the affair outside? Did you meet someone special next to a big oak? If you can't relate that tree to anything that happened, accept defeat and try, try again. Do not give up too easily. Do you think Nostradamus gave his first prophecy perfectly?

When you are finished with your scrying session, put your scrying object away, and put everything back in order until the next time.

Session Two

Follow the same instructions for preparation as for your first session, but decide whether you merely want to see what images appear or to ask questions. If you ask questions, do so when you feel relaxed and confident. After you ask a question the images should appear that provide the answer.

The second time you do a scrying session, after you focus your eyes, see if you can start to visualize a cloudy mist. (Of course, this can happen the first time around, but it is very unlikely.) See if the mist forms itself into any shapes or if anything seems to be going on just behind the mist. Even from these vague appearances, you can receive much information. Although the following qualities are not scenes or recognizable images, they may give you some information about the question you have or the future event you are imagining.

- ◆ **Glistening and silvery impressions**—Good sign, prosperity
- ◆ **Milky color**—Unstable circumstances
- ◆ **Dark and cloudy**—Trouble
- ◆ **White mist**—Positive signs
- ◆ **Black mist**—Negative associations
- ◆ **Shades of violet, blue, or green**—Happiness and satisfaction
- ◆ **Shades of red, orange, or yellow**—Danger, illness, or disappointment

If you see simple symbols or one image, use your common sense and take the image for what it is. Some scryers feel that images have metaphorical or symbolic meanings, like in a dream. Under this way of thinking, for example, a train could mean travel or possibly something more associative, such as "training" for something. I feel the images in scrying are more literal, meaning that if you see a train, you will have an actual connection with a train. It could be taking a trip by rail or buying a model railroad, but it will have something to do with an actual train.

Asking "Yes" and "No" Questions

If you need a simple "yes" or "no" answer, there is a quick and accurate way to receive your reply by scrying. Focus on your mirror or crystal ball as usual and ask your question aloud or silently. You should eventually see vapors or cloudlike images. If the haze ascends, it's a yes. If it descends, it's a no.

General Questions

When you are proficient at scrying, you can target specific areas of your life:

- Health
- Love
- Money
- Career
- Pets
- Spiritual messages
- People who have crossed over to the other side

Eventually, you should be able to pick up actual scenes and keen impressions by simply thinking about these topics. You will also be able to ask about things that happened in the past. Just silently voice the question to yourself (or aloud, if you prefer): "Did Sheila really forget to call me, or did she go to that party instead?" You may get an image of Sheila dancing the night away.

Feel free to get very specific in the present as well. Ponder, for instance, the idea that you would like to know what your boyfriend is doing right this minute. You may be surprised, so be prepared. He could be in the shower!

I once wanted to know why an editor wasn't returning my e-mails, so I took out my black mirror. I kept seeing her at her desk continuously grabbing something white. Later, I found out she had a cold and told me she kept sneezing and grabbing for Kleenex from her desk all day long.

In other words, you can pick up actual ongoing episodes. Some will be obvious, and others will be just a tad foggy. This is like reality television with people you know.

> **Visionary Insights**
>
> If you are scrying for someone else, keep that person at arm's length away from you. You should also not have more than two people in the room, to avoid too many energies complicating the situation.

A Phone Call Without a Phone

Another use for this skill is to communicate with someone else who is far away. Each person must have a scrying mirror or crystal and know how to gaze properly. One person gazes into his or her scrying object and silently asks the other person to send him or her a message. The other person, if at home, should be able to sense that someone is trying to connect and should go to the mirror or crystal and respond.

Later when they can both talk or e-mail, it is interesting to see what the results were. Talk about wireless!

The Least You Need to Know

- ◆ Crystal gazing is a form of clairvoyance, seeing beyond the physical.

- ◆ You need a clear reflective object in which to gaze. The most common tools are crystals, crystal balls, and black mirrors.

- ◆ Nostrodamus, a famous scryer, predicted many accurate events of his time as well as of ours.

- ◆ Scrying requires more practice and patience than most forms of divination. Don't try too hard, or it will be counterproductive.

Chapter 18

Palmistry

In This Chapter

♦ Palms of the past

♦ A closer look at your hand

♦ Mount up

♦ Fingers and nails tell tales

♦ Life, head, heart, fate, love: the major lines on the hand

♦ Other marks found on the hand

Whenever I go to a party and people hear what I do for a living, they frequently stick their hand in front of me and say, "Read my palm." Personally, it gets a bit tiring. Therefore, the more people who learn to read palms on this planet, the less pressure there will be on me and others like me.

Consequently, in this chapter, I teach you the simplest way to get a grasp of the general ideas of palmistry. You will learn the basics on how to read the palms, the fingers, the nails, and the major lines on the hand—and you'll even learn to spot the good omens from the not-so-good omens. Also, if there is someone's hand you want to hold, it's a great excuse!

Give Our Ancients a Hand

It is commonly said that your palm print is the "blueprint" of your life. It can tell everything about your past, present, and future. The observation of the palm, also referred to as *chiromancy* or *palmistry*, is not a new study. Cave paintings of hands were found in prehistoric caves dating back to the Stone Age. How do you think Fred Flintstone and Barney Rubble charted their life through Bedrock? It wasn't with Tarot cards!

The study of hands as a way to understand oneself and relationships with others can also be found in ancient Hindu writings.

Palmistry was practiced during the time of the early Greeks and Romans from around 400 B.C.E. to 40 B.C.E., and continued to grow into the Middle Ages. Obviously, for centuries, everyone had their hands out.

def•i•ni•tion

Chiromancy or **palmistry** is the practice of predicting future events for a person through the study of their palms. The lines, fingers, fingernails, and all sections of the hand can determine past, present, and future occurrences. All these areas have meanings and give us an indication of a person's character. Palmistry has been practiced all over the world, although numerous cultures have different variations of the process.

Take My Hand

Generally, when you first begin to do a palm reading, you look at the size of both hands in relation to the size of the person for whom you are reading. Next, you get a general feel for the palms. Determine what the overall look is showing you before you start detailing lines, mounts, fingers, and knuckles.

What's Your Size?

For simplicity's sake, we will look at only three general hand sizes: small, large, and medium. We are looking for the overall size of the palm and fingers in comparison to the rest of the body. Use common sense: if you never thought your hands were too large or too small for the rest of your frame, they are most likely average or medium. If you always thought your hands were a little on the big or small side compared to the rest of your torso, you would have noticed by now. There are exceptions, but those need to be investigated in more advanced books on palmistry.

- **Small**—To most people's surprise, those with small hands have big ambitions. They are leaders and take-charge individuals, and are not detailed-oriented. They look at the big picture and have no patience for trivia.

- **Large**—These folks are the opposite of our small-handed friends. They love details and have patience for minor aspects of a job. They are team players and would rather have someone else be the boss so they don't have to worry about the shop after a day of work. It's amazing what those big hands can skillfully do.

- **Medium**—This in-between size of hand is attached to someone who can be a leader or a recruit. These people do whatever it takes to accomplish a goal, without going to extremes. They are easy to live with and can understand all sides of the spectrum.

Enlightening Extras

As you search deeper into the art of palmistry, bear in mind that your reading must be an accumulation of all the aspects of the hand. For example, if someone's palms indicate that he is cheap, but other details say he is very generous, you must analyze the situation. It may mean that typically the person is generous, yet when it comes to spending money in a certain area, such as valet parking, he won't open that wallet.

Palms Away

The feel of the hand also provides insights:

- **Tender and fleshy**—This person tends to take the easy way out in all things through life, if possible. This person is not a good choice as a helper in anything that is difficult. Also, he or she has a tendency to overindulge in the better things life offers. (So what's wrong with that?) Still, this person can be good-natured and doesn't take daily occurrences too seriously.

- **Solid and lean**—Does the term *penny-pincher* ring a bell? This individual isn't naturally cheap, but for some reason he or she is concerned about never having enough money at hand.

- **Firm**—This is the ideal hand. This person is ambitious and successful, someone who works hard and smart, with balance in his or her life.

- **Concave or hollow**—This is not a good businessperson and should not pursue such paths. This person may tend to struggle in life to achieve the material pleasures many are looking for. He or she gets by, but to go to another level may take a bit longer. (But it's not impossible.)

Now that we have essentially looked at the hand as a whole, it is time to move on to the more detailed areas of palmistry.

I Have to Hand It to You

Before you actually start to read the palm, you have to determine which hand you read and for what purpose. Read the left palm for future conditions, feelings, and private wants and wishes. Ordinarily, this is the best choice. Read the right palm for things of the past and family traits.

> **Notions Through Time**
>
> Destiny has two ways of crushing us—by refusing our wishes and by fulfilling them.
>
> —Henri Frederic Amiel, Swiss philosopher

The pads of flesh that go around the edge of the palm are known as the *mounts*. These mounts are named after seven planets. They are indicated on the following diagram. If the flesh of a mount is much higher than the others or if it protrudes, it is overdeveloped. If you can barely tell there is a mount present or it is sunken, it is weak or underdeveloped. If it is a little elevated and not flat, it is normal.

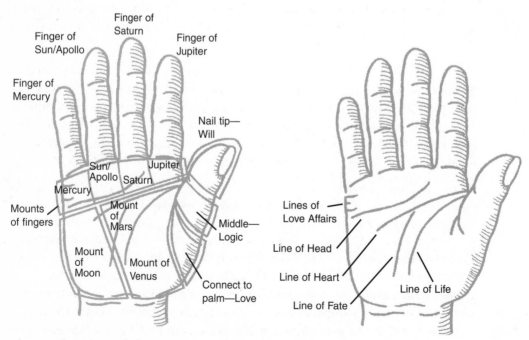

An at-a-glance key to the lines, mounts, and symbols of the hand.

Use the following explanations of the mounts as an additional part of the entire reading you will later form:

- **Mount of Jupiter.** Location: The base of the index finger, or Jupiter finger. **Normal development**—Associated with achievements, leadership, wisdom, and possible religious aspects. Lover of food and the outdoors. **Overdevelopment**—Associated with jealousy, being overbearing, and not being well liked. **Underdevelopment**—Associated with lack of religious or spiritual beliefs. Family problems not easy to amend. Not reliable.

- **Mount of Saturn.** Location: The base of the middle finger, or Saturn finger. **Normal development**—Associated with loners, deep thinkers, and few friends. Lover of classical or meditative music; dominant mathematical abilities. **Overdevelopment**—Pessimism and financially out for oneself. Work and money come first, at anyone else's expense. **Underdevelopment**—Someone tending to be depressed and morbid—a party pooper, to say the least.

- **Mount of Sun/Apollo.** Location: The base of the third ring finger, or Sun/Apollo finger. **Normal development**—Associated with beauty, art and the artistic temperament, joy, fame, and positive public attention. **Overdevelopment**—Affectionate, classy, great vanity, and a tendency to overdo, as in gambling and believing flatterers. **Underdevelopment**—Shyness; a career in show business most likely will not work. Reckless money habits. Sometimes a colorless lifestyle. Everything average and ordinary.

- **Mount of Mercury.** Location: The base of the little finger, or Mercury finger. **Normal development**—Associated with affluence, much traveling; easily picks up languages. Careers such as lawyers, inventors, and scientists are dominant. Loves "the game." **Overdevelopment**—Uses intellect to take advantage of others. Thinks too much and needs to relax, or can get in trouble of a legal nature. **Underdevelopment**—Not a business-oriented person. Lacking people skills and fears speaking in public.

- **Mount of Venus.** Location: The fleshy base of the thumb area. **Normal development**—Associated with passionate experiences and many love affairs prevailing. Loving the "good" things in life. An attractive and charming person. **Overdevelopment**—Not faithful and may tend to go from lover to lover, making no excuses. Attractive, but with high levels of sensuality, showing little respect for a partner. Sex is the number one priority, before family, work, or education. **Underdevelopment**—A serious sort, in which love has little chance to tear down the emotional walls. Little to no sex drive, and could care less about such things.

- **Mount of the Moon.** Location: Down the outside of the palm, between the heart line and the wrist. **Normal development**—Associated with traveling to unusual places, interest in the mysterious things in life. Good-natured but should be aware of being in dangerous situations due to curiosity. **Overdevelopment**—Someone creating their own problems and feeling sorry for themselves as a result. **Underdevelopment**—A lack of imagination and vision surrounds this individual.

- **Mount of Mars.** Location: Between the thumb and Mount of Jupiter. **Normal development**—For men, the women are crazy about them. For women, they attract men you find in romance novels. For both sexes, their relationships are strong, romantic, and exciting. Lovers of excitement and intrigue. **Overdevelopment**—Pushing people around is part of their makeup. Bragging about being in control is part of their fun. **Underdevelopment**—Someone who is nonconfrontational to the point of cowardice. The best word to describe this person is *wimp*. (Sorry.)

Some of these interpretations may seem a bit harsh. But remember that you have to combine the other influences around a person to create a proper reading. Someone could show a trait indicating an anger problem, but next to that line or mount is an aspect that shows he or she is overly gentle. Therefore, the person is balanced. Put together the puzzle. Do not look individually at traits.

The Fickle Finger of Fate

The fingers of your hand are important factors in fortune telling. Fingers are one of our liveliest parts, after the eyes and the mouth; your fingers communicate many things about you and can be used for every form of expression. From the impatient drumming fingers of someone delayed, to the single finger held to one's mouth to indicate quiet, fingers communicate and express our feelings all of the time. It's no wonder that they have drawn so much attention to themselves over the years, as fortune tellers seek to understand the strengths, weaknesses, and overall character of their subjects.

Look for many general characteristics when inspecting the overall look of the fingers on the hand. When reading fingers, it is not important which hand you read, left or right.

> **Visionary Insights**
>
> When conducting any type of palmistry, consider using a magnifying glass. This is not just for those who are visually challenged, but for all. It makes the process easier.

- **Short fingers** indicate an impulsive, enthusiastic, and hasty attitude of someone who is quick in action and thought, and who has strong intuitive capabilities.

- **Long fingers** show a tendency to be curious but analytical and someone who is inclined to worry. The long-fingered person is considered loyal and takes pride in a job well done.

More finger shapes should be investigated if you decide to pursue palmistry in detail. Consider exploring *The Complete Idiot's Guide to Palmistry, Second Edition* (Alpha Books, 2005) for specific information about this extensive subject.

Here's a Tip

The finger is generally divided into three sections: the tip, the joint, and the base that attaches to the palm. Let's start with the tip, which is considered the first section of the finger:

- **Flared fingertips** are those of adventurers who enjoy a challenge and tend to throw themselves into their work.

- **Square fingertips** are those of a conservative and traditional person who likes to stick with tried-and-true ventures that show results.

- **Round fingertips** are the mark of someone who makes people and relationships their priority. These people enjoy learning new things and may change careers several times in their lives.

- **Pointed fingertips** are the indication of an artist, a poet, or someone who feels things deeply.

Nice Joint You Have There

The second section of the finger is the joint or knot. Look at the joints of the fingers. If they stick out and cause the fingers to look irregular, they are considered large. This indicates that the hand owner is organized and thinks before making decisions or acting in haste. When the fingers are smooth with no obvious joints, the individual is spontaneous and a free-spirit type with artistic tendencies. That's knot bad!

Let's Get Connected

Now look at the size of the base of the finger that connects to the palm. Is there any difference in its size compared to the other two areas? Noticeably larger means the individual has no patience for negativity in life and focuses on pleasures. Smaller or flat signifies someone who can "go without" in life for a long time in order to achieve his or her ultimate goal. A size that is uniform to the other sections means the individual enjoys comforts but is not self-indulgent; he or she can make sacrifices to achieve an objective but does not suffer excessively to do it.

My Fingers Have Names

Each finger has a name that is drawn from the name of the mount of the palm below it. The Finger of Jupiter is the index finger, the Finger of Saturn is next, the Finger of the Sun/Apollo is the ring finger, and the Finger of Mercury is the pinkie. The thumb is split into three segments: (the tip) Will, (the middle) Logic, and (part of the palm) Love.

- **The Jupiter finger** (the index finger)—A long Jupiter finger indicates leadership qualities in a person who is confident and excels while drawing attention to oneself naturally. A short Jupiter finger is the sign of a giving person, one who likes to be supportive and tends to work hard in the background as a strong team member who loves to pitch in and help.

- **The Saturn finger** (the middle finger)—A long Saturn finger indicates someone who is cautious and likes to investigate fully any venture or undertaking. Preferring security and comfort, this person tends to like a predictable existence and routine, content with old friends and familiar surroundings. A short Saturn finger is a characteristic of the free-spirited soul who likes new experiences and resists being tied down. Although this person will eventually settle down, the need for change will lead him or her to experiment with new things throughout life.

- **The Sun/Apollo finger** (the ring finger)—A long Sun/Apollo finger marks a creative and artistic person given to joyful and intense dedication to special projects. Passion radiates, making this person attractive and fun to be around. A short Sun/Apollo finger is found on a shy person who is somewhat lacking in confidence. Very likable, this person needs to be drawn out by friends to reveal the understated charm and contentment underneath.

- **The Mercury finger** (the little finger)—A long Mercury finger is an indication of a persuasive and convincing personality who is both charming and determined. This is often the mark of a salesman or politician, or anyone who might move up the ladder into leadership by moving people to be supportive through character and good judgment. A short Mercury finger can be found on the down-to-earth, earnest, boisterous, and often blunt person who prefers to rub elbows with the little people. A champion for the working class, this person may tend toward righteous indignation and jump to the defense of the underdog.

Thumbs Up

In a class of its own, the thumb pertains to a person's drive. The definition of each section is listed next. If the thumb is ordinary and is in proportion to the hand, not too big or small, it means the person is fairly well balanced.

- **The Position of Will** (the tip)—A firm tip indicates a firm and constant power of will. A supple tip indicates generosity. A pointed tip indicates someone who is easily swayed.

- **The Position of Logic** (the middle)—A long, straight section of logic indicates a strength in abstract reasoning, while a short section indicates good sense with an inability to use it because of being easily swayed. Thinner implies intellectualism, while a more robust section implies a forceful nature.

- **The Position of Love** (the base and the upper part of the palm just above the mount of Venus)—This indicates one's power of emotions. A heavy section indicates sensuality, a long one indicates passions that are idealistic, and a short section foretells of an earthy nature. Angular joints at the section indicate musical abilities.

- **A long thumb** is an indicator of success and motivation, someone who is able to sell oneself and one's ideas. Determined and goal-oriented, this person is an achiever with a creative flair for bringing good fortune to himself.

- **A short thumb** is an attribute of a hard worker who needs the approval and support of others in order to stick to goals. This person gets sidetracked easily when involved in personal tasks, but when assisting a leader or cause he believes in, he gives his all and will be an asset to any team.

Nailing the Process

Most people who do not study palmistry think it is only the reading of the palm, which isn't true. It is important that you flip the hand over and take a look at those nails, which point out personality traits.

Next you should look at the shape of the nails. These should be as natural as possible and not manicured or altered.

- **Round nailbeds** signify a performer or a creative person who sees things in a new way. These nails indicate a warm personality who loves socializing and is friendly and easy-going.

- **Square nailbeds** are the sign of a detail-oriented person who tends to be a perfectionist and very organized.

- **Large nailbeds** are a sign of strength and both a hardy and steady personality. The subject tends to be a physical person who likes to work hard and has an abundance of energy.

- **Short nailbeds** tend to show a practical, constructive person who follows through and likes to get things done.

You may want to investigate other types of nails in the future on a more intermediate level.

Major Highways of the Hand

The best way to read the palm is to have it open and flat. The palm should be thought of as a chart of your life. At a glance, you will notice the three main lines on the palm.

These lines represent the major highways. In order of importance, they are the life line, the head line, and the heart line. These three lines should be the given the most notice and should require your greatest consideration.

Look at both hands when deciphering the three main lines (refer to the previous diagram of the hand to see the major lines).

Life Line

The life line is located at the base of the index finger or first finger and the thumb. It curves down the palm and encircles the mount of Venus. To read the life line, start above the thumb and read down.

This line tells of the health and the physical nature of the possessor, as well as special occurrences in one's life. The life line addresses the quality of life you will have through your years, not necessarily how long you will live.

- A well-marked line that runs down the hand without breaks or loops means a balanced life with no major health concerns. Even if one has illness and surgery, there is nothing that will not be solvable. This person will age peacefully.

- If the line is not very visible, it means the quality of life is undetermined. Not bad, mind you—just not known at the time.

- If the line varies from thin to thick, this indicates different levels of fortune, happiness, and health—an up-and-down type of thing.

- Breaks in the line mean that some serious matter may need to be addressed and may come and go. This does not mean death—that is a misconception! Also, it is a warning that you need to take care of yourself. Think in terms of preventative medicine. All things can be reversed.

- A *fork* in the middle of the line moving toward the end of the life line denotes someone who likes to travel and most likely will pursue that interest.

- *Branches* that ascend from the line are good luck because of this individual's drive.

- A *chained* life line may point out delicate health. Fringe-type lines at the end mean a peaceful old age.

The more the life line extends out into the hand, the more energy the person has. The closer the line is to the thumb, the less energy the person has.

def•i•ni•tion

A **fork** is a line that ends with two or three other lines at the end. **Branches** are straight-type lines with little lines ascending or descending from them. **Chained** is literally looking like a chain. Some readers call it netted because it can resemble a line of net.

Head Line

The head line is the second most important line to the life line. It is the second horizontal line of the two main horizontal lines on the palm, located below the heart line. It typically starts between the thumb and the first finger, which is between the Mount of Jupiter and the Mount of Mars.

This line represents your intelligence, comprehension, attitude, self-control, and philosophy about life. The head line can start in one of three places. Each gives insights to the personality.

- **Starting low, below the life line**—Someone who is dependent, weak, oversensitive, and needy. This rarely is found, lucky for all.

- **Directly joined to the life line**—A person who is lacking self-esteem and does not speak out for themselves. However, as the line starts to split and is no longer attached, the person becomes independent and self-confident. This is the most common, perhaps showing up in childhood and entering into adulthood. Some of us grow up faster than others.

- **Starting high above the life line and not connected from the beginning**—Someone who is independent and can be considered wild or not cautious, depending on the size of the space between the head line and the life line.

- The head line that starts under the index finger indicates an intellect superior to most.

- If the line is straight, the person is logical and even-tempered.

- If the line sloops downward, it shows idealism and a vivid imagination.

- A slight sloop with a fork on the end tells of creativity such as writing and other like endeavors.

- A wavy line shows a limited attention span, whether the person is highly intelligent or not.

- A chained line suggests someone who is "wound tight."

- The average lines end under the index finger. Hence, if the line runs nearly to the edge of the palm, that person is blessed with a good memory and thinks before acting.

- Too short of a line implies someone who is lacking shrewdness and is not a deep thinker.

Heart Line

The heart line is located on the upper palm. Simply put, it is the higher line of the two larger lines that run horizontally.

This indicator deals not only with matters of the heart, but with all emotions. The line starts and ends differently on all people.

♦ If there is no heart line, there will most likely not be a great love in this person's life because this individual is too doubting to allow anyone into his or her heart.

♦ A curved line is dynamic in romantic matters and forward in love.

♦ A straight line can be romantically idle and not too aggressive, but can be responsive.

♦ If the heart line starts between the first and second fingers, not broken or looking chained, this means loyalty and an even disposition. These qualities will bring happiness and love.

♦ A broken heart line shows that the owner will have one major heartbreak or more. If you see a new line overlapping the broken one, or if the end of the broken line is covered by a square, the heart will mend, or already has.

♦ If the heart line forks at the beginning onto to the Mount of Jupiter, with the other part of the fork running between the first and second fingers, the person is not on an even keel emotionally. This person may tend to become overexcited or obsessive about people and things he or she enjoys.

♦ If the end of the heart line turns up toward the Mount of Mercury of the little finger, this person takes money into account when looking for love.

♦ If the heart line is chained, the person tends to be flirtatious and is a player. This is usually someone who "only does casual."

> **Enlightening Extras**
>
> Many palmists find that people who enjoy happy marriages or longer-term partnerships have heart lines that are similar or nearly matching.

Fate Line

The palm has so many lines that it's hard to determine which to include in a restricted version of palmistry. I chose to add the fate line because it is quite predominant on the palm. This line runs up the palm, nearly dividing it in half. It travels toward the middle or the Saturn Mount.

Look to see where the line starts.

- If there is no fate line, which is not uncommon, it indicates that the person who has this void is not necessarily negative. Nevertheless, this person tends to be care-free, hoping others will help. These people do not actively pursue special interests and simply get by. They can have interesting lives and find great happiness, yet financially they may not become what one would call successful. But not all happiness is judged by how much money we have in the bank. This character just doesn't always make cents.

- If it starts as low as the wrist, it indicates someone who has self-made success, is logical, and doesn't take risks. That individual has to work hard to achieve that favorable goal—but he or she will achieve it.

- If the fate line starts at the Mount of the Moon and runs diagonally up the palm, careers in show business and creative work are present. It also indicates that there will be uncertainty in these trades, along with many changes.

- If the fate line starts higher up on the hand near or above the head line, this could be someone who is a "late bloomer"; accomplishments will take place, but the road might be a little challenging.

- If the fate line ends at the head line, it means that the hand owner will possibly become puzzled about life and what he or she is doing between the ages of 30 and 40.

Broken fate lines mean difficulties in careers and finding a niche in life, though it doesn't mean one will never find that niche. Some of us just don't know what we want to be when we grow up.

The best fate line you could have does not depend as much on where it rises, but on whether the line is unbroken and clear, and doesn't fade and thicken. If this is the case, you will most likely be successful in a chosen career. If the line turns and points to a specific mount, you will be led toward a career that the mount signifies.

Love Affair Lines

Your character is one thing, but most of us want to know about the "love stuff." Some classic palmists look for what they call marriage lines. But in this day and age, it seems the more contemporary readers are calling them love affair lines. Works for me!

Turn the palm outward and look for lines under the little finger above the heart line and the base of the little finger. You will find horizontals lines. These lines are faint and small. This is where a magnifying glass will come in handy. These lines will tell you how many love affairs you will have.

Love affairs can also mean marriage. The deeper the line, the more important the affair. These deep lines may well show the actual marriage or, unfortunately, marriages (plural).

Note that the lines on the left and right hands may not match.

- The lines on the right hand denote people who are in love with you.

- The lines on the left hand denote the people you are in love with.

If the number of love affair lines is different on the left and right hands, there will be romances that are not reciprocated one way or the other. For example, if you have two lines on the right hand and three on the left, you will probably encounter a case in which someone you may love doesn't love you in return.

Ahhhh … don't worry—we all have more than one soul mate.

> **Notions Through Time**
>
> If you love somebody, let them go, for if they return, they were always yours. And if they don't, they never were.
>
> —Kahlil Gibran, Lebanese novelist, poet, and artist

Other Marks on the Hand

I will not call these marks bad omens because they're not *that* bad (I've seen worse). You may find them interesting:

- **Cross on the middle finger**—People tend to gossip about you.

- **Square on the index finger**—Because of jealousy, you may find yourself changing careers.

- **Triangle on the little finger**—You love someone already married. Oh my! Didn't you know?

- **Circle on thumb**—Business failure. Oops, try something different.

- **Star on the thumb**—Problems within the family. Gee, who doesn't have those?

Look twice as hard for these little insights that may be good omens:

- **Cross on the index finger**—You will achieve a high standing socially and financially in life.

- **Square on ring finger**—You may become famous.

- **Star on index finger**—Success awaits you with no doubt.

- **Triangle on middle finger**—Your children will achieve greatness and you will be happily married.

- **Circle on index finger**—You will have a beautiful love affair in which love is returned with sincerity. Oh, I love a happy ending.

These omens are found only on the fingers. These symbols found on the palms have meaning, too, but are more complex, depending on specific locations. The art of reading palms is a study well worth pursuing. We have only touched the tip of this skill. If you are curious about the finer points of palmistry, I highly recommend you take the time to probe beyond the surface.

The Least You Need to Know

- Palmistry is an age-old practice that is still popular today.

- Palm reading provides insights into your character, where you have been, and where life may lead you.

- At first, simply learning to read the major lines—life, head, heart, fate, and love—can launch you into conversation with those who are like-minded.

- More detailed information is revealed in the fingers, nails, and overall size and shape of the hand.

Signs and Symbols

In This Chapter

◆ Are signs real or not?

◆ The sign said stop; the symbol means go

◆ Common symbols

◆ Signs from the "other side"

Are you one of those people who is always looking for a sign or symbolic message from the heavens to confirm a thought to validate that a future wish will come true? You think about someone you like, and all of a sudden you see a shooting star. You wonder if you will make that move to Virginia, and you suddenly hear a bell. You wonder if your diet will work this time, and a feather falls to the ground. Are these signs from a source that can't verbalize messages to us and thus uses physical objects, sounds, and other elements as a mode of communication?

Every day we are surrounded by things that can be considered signs as a way to answer our questions or to give us guidance. Knowing how to determine what is a sign and what isn't—that is the difficult part.

How often have you wanted to know how a dead loved one is doing on the "other side"? Then again, maybe you never did and never will. But for those of us who have that type of curiosity, the question is, how do you talk to that person? There is a way.

Is It Just Coincidence or Is That a Real Sign?

If you are a skeptic, you will say that there are no signs from the universe and that everything is just coincidence unless it can be scientifically proven. Still, some of us are opened-minded and don't live in a cold world where only logic is involved. We are the ones who can see the signs and use them to our advantage. And even if we are wrong, it's still a lot more exciting than being overly analytical and living on a one-dimensional planet.

> **Notions Through Time**
>
> When you live your life with an appreciation of coincidences and their meanings, you connect with the underlying field of infinite possibilities.
>
> —Deepak Chopra, author

Not everything in life is a sign, and, yes, of course, coincidences happen as a regular part of our life. However, when we see extreme coincidences, we have to take notice.

For example, if you were just thinking about Judy and you suddenly see her at the store, that's interesting, but most likely not a sign from above about anything relevant. On another note, if suddenly for no reason you started thinking about Judy, who moved to Australia five years ago, and heard nothing of her since, that could be considered remotely of interest. Yet, in addition to thinking about her, if you found yourself actually dreaming about her three days in a row, that could take on some significance. And again after that, if someone at the cocktail party you attended last night asked you about her, and *then* you saw her in the store, that could be an entirely different ballgame. Why? Because her vibration was coming your way via dreams, thoughts, and another person's pondering. You were "picking up" her energy. It was a sign that something important would come from a conversation with her.

Perhaps when you saw her, she shared with you the fact that Alex, that married guy who never liked to work for a living but whom you always admired, is suddenly single and moving back to your neighborhood. Or maybe Judy just moved back from Australia to the United States to start a business in which you can participate.

Then again, she might have nothing to say except the normal chit-chat two people make when meeting in a store. But most likely, it's the former and there is a purpose in running into her. You may not see it immediately, but be patient. The opportunity will show itself.

When you get three "hits" and then see someone you haven't seen for several months or longer, there is usually a message. Here we had three hits with Judy: thoughts, dreams, and another person's query. Remember the *three hit rule* when meeting someone you haven't heard from or seen for a long time.

def•i•ni•tion

The **three hit rule** pertains to seeing people you have lost communication with for a long time. You start thinking about them a lot in any form, including daydreams, nighttime dreams, or reminders in places you visit. Things like photos falling off shelves, songs that bring back memories, other people talking about them, and similar reminders or any kind of suggestion of them count as a hit. If you can count three (without forcing them), you will most likely see that person or hear news of him or her that will benefit you in some form. In my experience, and from researching others' experiences according to this theory, this usually is a positive encounter, not a negative one.

Other signs that appear to be coincidences are not only your own thoughts, but the actions of others. A client of mine named Dorothy always wanted to have a booth in a busy flea market near her house. She needed an inside booth because her merchandise had to stay out of severe weather, but an inside booth never was available. One day as she was cruising the flea market, her eyes kept turning to a particular booth. This booth sold old army relics of which she had no interest, but it was always filled with people. That night, for no reason known to her, she kept thinking about that booth, which had been there for many years, just like many of the others. The next day, she called the office to see if any booths had opened up, and she got the same answer she had for the last two years: "No, but we will call you if anything becomes available." She assumed that her thoughts were just thoughts and meant nothing.

Later that month, her grandson came to visit her and said he was going to check out the flea market. He came home with an army knife from that same booth. The next week, when she opened her newspaper, there was an ad she had never seen before advertising the old army relic booth at the flea market. She already thought this was getting too coincidental, but nothing seemed to be happening immediately, so she disregarded these signs. Two days later, the flea market manager called her and said the space that sold the old army relics would be available at the end of the month. This was the first time a booth had become available on the inside of the building for two years. Dorothy took the booth and has been there ever since. The time frame for these situations that took place was approximately one month. Was that coincidence or not? You decide. I think she was "meant" to have that booth, and the Universe was dropping hints along the way. Regardless, because it didn't happen the first day she started thinking about that unit, she disregarded the signs.

Notions Through Time

Adopt the pace of nature: her secret is patience.

—Ralph Waldo Emerson, American essayist, philosopher, and poet

Pay more attention to the things around you and events that seem to keep coming back to the same person, place, or thing. Document these occurrences, if you like, and see what the final outcome brings.

The Physical Evidence

"Oh please, oh please, give me a sign. Anything. A spark, a rainbow, a horn—thunder would work, too. Please, please, I will believe anything." The unspoken truthful part of that thought that should be added is, "because I'm so desperate for confirmation!"

Well, I hate to confess to being human, but I have spoken these words before—and you may have, too. Most of us do at some time. Okay, I know some are reading this who can honestly say, "I have never done anything like that." Well, to you I say, "Congratulations, you've been spared," because when you want something bad enough, you can get a little loony. You look for any sign from a higher source that will give you hope for the future—the future you think you need or think you should have. Therefore, we see false signs and symbols, or we try to make something work that isn't really a sign at all. Don't try to put something there that isn't.

Pick Your Own Sign

An interesting thing to do is to create your own good omen or "sign." Think of something personal to you. For instance, it might be three sevens in a row: 777. Some people use a rose, an angel, a tire, a flag, and so on. It can be anything. Just pick a symbol that you relate to, and if you see it in the course of one day, three times, good luck is coming your way. You typically will forget about your personal sign until you see it. Don't pick something too common, like a car or a tree. Be a little unique. It means more that way. How many times do you see an ostrich or a picture of one in the course of a day? (Unless you live on an ostrich farm.) Now there's a good sign. Have fun with it.

Recognizing a Sign

In the world of signs and symbols from a higher power, it is tricky to decipher what is real and what isn't. No one can say for sure what comes in the form of a symbolic message and what doesn't. But here are some ideas you might want to experiment with when looking for a sign. This method has worked for many individuals and may work for you—or it may not. That's why this is all about experimenting. Eventually, you will be able to recognize what signs and symbols work for you as a form of a sign.

1. If you need confirmation about something, take a walk in a safe area. This can be a city, the country, the mountains, or the desert.

2. Think of your concern or what you need confirmation about. For example: will I get that job this week?

3. Without trying too hard, look for what you feel will be your base sign or symbol. For example, if immediately after you project your thought, you see a bird, then a bird is your base sign. If you see a "stop" sign, then red or the word *stop* is your sign. If you see a dog barking in a window ... well, there's your sign!

   If you see a real dog, the next sign can be a stuffed one in a store window, or just something similar. If you use a stop sign, the next sign can be a poster of a stop sign, and so on.

4. Continue to walk without making a huge attempt to find this sign again. It's cheating if you see a stop sign and then take a left turn because you know that on Main Street there is another one.

5. After you have walked for about five minutes, turn around and walk home or back to where you started. If you don't see your sign three times in that period of time, you may not be getting what you wished for.

Some people do this while driving, but I do not recommend it because you should concentrate on your driving and nothing else. Your own safety and that of others is irreplaceable. Act responsibly: don't sign-search and drive!

I Never Looked at It That Way

Symbols are fascinating, yet they can have standard or mundane definitions or meanings attached to them, as well as esoteric meanings. For instance, a circle is a significant symbol that represents universal oneness. In mystical rituals, it is known that everything is safe within a circle. So if you see a circle when thinking of or asking for a sign, think safety, oneness, and conclusion.

Here are a few more common symbols that are food for symbolic thought:

- **Seeing or hearing a bell**—Positive symbols of dispelling negativity. Ringing in a beautiful future. A "yes."

- **Birds flying past**—Messages about your concern coming soon. These could be good or not so good. What kind of bird do you see? For example, if you see eagles and you like eagles, you will associate them with something good or a good sign. Then again, if you don't like eagles it is something unfavorable. You cannot assume here that there is a standard of good birds and bad birds. What do certain birds mean to you?

Visionary Insights

Sometimes we see 'em and sometimes we don't. When you ask for a sign from whomever or whatever, and you don't receive one, don't lose faith. The first thing you might take into account is that the Universal Life Force, God, Buddha, or whomever you recognize as your higher power isn't at your beck and call.

- **Lightning**—Raw power. You will catch the spark you want.

- **Lights flickering**—There will be a struggle in getting what you want.

- **Thunder**—A good sign: power and taking charge. Don't fear the thought.

- **Whistle of a train**—Things moving in the right direction in your life.

When you think you are receiving a sign, think about what it means to you, not to other people. If a black cat walks across your path, do you see it as a bad omen? This is a common superstitious belief. On the other hand, do you see the cat as a good sign because you draw animals to you who trust you or are just attracted to your kind spirit?

Be your own symbol interpreter. Does the sound of a gentle rain mean a cleansing, or does it mean gloomy days ahead?

Those Who Have Passed to the Other Side

Some of us have had many people we know pass over to the other side. Some of us perhaps have had no one special we want to particularly get in touch with.

But most people have a curiosity about communing with souls who have passed over. Some television personalities and a variety of psychics and spiritual leaders claim they can talk to these souls. I believe that some can and that some think they can but can't. Therefore, the best way is to try for yourself. I think that if your mind is strong and your intention is pure, you have a shot at communication. It may not be as clear as a professional who has been doing this for years, but even a little communication can give you great comfort and satisfaction.

If this seems creepy to you, don't do it.

Signs from the Spirit World

Often when we are not looking for any signs or evidence of departed loved ones, they can come to visit. What brings this on and how do they come back? I really don't know. There are as many theories as there are gravestones. This is one of those subjects of tremendous fascination that you might want to explore further. But I will give you my personal belief after much research and experience with such things. (That being said, this doesn't make my speculation true. It is just one to consider.)

I feel that when people pass over, it takes them several weeks to adjust to the other side. I think the day they pass, they may stop by to say good-bye by appearing at the end of your bed or in a room. They can't speak, but the apparition you see is supposed to be their good-bye letter. I also feel that they may leave a sign, like a clock that suddenly stops, something falling down, a telephone ringing with no answer, or a computer shutting down or turning on by itself. (Those are your more high-tech spirits.) Electricity might act strangely, a storm could brew, or a rainbow may appear in the sky.

Enlightening Extras

A common belief or myth is that to see an owl in the wild is a bad sign. They are said to be messengers of death or prophets of doom. Give the owls a break! I don't necessarily give a hoot about what the common thought is because more positive people see them as wise creatures and dispatchers of spiritual messages and good tidings. I never saw an owl that didn't bring joy and happiness. Think about "who ... who" you want to believe. Poor little guys. No wonder they come out only at night with a reputation like that! I just screech when I think of their self-esteem. It must be as dark as night.

I do think that you receive some type of message telling you they made it over or are on their way with an easy road ahead. Look for personal symbols they may use to tell you "adios." It could be any thing from a favorite song playing to a cat staring at a picture of them in the living room for no reason. These are obvious signs and can be a little disturbing, but nevertheless, it happens.

Once you feel you have a sense of someone on the other side or feel that the spirit has "settled in" to its new dwelling in the afterlife, the spirit may attempt to contact you via a mode of divination. It carries information about the future you do not have. Since it can't e-mail or call you, it may be able to help you in your divination to foretell future events in order to advise you.

When conducting any form of divination, if you feel you have someone special on the other side who may be trying to support you, give that spirit permission to guide you. Without permission, the spirit may feel it is an intrusion to the living. For example, you can say to yourself, "Uncle Jim, I give you permission to help me in this reading." You may find that your impressions come to you more readily.

Dreams

Symbols in dreams are a more relaxing way of getting signs from those on the other side because when you wake up, it's only a dream. It's not like actually seeing an image at the end of the bed. So if you know someone who has passed over and that person knew you would be the type who would get spooked if he or she showed up in illuminated glory, that person may prefer to come to you in a dream. This could save you from a heart attack. Dreams are good.

> **Notions Through Time**
>
> Pay attention to your dreams—God's angels often speak directly to our hearts when we are asleep.
>
> —Eileen Elias Freeman, *The Angels' Little Instruction Book* (1994)

If someone who has passed appears to you in a dream, it is usually *really* that person. Not just an image sent from your subconscious—it's him or her. Say hello! If your loved one looks happy, he or she is happy. If the person's face looks sad or drawn, he or she is giving you a message to pay attention to things going on in your life.

It may not be a disaster, but it could be as simple as the fact that you are overspending your financial position, or as complex as the fact that your boyfriend is a no-good bum running around with the receptionist at the cable company. Don't underestimate your dreams—they are links to the other side.

Face West for a Psychic Telephone Call

It's one thing to have someone come to you from the other side, but what if you want to contact someone? Do you e-mail, telephone, or use angel communication? Can you send a sign telling your loved one to pick up the celestial phone?

Many feel that you should not force communication with the dead and that they can only come to you. Hence, you have no way at all to call upon them. I agree with this, to a certain extent. Since we don't know what goes on "over there," it might not be right to yank someone back to earth for a social call (although I do think there is a happy medium—no pun intended).

If you need to talk to someone who has passed away, you need to call to the west. The direction west is the portal to the other side. This is where the sun sets and sleeps for the night. This is where the door to the other side opens and closes. This is where the spirits can move freely without restrictions.

To attempt to communicate with people who have made the transition, follow these steps:

1. Sit facing west.

2. Visualize yourself covered in a protective cloud of white light.

3. Think about the person you are trying to contact.

4. Ask in your own words if the person would like to give you a message of some kind. Let the person know that you give him or her permission and that you will not be frightened by thoughts that may come to mind.

5. Sit and wait for at least 15 minutes.

6. If you do not get a message, try again some other time.

7. If you just cannot seem to pick anything up after several attempts, ask the person to come to you in a dream or to give you a sign of some nature so you will know it was your loved one.

8. Pay attention to your dreams for the next nine days and watch for any signs or symbols that would make sense to you concerning them.

If you still don't receive anything, don't be discouraged. It most likely indicates that this was not a good time to attempt this call. Try again in a few more weeks. You will eventually break through.

When you are done with the procedure, wash your hands. This is a way of washing away any lingering energy that you may have grasped onto in the process. It's affiliated with ending a process as well.

> **Visionary Insights**
>
> You can do this method with another person as long as you are both serious and open-minded. You may both receive different messages, which naturally is just fine. Sometimes there is more power in numbers. Three is particularly good because it stands for multiplication, and the energy set forth is multiplied.

The Least You Need to Know

◆ We can receive signs from a higher power—be open and pay attention to the message, whether it is visual, audio, or just a gut feeling.

◆ Remember the three hit rule: three hits, and something is going to give. Remove coincidence from your thoughts.

◆ Signs come in all sizes and shapes. Pay attention and don't analyze your signs the way everyone else does. If a standard interpretation doesn't seem right for you then use your own instinct.

◆ When trying to contact those who have crossed over, face west. When using forms of divination give them permission to assist you.

Part 5

Methods of the Ancients

The voice of the past can only whisper, but because of these hushed tones, we often listen more closely. And there is an understanding about what our ancients viewed through myth and mysticism that we now see scientifically.

An eclipse now has an understandable reason for this occurrence. But to the ancients, it was perhaps a sign of a shrouded event. Yes, many things that they thought were due to magic or the occult have logical explanations. But not all ... not all. How is it that some forms of divination survived time, disbelief, and even accusations of illegal wizardry?

Chapter 20

Runes

In This Chapter

- ◆ Runes of time
- ◆ Buying or making a set of runes
- ◆ Definitions from the past
- ◆ Three basic ways to lay out the runes

There's nothing wrong with rune-ing your life—it's a great way of fortune telling. So where did these little stones with symbols on them come from? I'll tell you. Are the runes some type of alphabet or just symbols someone thought of? I'll tell you. How do you know what the symbols mean? I'll tell you. Are there certain layouts you use, or do you just pick a stone? You guessed it—I'll tell you!

The Tradition Behind Runes

Several theories surround the origin of *runes*. No one can determine, without a doubt, the actual people who originated these symbolic tokens. The theory that the Goths and Germanic tribes of northern Europe created them around 100–200 C.E. seems to be the most widespread.

def•i•ni•tion

Runes are an ancient Germanic alphabet. The word *rune* derives from the Gothic for "mystery." These symbols were inscribed on rocks or wood as a form of writing. The runes were made up of straight lines, which apparently made the engraving easier. When individually inscribed on pieces of stones or wood, they became a form of divining and were used for magical practices. Runes have no lowercase letters and were read left to right as well as right to left.

Obtaining Your Runes

Working with runes is a very mystical journey into the unknown. It should be a part of your fortune-telling adventures. Hopefully, you will give it a chance. To skim over this section would be a misadventure on your course of mystical induction, so I recommend giving it a throw.

To make them or not to make them? That is the question.

Buy 'Em

Runes can be purchased anywhere you find metaphysical or new-age items. Sometimes they can be purchased as a part of a book set in larger book stores.

You can find runes in numerous materials, including wood, stone, and plastic. The advantage to buying them instead of making them is the obvious: it's just easier, especially when first starting out. We all walk a different avenue, so ponder this idea and make a decision.

Make 'Em

Okay, I know I said buying runes is perfectly fine—and it is. But there is just something about creating a set from scratch that makes their energy fly up into the heavens.

When working with runes, you can easily imagine their mystic qualities in a historical sense. Envisioning primitive people casting their runes in the light of a fire can help you feel the connection that carries across the ages. Feel the desire of humans to tap into the great unknown and to seek answers and assistance in their daily lives.

To be really creative in making your own runes, consider the types of tools and supplies these primitives may have used to create their runes. Nature should be your first resource for rune materials: wood, bone, stone, shells, seeds, beans, and other easily acquired natural supplies make the best runes. Choose items that are by nature similar in size or that can be shaped to make fairly uniform runes.

The next step is to transfer your rune symbol onto the item. Painting the symbols may be the easiest way to do this.

In a short time, you can have your own set of hand-painted runes. This is a very popular way of doing it. You can use markers or paints of your choice. Once you paint your runes, you can buy a spray-on sealer found at crafts stores or use clear nail polish so the markings don't wear off too easily.

If you want to be more traditional, cutting or burning the symbols into your material more closely matches the way primitive people created their runes. Modern tools make this far easier than it was for early mystics, and there is a stronger sense of permanence to runes that have been created by these processes than those that have been simply painted.

In addition, carved or inlaid runes have a pleasing feel in one's hand. The tactile quality brings you more closely in touch with your runes in a physical way. And I am all for getting physical (spiritually speaking, of course … ahem).

Following are several examples of how to make your own runes. You will need 24 of whatever type of token you select because there are 24 runes. (You'll see all of the runes pictured later in the chapter.)

Stones or Shells Work Well

Admittedly, the following process is for the artsy-fartsy types. Nothing wrong with that—those are my favorite people!

1. Start by gathering your materials:

   ◆ Stones, shells, or other material. Cowry shells are the best shells to work with because they roll nicely yet have definite up and down sides. The shell is smooth and egg-shaped, with a long, narrow slitlike opening. Soapstone is easy to work with, but you can also use stones found in creek beds (they tend to be smooth) or those highly polished bits of colored stone found in rock shops and New Age stores. With bone, you want to choose something very clean and dry that can be cut into finger length pieces and smoothed down. Because ivory trading is illegal, ivory is not a consideration. But if you are really set on the look of ivory, find plastic blanks slightly smaller than dominoes and use them instead.

◆ Something with which to engrave. You can scratch your symbols into softer stone, if you like, but I prefer to use an electric hand tool made specifically for crafts. These tools have interchangeable bits that can grind and polish and make the work go quickly.

◆ Nonhardening clay. Use the plastic type you can pick up in most craft stores. It is reusable and should be stored in a zip-lock bag when done.

◆ A pen to trace your symbol.

◆ Eye protection. Always use protective eyewear when grinding, just in case a chip flies off.

◆ Paint, polish, or a similar substance to fill the engraved area (optional).

2. Assemble your supplies in a place where you can spread things out a bit. Trace your symbols onto the surface of your stones. Squash a golf ball–size chunk of clay onto a hard, stable surface (if you are working on a table top, remember this clay can mar wood finishes).

3. Press your rune into the clay with the intended symbol side up. The clay acts as a clamp, securing your runes so they don't move. Put on your eye protection. Using a pointed grinding bit on your electric hand tool, carefully trace the symbol into the stone. You may want to have extras for practice, to get the feel of the stone and the amount of pressure you need to apply to achieve the results that you want. You may also need to retrace the symbol with the grinder several times to get the depth you want.

4. When you have finished, you may want to polish the engraved areas with a polishing bit on your hand tool to smooth rough edges. Once your runes are engraved and smoothed down, you can force either paint or a colored polish into the engraved area, buffing off any that spills over onto the stone. A waxy polishing paste in gold or silver is nice, although black paint may be more visible.

5. Allow your runes to dry. Then put them into a pretty velvet drawstring bag for safe keeping.

When your runes are engraved, you can use your imagination for how to decorate them. For example, you might trace the engraved symbol with glue and fill it with colored sand, glitter, tiny gems, or a contrasting color of ground stone. You might use the drill to put in accent areas on the runes to fit with gems or other decorations. You might even make holes so that you can string your runes on a silken cord.

Wooden, Nut, Bean, or Seed Runes

Geez, these runes sound edible, but don't try it. This isn't rune soup, so don't combine materials, either. Make your rune set from only one of this group.

Here's what you will need:

♦ Pieces of wood or other items that had life. You can buy or cut found pieces of wood to a uniform size. Using aromatic wood such as sandalwood or cedar adds an extra pleasing touch to your runes. If you use beans or seeds, be careful to keep them dry, or you wind up with sprouting runes! Obviously, you will need larger, extra-hard beans or seeds to make this work. Here in Florida there is an invasive plant called "snicker bean" that has a very hard, nut-type seed that works wonderfully. But if you aren't here in Florida, look to other choices.

♦ Something with which to engrave. Again, you can scratch your symbols into wood, if you like, but it is easier to use an electric hand tool for grinding, as described previously, or a wood-burning tool.

♦ Nonhardening clay.

♦ A pen to trace your symbol.

♦ Eye protection.

♦ Paint, polish, or an item to fill the engraved area (optional).

Assemble your supplies and follow the previous instructions for making stone runes if you are using an electric engraving tool. A wood-burning tool will give you similar results, but you will not need to fill the engraved symbol because the burning tool will darken the wood naturally. Remember to use practice pieces to get a feel for how the tools work, and follow the safety precautions recommended for them. I don't want you to ruin your good pieces.

Visionary Insights

Other things can work for home-made runes as well. Metal blanks or similar items can be engraved or embossed. Animal teeth (such as shark's teeth) can be used, as can large, flat buttons, beads, or bits of jewelry with an appropriate size and surface. They can be made from clay and glazed, fired, or painted onto ceramic tiles. I know of one case in which beer-bottle caps were used. The person first cut symbols out of thin black plastic using an Exacto knife. Placing each symbol in a bottle cap, he filled each cap with clear polyurethane and allowed it to dry.

Rune Definitions

Make an effort to become familiar with the meanings of the runes before you even begin to conduct a reading. This will allow you to be more relaxed when you actually start to read the spreads. Hold your runes in your hand one by one as you read the definitions. You will form a type of bound with them.

Keep your runes out for a while near your desk or an area where you can pick them up occasionally and try to remember the meanings. After a while, you will have the definitions memorized (although not required) without too much effort. When you actually cast your runes and see the corresponding definitions, it will not be a totally new thought, and you can make more of a psychic story of the final results.

Some of the runes have reversed meanings, and some do not. This is because many of these pieces, such as an X, look the same whether they're right side up or reversed.

Fehu

Meaning of symbol: Domestic cattle, wealth. Divinatory meaning: Prosperity and financial security. Desires and passion satisfied. Reversed meaning: Disappointments in matters of the heart. Arguments and money concerns.

Uruz

Meaning of symbol: Wild ox. Divinatory meaning: News from a distance. Strength of body, sexual desires, high levels of energy. All things successful. Reversed meaning: Obsessive behavior, opportunities possibly lost if you delay, illness, and failings.

Thurisaz

Meaning of symbol: Giant. Divinatory meaning: Things that are changing. Do nothing because a situation of concern will work itself out. Reversed meaning: You might later regret a decision made in haste. Someone who is not a good person. Hatred and great negativity.

Ansuz

Meaning of symbol: God—that is, Oden. (Oden was considered the most supreme of all the gods.) Divinatory meaning: Advice from someone who has great wisdom. Messages, good health, and blessings. Reversed meaning: Someone may interfere in your life. Miscommunication, vain pursuits, and duplicity.

Raidho

Meaning of symbol: Wagon or chariot. Divinatory meaning: Travel or a journey of a pleasant nature. Change of residence. You will finally make a decision that will project into a brighter future. Reversed meaning: You are wandering in life and need to get organized and decide what you want. A journey may be delayed or completely canceled.

Kenaz

Meaning of symbol: Beacon or torch. Divinatory meaning: Fiery ventures that spark you forward. Sex, passion, artistic endeavors, and mental frustration. For women, good luck and a gift from a man. For men, lust for a woman. Reversed meaning: Banishing things from the past, endings, breakups, and lost hope.

Gebo

Meaning of symbol: Gift. Divinatory meaning: A fair exchange of energy and balance. Gifts given and accepted. Solid partnerships and relationships. Love! Reversed meaning: None.

Wunjo

Meaning of symbol: Joy. Divinatory meaning: Realization, happiness, and prosperity. However, be warned of excess pleasures, especially those of the flesh! Reversed meaning: Be careful of business concerns for the next four days. Do not push a deal. The "big picture" needs to be seen. Keep your eye on the prize and don't detour.

Hagalaz

Meaning of symbol: Hail. Divinatory meaning: Nature at her finest. Weather conditions you cannot control must be considered when planning. Risky business and upsets that are out of check. Spiritual testing and complications. Reversed meaning: None.

Nauthiz

Meaning of symbol: Need. Divinatory meaning: Determination, restraint, limitations, and self-searching. A good time to look at your faults and your fears and correct them. Reversed meaning: Loneliness, emotional void, and financial distress. Caution for wrong decisions that can set you off course for a long time.

Isa

Meaning of symbol: Ice. Divinatory meaning: Someone who is cold-hearted. Mental blocks that need to be overcome and investigated. Withdrawal from reality. Reversed meaning: None.

Jera

Meaning of symbol: A year, a good harvest. Divinatory meaning: A period of one year. Legal issues, business professionals, responsibilities. Hope for a better life and promised opportunities coming into fruition. Success and rewards for a job well done. Reversed meaning: None.

Eihwaz

Meaning of symbol: Yew tree. Divinatory meaning: Problems solved. Matters that were stressful are now put to rest. Goals can be achieved. Enlightenment, dependability, and safety. A man you can trust. Reversed meaning: None.

Perthro

Meaning of symbol: Womanhood. Divinatory meaning: All issues involving female topics. The occult, mysterious situations, intuition, and secrets. Seduction, art, and emotions of joy and caring. Reversed meaning: Betrayal, depression, confusion, and broken promises.

Algiz

Meaning of symbol: Protection. Divinatory meaning: Psychic protection from entities not of the physical realm. Spirituality and enlightening realities. A change of careers or jobs due to your own efforts. (No free rides.) Reversed meaning: People may take advantage of you. Stand up for yourself. Be cautious in all things. Don't forget your spiritual side. Weakness and fear.

Sowilo

Meaning of symbol: The sun. Divinatory meaning: Time for relaxation, rest, and deep thinking. Achievements are on the horizon. All good things that bring sunshine into your life. Reversed meaning: None.

Tiwaz

Meaning of symbol: Victory. Divinatory meaning: Accomplishment and attainment of goals. You are in touch with your inner self, so use it to your advantage. Leadership and honor. Winning legal matters. If a woman, love will be knocking at your heart. If a man, love will befall you quickly with the pierce of Cupid's arrow. Reversed meaning: Failure, war, lost battles of life if not careful. Uncertainty in romantic predicaments. Lack of trust. One may have to give up the idea of making a relationship work.

Berkano

Meaning of symbol: Growth. Divinatory meaning: Birth and rebirth. New beginnings and ideas for the future. Family, fertility, and close friends. A new love affair will develop with time. Reversed meaning: Troubles with family members and lack of communication in the household. Things that will not move one way or the other, stagnation.

Ehwaz

Meaning of symbol: Horse, two horses. Divinatory meaning: Any mode of transportation. A better lifestyle and improvements around the abode. Progress to a more positive future. Things getting progressively better. Teamwork and a marriage made in heaven. Reversed meaning: Positive change coming soon that has been delayed. Travel on or across water. Knowing when to take action and when to stand still.

Mannaz

Meaning of symbol: Man, mankind. Divinatory meaning: Knowing how to deal with others. Acceptance of "the self." Indecision in matters regarding legal documents. Reflection about one's life and how to proceed with humility. Reversed meaning: Self-absorption, ego, and a tendency to manipulate others.

Laguz

Meaning of symbol: Water. Divinatory meaning: All things that flow: psychic abilities, creativity, emotions, travel, and dreams. Fantasies, the esoteric, and the hunger for the unknown. Reversed meaning: Recognizing limitations and not ignoring them. Giving up hope and becoming depressed. You can change this.

Ingwaz

Meaning of symbol: Virility. Divinatory meaning: Things of or pertaining to a masculine energy. Love for family, home, and self. Being able to finally take another step forward on your trek through life. Reversed meaning: None.

Dagaz

Meaning of symbol: Day or dawn. Divinatory meaning: Security and safety. Stepping up to the plate and taking charge of your life. Growth and a new outlook on life. New plans, business, relationships, and health realizations. Reversed meaning: None.

Othala

Meaning of symbol: Property. Divinatory meaning: An inheritance or something given. It should be noted that someone does not have to necessarily pass on for you to inherit something. Land, real estate, legal documents. Spiritual guidance and wisdom from those who want to help you through their life experiences and knowledge. Reversed meaning: Beware of not having order in your life. Faulty craftsmanship. Tools and mechanical items that may break down.

Some sets of runes have 25 pieces instead of 24. They use an additional blank rune. However, no constituting history or evidence can prove that a blank rune was included in this type of divination. Because the piece was added to some sets in the early 1980s, in my opinion, it should not be noted. The good news is that if you buy a set and lose a rune, you can use the blank as a substitute and draw the symbol on it yourself. If you like the idea of the blank rune, then use it in your rune casting. Modern-day rune readers say it means karma: "What goes around comes around." Supposedly, it can also mean an ending.

Laying Out the Truth

As with many oracles, such as the runes, there are many kinds of layouts. For our purposes, I provide three basic spreads that will give you the elements with which to start reading with runes.

Single Rune: Pick a Rune, There's Your Answer

It doesn't get easier than using the single-rune layout. Lay the stones down in front of you and shuffle them on the table or platform with the symbols facing down. Think of your question or a general message you would like to receive. Pick a rune, turn it over, and find the meaning. This is short and to the point. Not too much contemplation, but it's very good for a quick response. Set the chosen rune to the side and ask the next question, if you have one. Do not

Visionary Insights

If you are joined by other people, each person should start with the full set of runes. Do not pick a rune from the pile and then have someone else pick from the same pile. The runes should be shuffled in their entirety for each individual person. If not, your energy and that person's may get commingled, and the reading will be ineffective.

put the rune you have just chosen back in the pile. You can ask several questions using this procedure, but do not repeat the same questions.

Three Runes: Three Different Methods

Different ideas have arisen about casting three runes for a reading. First, choose one of the following methods that you like, and then find the definitions and interpret the meanings. For all three methods, use the same approach: mix up the runes on the table face down, and then select three. One by one, place them in a line left to right, turning each over as you select it so the symbol faces up.

 ◆ Method One:

   Rune #1 involves the circumstance around the question.

   Rune #2 reveals the course of action that should be taken.

   Rune #3 gives your final outcome.

 ◆ Method Two:

   Rune #1 tells your past situation regarding this matter.

   Rune #2 describes your present situation, where you stand now.

   Rune #3 tells your future outcome if you don't change your course.

 ◆ Method Three:

   Rune #1 addresses the circumstances that prompted you to ask this question.

   Rune #2 explains the future you will be facing.

   Rune #3 reveals the present situation. It also may tell you of choices you can make to better your outcome.

Five Runes: Cross

Mix up your runes on the table face down. Ask a question while shuffling your runes. For a general message, just ask your higher source for insights to your future.

Select five runes, keeping them face down. You will be making the shape of a cross:

 ◆ Place the first rune in the center.

 ◆ Place the second rune above the first rune.

- Place the third rune below the center rune.

- Place the fourth rune to the left of the center rune.

- Place the fifth rune to the right of the center rune.

Then follow these steps to read the runes:

1. Read the rune in the center first. This is what surrounds the question, or the basis of the message that is meant for you.

2. Read the top rune above the center rune. This is what will possibly be a part of your future.

3. Read the rune to the left of the center. This is something that soon will pass or things you are dealing with now.

4. Read the rune at the bottom, or below the center rune. This is anything that you are trying to prevent, that you do not like, or that you do not want to take place. It may even be an individual.

5. Read the rune to the right of the center rune. This is your future or final outcome.

If you don't like the final outcome of a matter, don't be discouraged. Using the runes as a projection of what may happen in the future, do what you can to change it. We can change our fate.

Runes are a very complex type of fortune telling. This is a subject that is much more complicated than presented in these pages. Therefore, if you have an interest in more detailed information, a great deal more is available—and it's well worth the exploration. One book you might enjoy is *Empowering Your Life with Runes* by Jean Marie Stine (Alpha Books, 2004).

Notions Through Time

The future is called "perhaps," which is the only possible thing to call the future. And the only important thing is not to allow that to scare you.

—Tennessee Williams, *Orpheus Descending* (1957)

The Least You Need to Know

- Runes are an ancient Germanic alphabet. This set of symbols seems to have been rediscovered in this day and age and also serves as a form of fortune telling.

◆ You can make your own runes or buy them. Homemade runes carry with them your personal vitality, but purchased runes can also take on your particular energy.

◆ There are 24 runes; each has a meaning. Put together in groups they can form a more specific rendering or outlook about your matters of importance.

◆ Certain layouts contribute to a more interesting reading. You can inquire about a specific topic or get general information about the past, present, or future.

Chapter 21

Pendulums and Dowsing

In This Chapter

- ◆ Prophesying with pendulums
- ◆ Swinging for answers
- ◆ The mysterious art of dowsing
- ◆ Using Y-rods, L-rods, and pendulums for dowsing
- ◆ Dowse in your everyday life

A pointed piece of stone swings from a cable being held above a flat surface by a woman's hand. You see it go back and forth and around in a circle. What is that? That's a pendulum. It can give you answers to simple questions. Is this really a form of mystical fortune telling? Or do the answers come from the way we move our hands? Well, we'll talk about that later.

But now what's that fellow over there doing with that Y-shaped branch? Is he pointing at snakes in a desert? No, silly, he's dowsing for lost objects, water, metal, or maybe even a person or animal.

How do you do all this, and why even bother? All is revealed in this chapter.

Getting Into the Swing of Things

A pendulum is a weighted object attached to a string or chain, which is used for divination. Typically, a quartz crystal or another type of gemstone such as amethyst is used because of the magical properties of the stones and the vibrations they emit, but any weighty object can be used.

Pendulums bought at a magical-arts or New Age store are the easiest if you plan to use them often, because they are balanced and all set to go. However, you can easily make your own if this is your first experience with pendulum work and you want to just try it out. A necklace with a pendant and chain also works quite well.

Making a Pendulum

Constructing a pendulum does not require any special artistic talent. If you can tie a knot, you're home free. Simply get a 6- to 9-inch piece of string, chain, ribbon, or yarn, and a weight for the end: a pendant, pin, heavy earring, stone, seashell with a hole, or washer (no, not the kind at the Laundromat). Be creative and find something unique to tie on the end of your string. Once you find a weight, make sure it's fastened in such a way that the knot isn't off to one side. The idea is to make it hang straight. Ta-da! You have an official pendulum.

Yes/No or More?

The pendulum is best used for receiving "yes" and "no" answers from your inner self or subconscious mind, helping you to make decisions and to get clarity. It is also excellent for getting insights on whether someone is telling you the truth about a given situation.

People often use pendulums to foretell future events, but this is something I do not recommend unless you have a distinct aptitude for *precognition*. Why? Because you can influence the movement of the pendulum so easily (because you have so much control over the device), it's difficult to access the deeper recesses of the subconscious mind, where future events are likely to be accessed. So with this tool, you're more likely to be accessing intuition about the present or about things that have already occurred. However, if you suspect this is something you may want to examine, use the tool in any way you want. Delve deeper into the subject

def•i•ni•tion

Precognition is the ability to foretell future events.

through further research. But for most people, especially beginners, a pendulum is most useful for answering questions pertaining to the past or present, not the future.

When you think of divining with pendulums, think "simplicity." Here are some example questions:

- Is the man I am seeing serious about our relationship?

- Should I move out of the place where I am living?

- Will I be happy if I take that other job offer?

- Is the lady I am seeing now going to change jobs and move to be with me?

- Would it be beneficial for me to start that new venture?

- Should I be following a more spiritual path at this time in my life?

This tool is a springboard for tapping into your subconscious to find out what you really want in life. Hopefully, it will help lead you to true happiness and fulfillment on all levels. The pendulum is such a wealth of information about present situations, events, and general decision making that you will feel greatly relieved because you will no longer have to obsess about people and choices. To put it in a nutshell, use your pendulum when you can't decide what to do about something or when you want to know if someone is telling you the whole story about a situation.

If you do ask a question about the future, the pendulum may tell you only what your subconscious *wants* to transpire, not what will happen. Therefore, you may be disappointed. Use it properly, and you will see the great value and potential in front of you.

> **Notions Through Time**
>
> Quality questions create a quality life. Successful people ask better questions, and as a result, they get better answers.
>
> —Anthony Robbins, motivational speaker and author

Although I encourage pendulum use strictly for "yes" and "no" answers for beginners, it can be used for dowsing, the art of searching for things, as well. In this case, the pendulum takes on a whole new meaning. We talk about dowsing later in this chapter.

Using a Pendulum

You can use a certain amount of ritual or procedure before you work with your pendulum. These are only ideas and options, though: try one, all of them, none, or create your own. There is no right or wrong, as long as your intention is focused. However, as you begin, the hanging pendulum must point directly at a target. Therefore, you will need a *target card* or a focal point.

def•i•ni•tion

A **target card** is any piece of paper or cardboard with a circle drawn on it—the heavier the paper, the better. This will be used as a starting point for your pendulum. If you do not want to create a target card, you can use a quarter, button, or any object that can be viewed as a bull's-eye.

As you work with a pendulum, it is very important that things be tranquil all around you. You might want to meditate before you begin. You may also want to wash your hands or even take a shower to cleanse your energy field of any impurities or outside influences that may have attached to you over the course of the day.

Light a candle and place it in front of your target card. You can use a combination of candles as well. Choose a color that is appropriate for the nature of your question. (See Chapter 4 for the meanings of different colors.) If you are using two candles, place one on each side of the target card. If using three candles, create a triangle with two candles in front of you on a table or platform, and the point of the triangle at the top. There is power in threes because it is a number of multiplication and abundance. Keep the lights dim, and keep your focus on the pendulum and the target card, and let everything else fade out of the picture. You may also want to play some soothing music. Ask your higher power or inner voice to allow the information to flow through you.

Most often, you'll want to work with the pendulum by yourself. But working with another person or people is fine, as long as everyone is focused on the same question and not concerned about what they will ask when it is their turn. Having others involved can be very exciting and interesting. However, solitary use is recommended for serious matters. Try both and see what works for you.

There is more than one way to work with a pendulum. Here are two different methods to explore.

Basic Method

Set up your pendulum area using candles, music, or whatever you choose. Make sure you have no distractions. Now is the time to light the candles and put on the music. Turn telephones off, if possible. Place your target card in front of you, and hold the pendulum suspended from one hand, with the point approximately 1 inch above the center circle. You can bend your elbow or keep your arm straight. "Still" the pendulum so it is not moving. Sometimes saying something like "quiet," "still," or "stay" works. You can say this aloud or to yourself.

After you have steadied the needle, you need to determine the directions for "yes" and "no." These will be different every time. Therefore, do not write the words *yes* or *no* anywhere on the target card.

To determine the directions for "yes" and "no," ask a question silently or out loud that you know the answer to, such as, "Is my name _____?" If you give your real name, it will point in the direction that will indicate a "yes" answer. Then ask a question that you know has a "no" answer. The pendulum should swing in the opposite direction of "yes." If it does not, try again until you get clear directions for "yes"

and "no." Your directions may change daily, so do this procedure each time. It is not necessary to do it after each question, just every 24 hours or more.

After you go through this set-up procedure, you can ask all the questions you choose. However, don't go overboard! If you find that the needle of the pendulum is going in circles or in a direction that makes no sense, stop and start over. If this continues, put it away and try another day. For the most part, you should not have that problem.

If you notice that your hand shakes or moves a bit, don't be concerned. Your subconscious motivates the brain to send a type of electrical impulse to your hand, thereby moving the pendulum. Remember, this is a device to help you get in touch with your subconscious. If you want one thing and the pendulum tells you something different, you need to think about the message your inner self is trying to get through to you.

For example, say you ask the following question of the pendulum: "The man I have been dating for three years is a 'free spirit' who does not like to work, has no ambition, and uses me, and I think he sees other women occasionally. Regardless, I still love him and I can't help it. Is he the one for me?" It could be that you want a "yes" answer, but the pendulum is telling you a clear "no." The pendulum may be conveying the wisdom of your inner guidance, no matter what you think you want.

If you want the pendulum to say "yes" and it says "no," consider the reason for the different points of view. Maybe there is something you're not admitting, and you need to deal with it. I think you get the point!

Advanced Method

Put together a list of about 10 yes-or-no questions about what is presently going on in your life or situations around you. Before using the pendulum, write down what you think the yes-or-no answers will be.

Next, ask the same questions using the pendulum and write down the responses that you get. With the passing of time, and as things reveal themselves, see who was more accurate, you or the pendulum.

For example, you may ask, "Will I get a raise next week?" Your answer may be "yes," while the pendulum may answer "no." This may indicate that you know in your heart that it's unlikely you will get a raise, given the current conditions. On the other hand, you may ask, "Will Joe ever call me again?" Your answer may be "yes," and, happily, the pendulum's answer may also be "yes." You can expect that phone call!

Enjoy working with your pendulum, and use it wisely. After a while, it will help you develop your decision-making skills and your awareness of people, places, and things. At that point, you may not need it, so you can put it away for safekeeping—just in case!

The Art of Finding Things

Dowsing has been called many other names: water witching, radesthesia (conducting medical diagnosis and finding missing persons), doodlebugging (locating oil), and rhabdomancy (divining by a rod), among others. Generally, dowsing is the art of finding things—underground water, people, places, golf balls, and so on—with a tool or device. The tools used for dowsing are typically a dowsing stick, divining rods, and a pendulum.

def•i•ni•tion

Dowsing is the ancient art of finding things intuitively, using a dowsing stick or other tool.

No concrete evidence accurately identifies when dowsing originated. Yet much pictorial evidence from different cultures indicates that it has been practiced for thousands of years. In fact, wall murals were discovered in the Tassili Caves, which are a part of a mammoth system of caverns in the Atlas Mountains of North Africa, that identify tribesmen with forked sticks, possibly dowsing for water. These sketches are said to be up to 8,000 years old.

In other cultures, many petroglyphs and cave paintings portraying images of dowsing are proof that this art was alive and well many moons ago.

Ancient Egyptians and Chinese artists depict individuals holding objects such as Y-shaped branches pointed down to the ground. This is typical of a dowser using a divining rod to look for water or minerals. These scenes may have been documentation that the art of dowsing was in use for centuries. There may also be biblical evidence: for instance, when trying to find water, Moses and Aaron used a "rod" as a device to locate a reservoir.

Unfortunately, at times throughout the centuries, dowsing was considered the "work of the devil." That is where the term "water witching" derived. So what was wrong with trying to find water? It doesn't sound so evil to me. But to some, the use of what was seen as "unnatural powers" set off the fear that such powers might be dangerous. Even today, people sometimes ascribe a negative image to things they can't understand. For this reason, it's best to share information about your dowsing activities only with those you trust to be open-minded.

On a more modern note, there is a controversial account that the United States military engaged a professional dowser to instruct the Marines on how to unveil land mines and tunnels in Vietnam during the 1960s and 1970s. All over the world today, dowsers are used to dig for wells, find underground creeks, and locate drainage pipes and underground cables.

Enlightening Extras

A story told in dowsing circles reports that a famed water dowser, Vernon Cameron, supposedly told the United States Navy where U.S. submarines were located. To ascertain this information, he used map dowsing, in which the dowser holds a pendulum over a map. The point where the pendulum starts to circle indicates where the target object might be detected. Cameron reportedly also told the officers present where Russian subs were located. When the experiment was concluded, his findings were never confirmed one way or the other. However, he was barred from leaving the United States and could not obtain a passport because he was considered a security risk. Hmmm ... what was that all about, if he didn't know what he was doing?

Interestingly enough, skeptics say that dowsing has no scientific proof behind it. They claim that the dowsers who have a history of success are just lucky or have good instincts. Yet what are "good instincts" if not psychic abilities? Oh, well. Either way, there just isn't proof. So try for yourself and come to your own conclusions.

How Does Dowsing Actually Work?

At the risk of being vague, I have to admit that no one knows for sure how dowsing works. The theories and guesses are abundant. Some say it's just psychic intuition that uses a tool. Others say it's a connection between the dowser; the object, person, or location; and an energy force. They say the dowser is able to tune in to the vibration of the commodity or person. When this occurs, the dowsing instrument begins to move in the direction of the object of the search, to point out where this person, place, or thing might be. The dowsing device may also act as a radio antenna that boosts the energy, causing the rod, pendulum, or dowsing sticks to tremble.

Dowsing Equipment

You can use three basic tools to dowse:

- A **dowsing stick** or **forked stick** (Y-rod) is the most established device. This comes from nature, in the form of a small Y-shaped branch from a tree.

- **Divining rods** (L-rods) can be purchased online at dowsing sites such as www.naturesprite.com or auction sites such as ebay.com. The average cost is $10 to $15, depending on material and embellishments. Or you can make your own; I'll tell you how in a moment.

- A **pendulum** (as discussed earlier) is a weighted object that hangs from a string or chain.

People use many other tools to dowse, but these are the most common and have proven to be the most effective. These items can be bought or, in the case of a branch, borrowed from nature.

When you determine what you want to dowse for (meaning what you will be searching for), you can make your choice of what type of dowsing supplies will be best for you. Y-rods and L-rods are best for finding water, minerals, objects, people, and animals. They can also be used to locate physical problems. A pendulum is best used for finding locations and directions using a map, as in map dowsing.

You can make your own L-rods with wire coat hangers. This is an easy and inexpensive way to experiment with dowsing tools. You will need the following:

- One wire coat hanger

- Pliers

- A plastic drinking straw

Then follow these steps:

1. Using the pliers (or your hands, if you are a strong sort), straighten the coat hanger.

2. Use the pliers to cut the hanger in half. Another option is to use your hands to twist it back and forth in the middle until it snaps.

3. Hold one piece, using the long straight end as your pointer. Using the pliers, bend the shorter part into an *L*. This creates your handle.

4. Straighten the twists the best you can.

5. Do the same thing to the other piece.

6. Cut your straw in half.

7. Enclose the straw over the handles of your hanger as a sleeve. Because they are not glued or tightened, they will move freely over the wire.

8. When you begin to dowse, hold the plastic straw handles as your foundation.

You can create your own dowsing tools in several other ways. This is one of my favorite forms of divination and is certainly worth the investigation of detailed processes.

When you have determined what type of dowsing device you feel is comfortable, it is time to begin. Leave your mind open to all the possibilities. We all have the talent, if we go into the process without being judgmental or unbelieving.

You can recruit a friend or loved one to learn the process with you, if you see that he or she has the desire.

A-Dowsing We Will Go!

The best way to learn how to dowse is to be highly motivated by the desire to find something. So think about something you have lost or something that you have always wanted to find. You might try to find that pair of glasses that disappeared a month ago, for example, or you might go into your grandparents' yard and see if the buried treasure your uncle always talked about is really out there somewhere.

To start dowsing, you must select and have available your dowsing instrument, as described earlier. Different dowsing tools have different methods associated with them, so when you have determined what tool you will be using, you can start to practice, using the following guidelines.

Y-Rods

If you are working with a Y-rod to find a lost object, water, or a mineral, select a branch from a tree that is shaped in a fairly symmetrical *Y.* Hold the branch at the top of the *Y,* with one limb in each hand. The end is the pointer.

Select the location where you will begin to dowse by using the best information available about the general location of the thing you are searching for. Hold the branch or Y-rod gently, with your palms facing up and your fingers folded over the rod. The rod should be held parallel to the ground.

Visionary Insights _____

Several countries have associations of dowsers in which you can participate. The American Association of Dowsers (www.dowsers.org) has chapters in nearly every state. The Canadian Association of Dowsers also has extended chapters throughout Canada. You can find information about these organizations on the Internet or at your local library.

Take a few moments to breathe deeply and think about what you hope to find, focusing on the intention to find it. Ask a question to the spirit world, or the God of your understanding, or the Universal Life Force. For example, you might ask, "Universe, please help me find my lost watch."

Walk over the area to be explored with your dowsing rod, keeping it parallel to the ground and not letting it drop. Continue walking; when you pass over the object you are looking for, the rod will start to point downward. When the rod starts to descend toward the ground, this is when you should specifically investigate that area. If you are outside, you might even want to dig to see what is below the surface.

L-Rods

For this type of dowsing, you use two L-rods, one in each hand. Hold the short sides of the rods parallel to the ground and to each other. Your arms and hands will face each other in a pistol grip.

As you walk the area, the rods will swing apart or toward each other when they find their destination. This is really an exciting occurrence to experience. When they start to swing a certain way, start looking downward and unearth what the rods have led you to.

Map Dowsing with a Pendulum

Earlier in the chapter, I suggested using a pendulum for yes-or-no answers. However, when it comes to dowsing for directions and locations, you may want to try using your pendulum for that purpose as well. When dowsing for a location, you do not need to be there on the spot. Hold your pendulum over a map of the area and then ask your question about where you think something or someone is located. You can speak your question aloud or merely think it in silence. When the pendulum starts to swing in a circle around a given area, you have found your spot.

If your search is still too general, make your map more specific. For example, if you used a map of the United States and it tells you that Uncle Homer's safety deposit box is in Wisconsin, that's fine—but still a bit too general. So dowse over the state of Wisconsin. Then when you find that Uncle Homer's safety deposit box is in Lake Geneva, dowse over a close-up of Lake Geneva. Keep narrowing your map and getting more specific. At the end of the process, you should be able to locate the street and the bank where Uncle Homer had his account. Sounds too easy, doesn't it? You won't know until you try!

Dowsing is an art, as all types of divination are, but it is extremely mysterious. With practice, you will become better at it, though you may never understand why.

Dowsing is one of the best of all the divination skills to develop because it can help you in everyday life. You can use it to find your keys in the morning, ask where lost people or lost objects are, or whatever you want.

Now where did I put that manuscript for *The Complete Idiot's Guide to Fortune Telling*? Oh, there it is. Whew … glad I had my dowsing rods!

> **Notions Through Time**
>
> Faith is to believe what you do not see; the reward of this faith is to see what you believe.
>
> —St. Augustine, theologian

The Least You Need to Know

◆ A pendulum is best suited for answering "yes" or "no" answers about the past and present rather than for predicting future events.

◆ Dowsing is a mysterious art that has been practiced for thousands of years.

◆ A Y-rod, L-rod, or a pendulum can be used as a dowsing tool.

◆ Dowsing can help you in your everyday life to find lost objects and people.

Chapter 22

The *I Ching*

In This Chapter

- The ancient Chinese *Book of Changes*
- Understanding the hexagrams
- Using the *I Ching* as an oracle
- Interpreting the 64 hexagrams

Because the *I Ching* is such a complex work and practice, I present only its preliminary framework in this chapter. Some people devote their entire lives to learning the nuances of this form of fortune telling, and many people use it to make decisions about their day-to-day lives.

The great thing about the *I Ching* is that you can learn how to use it fairly quickly, but it also stands up to years of study. It surely has passed the test of time because it has been around for centuries, yet it has also been compared to a modern-day computer language. The simplicity of this form of divination is, therefore, deceptive. Its insight runs deep.

What Is the *I Ching?*

The *I Ching* is a book of ancient Chinese wisdom. The basics of two branches of Chinese philosophy, *Confucianism* and *Taoism*, have found their roots in this book. *I Ching* is commonly pronounced "ee ching" by most Americans. The Chinese pronounce it more like "ye jing." Either way, it simply means "Book of Changes."

def•i•ni•tion

Confucianism is the system of thought derived from the teachings of Confucius. These teachings emphasize passion for humankind and respect for social order. **Taoism** is a Chinese philosophy founded by Lao-tzu in the sixth century B.C.E. It is said that these beliefs and practices make up "The Way" or "The Path."

This Chinese manuscript was composed more than 3,000 years ago, making it one of the oldest forms of divination known to humankind. The *I Ching* offers a wealth of knowledge and insight, and proposes advice and guidance to assist individuals with their problems as they journey through life. Due to the depth of wisdom found in the *I Ching*, it has influenced science and issues of state in China throughout the centuries, and continues to do so into the present day.

Hexagrams–Not Something Witches Send

According to the wisdom of the *I Ching*, the universe is made up of two types of energy, *yin* and *yang*. yin is commonly described as the feminine aspect of this energy. yang is described as the masculine aspect. *I Ching* symbolism shows us that the symbol for yang is represented by a solid horizontal line (—). The yin symbol is represented by a broken horizontal line (- -).

(By the way, many people refer to the yin and yang as "*ying* and yang." No, nay, not. This is wrong, wrong, wrong. I have even seen books, T-shirts, bumper stickers, plaques, and posters with these inaccurate expressions. It is *yin* and yang—not like sing-song, ping-pong, or ding-dong! No *g* on the yin. Whee, now I feel much better.)

When six of these lines are combined, they create what is called a *hexagram*. Each hexagram can be divided into upper and lower lines of three each. These groups of three lines are called *trigrams*. The combinations of these lines can form a total of 64 hexagrams. For each hexagram, there is an explicit concept and interpretation. It is from these 64 hexagrams that you will be able to tell your future and gain an understanding of your life's path.

Just as an interesting point, the Chinese use the word *Kua*, which is pronounced "gwa," to describe a hexagram. So if you're talking about the *I Ching* with a Chinese native, be prepared to learn some new terminology.

At this point, you must be wondering how you pick and choose the hexagram, or group of them, that will allow you to discover the answers to your questions and tell you what your future holds. The traditional method was to use *yarrow* stalks, sometimes simply called "sticks." Yarrow is a plant that grows up to 2 feet in height. The Chinese used the stalks of the yarrow to cast their hexagrams because they thought the yarrow had magical properties, making it perfect for divination.

def•i•ni•tion

Yarrow is a plant said to have many medicinal uses. Its tall stalks were traditionally used to "throw" the *I Ching*—in other words, to randomly create the hexagrams that would be read to prophesy.

Generally, when casting yarrow stalks to find your hexagrams, 50 stalks are used, although the number varies in some sources. The stalks are thrown to the ground and, eventually, are grouped in a specific way, which defines the hexagrams. This is a time-consuming and complicated method. You may investigate this process in any one of the many, many books written on the *I Ching* if it appeals to you.

An easier way is to use sticks that have been purposely designed for the *I Ching*. You can purchase *I Ching* sticks from new-age stores and Internet sites. Typically, they come as a set of six plastic sticks with directions on how to use this contemporary method of casting *I Ching* hexagrams. The cost runs approximately $15 and up. A little later in this chapter, I offer an even simpler method, using coins, that is popular for consulting the *I Ching*. (And, no, the sound the coins make when you toss them is *not* the origin of the name of the book, although it's a happy coincidence—ee-*ching*!)

Whatever method you choose to throw the *I Ching*, the goal is to determine the three elements of the upper trigram and three elements of the lower trigram that make up your specific hexagram. For example, you may find that each of the three lower elements turns out to be an unbroken single line (three yang), and the three upper elements are a broken line, an unbroken line, and a broken line (yang, yin, yang).

The skill is to understand how the description of the hexagram you threw applies to the situation you are attempting to divine about. Sometimes the correlation is very clear. Other times, it is very cryptic. With practice, you will read more meaning into these seemingly simple hexagrams.

The *I Ching* as an Oracle

Understanding the history and uses of any fortune-telling method gives us more power to read it accurately. But because the history and uses of the *I Ching* are so varied and complex, it's a good idea to "cut to the chase" and learn the simplest and perhaps most popular method: throwing Chinese coins. Specialty stores sell *I Ching* round coins with square holes in them, a design the Chinese used for centuries. It's not as natural as using yarrow stalks, but it sure is neater—and more convenient, if you don't happen to have any yarrow growing nearby. In fact, you may not have access to Chinese coins, either, so pennies will do just as well.

Notions Through Time

When clouds form in the skies, we know that rain will follow, but we must not wait for it. Nothing will be achieved by attempting to interfere with the future before the time is ripe. Patience is needed.

—From the *I Ching*

Visionary Insights

When you find your special coins, keep using those same coins if they are working well with you. Keep them in a place of dignity, such as a soft velvet bag, a special box, or any container or holding place. Keep them somewhere you think they will be happy.

Pennies from Heaven

All you really need to "throw the Ching," as this divination method is sometimes colloquially referred to, is three pennies. How easy is that? If you live in Canada, three Canadian 1-cent coins are perfect. One reason the *I Ching* is called the *Book of Changes* might be that it is flexible enough to accommodate our modern-day approaches and still yield its ancient wisdom. (Or maybe it's because pennies are called "change." Nah.)

On a technical note, I highly encourage the use of copper coins, if possible. Copper is recognized to channel psychic "energy," just as it is similarly used as a conductor of electricity in the mundane world.

Whatever type of coins you decide to use, it is important that they feel good in your hand. You can wash them under water to clear out any negative energy they may have "picked up" while in circulation. The clearing technique is the same as mentioned in Chapter 17.

Heads or Tails?

Creating a hexagram with coins is contingent upon *heads* and *tails* interpretations. Most people know what "heads" and "tails" are when it comes to a coin toss. But because this is important and your future could depend on it, let's clarify.

When working with coins, traditionally the side of the coin sporting a bust of a ruler or other authority figure is called heads. The opposite side is then considered tails. In the currency of some countries (such as China), there may not be a literal head on one side of the coin. If this is the case, determine which is the stronger image, and use that as heads and the other side as tails.

Shake, Rattle, Roll, and Draw

Using a piece of paper, pen or pencil, and your coins, you can now start to build your hexagrams. Set yourself up with a surface you can write on, as well as a flat place you can throw your coins and see precisely how they land. By the way, it should be clean and free of little annoying things, such as utility bills and cookie crumbs. Personally, I like a tablecloth, a towel, or special fabric.

1. Set a mood using whatever enhancements—candles, incense, music—seem appropriate (see Chapter 4).

2. Take your coins in hand and concentrate on your question. This could take seconds or minutes. When you feel you are ready, you are ready. You can't make mistakes when it comes to "knowing" when you are set to begin.

3. Shake the coins in your hand (left, right, or both—it doesn't matter). Be comfortable. Throw the coins gently down on the surface you have selected.

4. With the first throw, examine the side of the coins that are "up." If you throw three heads, that's a yang (—). Three tails is a yin (- -). Two heads and a tail is a yang (—). Two tails and a head is a yin (- -).

> **Notions Through Time**
>
> Everything proceeds as if of its own accord, and this can all too easily tempt us to relax and let things take their course without troubling over details. Such indifference is the root of all evil.
>
> —From the *I Ching*

5. This first throw determines the first line of your hexagram, which starts at the bottom and works up. Draw the first line, whether it is a yang (—) or a yin (- -).

6. Continue with this same procedure until you have thrown your coins a total number of six times.

Your recording should look something like this:

First throw (which is the bottom line) is yang (—).

Second throw (which is the second from the bottom) is yin (- -).

Third throw is yang (—), and so on.

Draw the matching solid or broken line to create your hexagram.

Example after six throws:

- - (sixth throw)

— (fifth throw)

— (fourth throw)

— (third throw)

- - (second throw)

— (first throw)

You have now completed your hexagram, which should answer your question, afford you insights for decision making, and offer you guidance. Using the following interpretation key, find the matching hexagram and read the message.

Interpretation Key for the Sixty-Four Hexagrams

When you have found your hexagram via the lines you have drawn, you can match it to the corresponding hexagram interpretations. When you find the description of your hexagram, try to understand it in the context of the question you have asked. Look beyond the surface meanings and into the deeper significance of the universal pattern or flow of energy that is being described. Learning to "read into" the meanings of the hexagrams will give you deeper insight into the answers to your questions.

1. Ch'ien—The Creative

The power of creation, of life and fruition, is to be had by one who is wise enough to be open to it and apply him- or herself to opening doors and finding opportunities in an innovative way. Be aware of your surroundings, find beauty in all, and draw your energy from it—and you will be rewarded.

2. K'un—The Receptive

Success is possible for the wise person who works hard and is willing to follow the leadership of someone of higher rank (who is older, wiser, more experienced, and so on) without bragging or trying to take all the credit. Arrogance and self-importance will lead to failure in spite of one's hard work or talents. Being the support person, whether in business or in love, will bring you the best success, and you will both learn and be honored for your loyalty.

3. Chun—Difficulty at the Beginning

Difficult times lay ahead in a new undertaking; problems will arise, causing delays. Patience is needed; hurrying things will only bring failure. Remain steadfast to your ideals, in spite of the bleak outlook. Be willing to wait, seeking guidance from those who have been this way before. Pushing too hard for results ends in failure, while biding your time will result in ultimate success.

4. Mêng—Youthful Folly

Look for a mature person, whether for advise, employment, or love. Humiliation, disappointment, and failure will come to you if you foolishly seek out youth for youth's sake. Do not overlook the tried and true simply to be different. Taking foolish chances will bring misfortune, while approaching life with childlike wonder (or a new perspective on an old subject) will bring joy and fulfillment. Do not try to right a wrong with another wrong, but use both kindness and forgiveness (for yourself as well as others); take the higher path.

5. Hsu—Waiting (Nourishment)

Your waiting will be rewarded if you are sincere. You may have to endure trials before you achieve your goals, but as long as you stick to your ideals and are willing to work toward your goals, in time you shall achieve them. It is important, though, to remember that you mustn't be so single-minded that you lose sight of your day-to-day life. Enjoy the moments; do not delay satisfaction. Take pleasure in what each day holds, and take time to smell the roses. You will be surprised that your eventual success will be all the sweeter for the pleasures taken while waiting.

6. Sung–Conflict

Even though you are sincere in your desires, your path is blocked. Be willing to accept that there may be some things you cannot change. Be willing to change yourself instead, to accommodate whatever limitations or problems you must face. Fighting to change what you cannot change will bring sadness, while accepting will bring peace. Prolonged conflict destroys; there are no winners. Do not risk losing all for the sake of winning more. Keep your dignity intact. You will find freedom in acceptance.

7. Shih–The Army

Leadership is not a solitary role, but one that involves a partnership with those beneath you. Maintaining a relationship of respect and appreciation with those around you will strengthen your role as a leader, and teamwork, whether in business, family, or school, will gain the advantage.

8. Pi–Holding Together (Union)

Unity is key to reaching your goals. United and working together, persevering for the common good, these things will bring good fortune. Rely on others you trust to keep moving in the right direction. Uncertainty and confusion will bring disaster.

9. Hsiao Ch'u–The Taming Power of the Small

This is not the time to hurry forward. Instead, take an account of what you have, and make small improvements that will benefit you in the long run. Do not be greedy or pushy because this spells disaster. Consider your character, loyalty, honesty, and sincerity as strengths. Count your blessings and humble yourself.

10. Lu–Treading (Conduct)

There is danger for those who behave rashly and without conscience. Conducting yourself honorably and blamelessly will benefit you most. It is possible to overcome your weaknesses with sincere effort, and this will empower you. Plan carefully, be aware of the pitfalls, and then move forward slowly but with confidence.

11. T'ai—Peace

A time of peace is at hand, but use your wisdom to make the most of it. Avoid extremes, and be aware of the flow of things. Anticipate the ups and downs, and you will maintain more stability. Be flexible, and share your prosperity and joy with others.

12. P'i—Standstill (Stagnation)

Be conservative; things slow down and no progress seems to be made. Have patience and do not lower your standards, but instead wait out this time of difficulty. Keep in control, cut back, and abstain where necessary to maintain the well-being of others. Good things will follow.

13. T'ung Jên—Fellowship with Men

This is a good time for successful relationships. Partnerships, marriages, and friendships will benefit. Fellowship is important and should be a priority. Avoid making social distinctions, and treat everyone with warmth and kindness. Success will surround you.

14. Ta Yu—Possession in Great Measure

All is good, and prosperity ensues for those who remain alert and on top of things. This is a good time to start a new venture, but count your blessings and give thanks always. Be generous with your good fortune; share with those around you, and it will come back to you. Be honest in your dealings and avoid shame.

15. Ch'ien—Modesty

Balance is the key to success at this time. Be modest both in desires and in expression. Avoid excess and reduce want, bringing stability to your life. Act with humility; do not boast or seek praise. Good fortune is waiting for those who put arrogance behind them.

16. YuYü—Enthusiasm

This is a good time to set big things in motion. Remember to enlist the help of those who are wise and to show appreciation for the benefits they bring you. Include those around you in your successes; friends and family should benefit from your good fortune. Do not indulge in excesses; over-stepping can bring failure.

17. Sui—Following

This is a good time to allow another to take the lead. Guidance will bene-fit you. Do not feel that you need no assistance—you will cut yourself off from others' wisdom. Neither should you be complacent and helpless, for you will be seen as a child. An attitude of the student, willing to learn and make progress, brings the best success. Use your good sense to know what you should do; sound judgment is called for.

18. Ku—Work on What Has Been Spoiled (Decay)

Assess yourself and your life for areas that need improvement. Bad habits, poor attitude, and things that have been a thorn in your side need atten-tion now. Make changes for the better, and invest in yourself so that others will see the value in you. Do not let your past drag you down, but learn from it and try to set things right.

19. Lin—Approach

Success and good fortune are given to you as long as you proceed humbly and without arrogance. You will be most encouraging to those who help you if you proceed with gentleness and respect. Enjoy this time of success because it may be short-lived. Do not step on others' toes on your way up, and you will have their respect when the going is rough.

20. Kuan—Contemplation (View)

Take stock of where you are, and maintain a mature perspective on how far you have come and what needs to be done next. Keep your eyes open; do not let opportunities escape you. Strive for clarity in your goals, and seek the assistance of those in power to improve your lot. Do not forget to reward those who help you, and do not betray those who depend on you.

21. Shih Ho—Biting Through

Justice must prevail. Rules have been broken, and you must take your punishment. Accepting the blame for what you have done will clear your conscience. Correcting your mistakes will make things easier on you, and you may move forward. Delaying justice makes matters worse and causes problems and pain.

22. Pi—Grace

New beginnings and undertakings will be beneficial at this time, but be realistic and do not be deceived. Look for tranquility and happiness in the simple things that bring beauty and grace; they should be appreciated and not taken for granted. Wrap things up without an excess of fuss; to over-work things will bring dissatisfaction with the ending.

23. Po—Splitting Apart

Proceed with due caution; be reserved and do not act rashly. Misfortune awaits those who do not think things through. Stay close to home, this is where you are most needed now. Family matters may need tending. Allow things to flow naturally to their conclusion.

24. Fu—Return (The Turning Point)

A time of change is at hand, so anticipate new things. This is a return to good times and new friends. Things will be happening—perhaps travel or new scenery. Now is not the time to sit still and wait. Be ready to take a new path.

25. Wu Wang—Innocence (The Unexpected)

Expect the unexpected. Be prepared to take up the reins of a new venture (business, personal, or romantic), but do it with an open heart and mind, honestly and without guile. Be honorable and true, and you will be rewarded. Be willing to go with the flow; do not be too rigid, or all will fall apart.

26. Ta Ch'u—The Taming Power of the Great

Information and education are important at this time. You gain the advantage by being very knowledgeable. Learn from the past; its lessons will strengthen your discernment in the future. Discussions and debates with friends over meals will be fruitful, and being a social butterfly at this time is the way to go.

27. I—The Corners of the Mouth (Providing Nourishment)

Time for you to heed your health and diet. Do not implement just a fad or a spur-of-the-moment plan: a thorough contemplation of health issues is overdue, and you must consider the future for your own protection of your body. Slow down and make changes. Do not eat and drink with abandon, but consider your overall health.

28. Ta Kuo—Preponderance of the Great

The advantage is to be had by the self-sufficient; independence will bring you through trials. Courage and strength are needed at this time. Advice or assistance by someone more experienced can renew your strength. Do not fear obstacles, but be prepared to bear the brunt alone. Approach all with humility, and do not be arrogant.

29. K'an—The Abysmal (Water)

Be cautious; now is not the time to overextend yourself or take on big projects. Go slowly, being thoughtful and humble while making small gains in business. Be generous with yourself, showing others the way or mentoring another. Do not make rash decisions; it may lead to disaster.

30. Li—The Clinging, Fire

Take care of business on the home front, count your blessings, and look for the good in things. Take the approach of "the glass half full" rather than "the glass half empty," and you will have good fortune. You will be surprised by a new outlook and encouragement; things will go well for you. Plans made in haste will fizzle out; good preparation and groundwork lead to success.

31. Hsien—Influence (Wooing)

Be open to others, and new opportunities (for romance, business, or personal advancement) will present themselves. Take your time—now is not the time to rush. Encourage those around you, and it will add to your fruitfulness. Waiting brings advantage at this time.

32. Hêng—Duration

Make preparations for the long run, and your endeavor will prosper. Marriage, partnerships, and other relationships benefit from careful cultivation. Do not expect progress without hard work. Good fortune will come to you if you plan carefully and do not act in haste.

33. Tun—Retreat

Back off from new relationships or endeavors. Do so without making trouble; do not make enemies at this time. A graceful retreat allows you to retain your strength and does not create animosity. Do not vacillate; be firm but pleasant, and turn down new ventures or responsibilities that might prove too taxing. Do not bite off more than you can chew.

34. Ta Chuang—The Power of the Great

Proceed with caution; do not attempt to be innovative at this time. The tried and true will prevail, and it does not pay to try to change the "old guard" at this time. Wisdom dictates being diligent and thorough, without stepping on others' toes, and you will be successful. Give respect and appreciation to those who are your senior. Honor the past.

35. Chin—Progress

Take in the big picture. Good fortune is yours and things move forward, but there may be setbacks. Do not let them worry you; everything will move forward at its own natural course. Your family contributes to your good fortune; you will gain the support that you need. Be vigilant and honorable, and you shall receive your reward.

36. Ming I—Darkening of the Light

Have courage. Stressful times lay ahead. Be resilient and do not yield. Your strength may be sapped, but you will overcome. Retain your confidence and you will prevail. Do not let others undermine your faith; all will be well, and you will come through this stronger than before. Take heart. You will be proven right in the long run.

37. Chia Jên—The Family (The Clan)

All things to do with family should take priority. Happiness and good cheer should be cultivated in the home. Friends and family should be kept close and nurtured. Spend time together, and you will be greatly rewarded. Do not neglect those who love you—they are your future.

38. K'uei—Opposition

Troubles may come, but if you keep your head, you shall prevail. Do not scramble to correct things; wait and they will work themselves out through their natural course. You will meet a like-minded person who will be supportive and a good asset. Do not judge too quickly—all will be revealed later. Wait and you will be rewarded.

39. Chien—Obstruction

Your path will be blocked in many directions, but it is not your fault. Focus on self-improvement while matters take their own course. Be honorable and trustworthy; you will not be found at fault. At the end, good things await. If you are sincere and hard-working, you will persevere.

40. Hsieh—Deliverance

Do not be arrogant; this will bring failure. Pushing ahead without forethought is a mistake—step back and take a thorough accounting. Be forgiving, of both yourself and others. Admit errors and start again; ignoring them leads to disaster. Be humble and allow your superiors to take charge: you will gain their respect, and good things will come.

41. Sun—Decrease

Restraint and moderation are called for at this time. Do not indulge in excesses or allow your emotions to run rampant. Conservation now brings abundance for others as well as yourself in the long run. Being generous will be of benefit to all. A new venture will succeed, but only if you are willing to make the necessary sacrifices.

42. I—Increase

Kindness and goodness will bring success to the sincere of heart. Follow in the path of one who is a good example; learn from that person and do likewise. Do not let your weaknesses bring you down. Overcome them, and you will be successful in the future. Be gentle, honorable, and trustworthy; you will find favor with all, and your advantage increases.

43. Kuai—Break-Through (Resoluteness)

Do not turn back now, but an aggressive stance will not be fruitful. Stand tough, but with patience and good heart. Confrontation should be avoided. Be generous with your rewards; do not forget those who have helped you along the way. Your good standing will further your progress, as an ambassador smoothes the way for changes. Have courage, and you will be proven right.

44. Kou—Coming to Meet

Be watchful—a new situation should be monitored carefully. Do not allow things to get out of hand; put a stop to them quickly. You may be taken by surprise, and a seemingly benign person may prove to be a problem. Keep the upper hand, and do not let your leadership be challenged. If you remain in control, no harm will come, but be wary of those who would undermine you.

45. Ts'ui—Gathering Together (Massing)

Give proper respect and honor to those above you, and it will go in your favor. Appreciation and gifts are valued. Be sincere, and you will be rewarded. A new beginning will be fruitful; go forward with thankfulness, and all will go well. Prepare for the future, and it will go well for you. Those who you look out for will repay you in kind.

46. Shêng—Pushing Upward

This is a time of growth; change may be imperceptible at first look, but small improvements over time prove gainful and rewarding. Be honorable in all things, and the benefits will add up. Give others credit and be humble; repay those who have helped you, and strength will be on your side. Do not be afraid that you may not see where you are headed; be confident that your good character and hard work will take you to eventual success.

47. K'un—Oppression (Exhaustion)

Do what is right and what you believe in, even though the outlook is gloomy. If your heart is in it, it will succeed, but it may be a long time before you see the fruits of your labor. Be willing to make sacrifices for the greater good. Do not let others bring you down by their lack of confidence in you. You may need to put out more than you take in for a time, but you should succeed with hard work and perseverance.

48. Ching—The Well

Be aware of your place in the scheme of things; do not overvalue your own worth. Instead, appreciate those who assist you; value them, and you will be rewarded. Be encouraging and realize that you are in it for the long haul. Overlook the daily ups and downs, and focus on your goals; you will find success. Team effort produces greater works than a loose cannon. Stay focused, and time will work to your advantage.

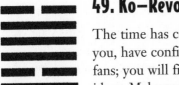

49. Ko—Revolution (Molting)

The time has come to strike while the iron is hot. Put your regrets behind you, have confidence, and push forward. Your persistence will win you fans; you will find that you have solid backing if you have faith in your ideas. Make preparations to follow through; hesitation will not help you.

50. Ting—The Caldron

Success is at hand. Very good things will come to you. Be upright in all things, benevolent, and gracious; you are a winner and should set an example. Take stock of yourself and your assets. Shed the things that hamper your success, and move forward; the prize is in sight.

51. Chên—The Arousing (Shock, Thunder)

Something dramatic is about to happen; keep your head and do not let it shake you. See to others affected, and let them know you are there for them. Act in good conscience; do not be led by selfishness. In the end, good things will come out of it, and you will benefit greatly. Be patient and unafraid.

52. Kên—Keeping Still, Mountain

Monumental things may be at hand. Stay focused; do not push forward or retreat. Take stock of the situation, prepare yourself as best you can, and wait. Action should be only to the immediate needs; you need inner strength, and your will may be tested. Remain steadfast, and you will prevail.

53. Chien—Development (Gradual Progress)

Growth and prosperity are ahead for those who are of good character. Love may flourish, and good times with loved ones and friends should be encouraged. Tame your wild side so that hearth and home may prosper. Do not take foolish risks for brief pleasures; instead, invest in the future and nurture what you have.

54. Kuei Mei—The Marrying Maiden

Appreciate what you have, and be aware that all is temporary. What is fruitful today may be barren tomorrow. Realize the magnitude of the universe and your small place in it. Do not covet what you do not have; your desires may be your downfall. What may look pleasing now may hurt you later. Be constant and faithful; you will benefit from both.

55. Fêng—Abundance (Fullness)

Abundance should bring happiness; beware the feelings of discontent. To overlook your blessings and grumble will be your undoing. The time of ripeness is at hand; do not waste it, or you will be filled with regret. Show gratitude and respect to all those who have helped you, and appreciate all that has been given you.

56. Lu—The Wanderer

Be careful in your dealings; do not stray into murky waters. Remain solid and forthright—honesty is the best policy. Your hard-won reputation could be lost by foolishly dabbling in crooked dealings. Do nothing that will cause you shame, and you will remain stable and without blame.

57. Sun—The Gentle (The Penetrating, Wind)

Walk softly and push slowly; change can be great through small things. Good things will come; continue in the direction you are going. Your plans are solid; proceed toward your goals at a slow but effective rate. Think in terms of miracles, and do not discount faith.

58. Tui—The Joyous, Lake

Happiness looms, but there are pitfalls. Don't let the little stuff bog you down. Make amends where possible, but beware of taking to heart too much past baggage. Success and joy will come when you let go of recriminations and bad feelings, and allow fellowship to be a happy and beneficial occasion again.

59. Huan—Dispersion (Dissolution)

A spiritual awakening is a blessing to you now. Shed the old, honor God, and you will be relieved of your burdens. You can disengage from detrimental relationships and habits; doing so will bring you good benefits. Do what you need to do to cleanse your soul so that you are without blame. Do not look back.

60. Chieh—Limitation

Knowing and accepting limitations brings peace. Striving beyond your capabilities brings failure and unhappiness. Acceptance can be liberating; do not chastise yourself for that which you cannot accomplish, but take pleasure in your strengths and talents. The duck cannot be a swan, nor the dog a bear. Happiness is not having what you want, but wanting what you have.

61. Chung Fu—Inner Truth

Contemplation of your character should be honest to be successful. Do not judge others too quickly or be quick to take offense. Allow things to unfold before making judgments; do not be rash, but take all things into consideration. Forgiveness and acceptance go a long way toward bringing you peace.

62. Hsiao Kuo—Preponderance of the Small

Be reverent, and do not take lightly anything that can bring damage to yourself or others. Consider with wisdom your situation before acting. Do not act in haste, or you may regret it in your leisure. Hold life in high regard, and act accordingly. Your character should be blameless; honor and virtue are highly valued.

63. Chi Chi—After Completion

Be aware that achieving your goal is not the end, but a beginning. Do not expect to remain on top if you do not prepare yourself to avoid losing ground. Prepare for the future; what you have may not remain for long if you are not careful. Do not take anything for granted; tend to things that are of great importance, or they may crumble and vanish.

64. Wei Chi—Before Completion

Do not be overconfident when you see the finish line. Maintain your stride; do not hold back or let yourself be turned aside. Achievement can be whisked away if you fail to follow through. Have respect for the challenges ahead, and do not become arrogant. Humiliation will result for those who fail to remain on course.

The Least You Need to Know

- ◆ *I Ching*, or the *Book of Changes*, can be used as a book of wisdom or an oracle.

- ◆ Hexagrams made up of lines create the symbols you will interpret.

- ◆ You can use coins or yarrow sticks to create your hexagrams.

- ◆ When consulting the *I Ching*, try to see beyond the descriptions of each hexagram, into the deeper meaning of these universal patterns.

Glossary

altered state of consciousness A deep sense of relaxation or more profound shift in awareness. It can sometimes be accessed in the time between waking and sleeping, right before drifting off into dreamland. Meditation and hypnosis can also produce an altered state of consciousness.

branches In palmistry, straight-type lines with little lines ascending or descending from them.

cartomancy The art of reading regular playing cards.

chained In palmistry, literally looking like a chain. Some readers call it netted because it can resemble a line of net.

chapbooks Poor-quality printed matter sold by venders peddling in the streets in the Middle Ages, usually addressing daily matters. *See also* tablets of fate.

cirrus clouds Very thin, white clouds with a wispy, feathery, or stringy appearance.

clairvoyance The ability to see into the future.

clairvoyant A person who sees clearly into the future.

concentration Focusing on an external object and seeing it in a physical form.

Confucianism The system of thought derived from the teachings of Confucius. These teachings emphasize passion for humankind and respect for social order.

cumulus clouds Billowing clouds with flat bases and a vertical doming akin to a "cauliflower-like" appearance.

Delphi A city in ancient Greece.

divination Another word for fortune telling.

divining To actively use a fortune-telling method, as in "I was divining my future using a pendulum."

divining rods Typically two L-shaped metal rods.

dowsing The ancient art of finding things intuitively with the aid of a tool or other device.

dowsing stick or **forked stick** A small Y-shaped branch from a tree.

elements Earth, Fire, Air, and Water. Considered to be the basic components of our planet. They appear in the esoteric teachings of cultures all over the world, from Hawaiian huna to Celtic druidism, to medieval alchemy, to Siberian shamanism, as the root material of our existence and the key energies of what is sometimes called magic.

energy body The area around your body that life force radiates into. It is thought by some to be the source of the "sixth sense" of psychic awareness.

esoteric Relates to things that are known and accepted by a limited number of people. Usually things pertaining to mystic and supernatural experiences.

extrasensory perception (ESP) The ability of an individual to perceive someone's thoughts, distant circumstances, or events—sometimes even in the future—without having any sensory communication or physical association.

fork In palmistry, a line that has two or three other lines extending from it.

gyromancy Involves printing the alphabet on the ground in a large circle. Participants dance or spin until they become dizzy and stumble upon the letters. This goes on until an entire message is recorded or suggested.

hexagrams The six-line symbols that result from the combinations of Yin and Yang that appear when using one of the methods for setting up the *I Ching*.

I Ching A book of ancient Chinese wisdom. The basics of two branches of Chinese philosophy, *Confucianism* and *Taoism*, have found their roots in this book. *See also* Confucianism and Taoism.

inkblot test A psychological test in which a subject analyzes a series of inkblots using his or her own interpretations.

left-brained The part of the brain dominated by logic and analytical thought, with lots of verbal communication. *See also* right-brained.

magick Sometimes spelled with a *k* at the end of the word, as opposed to the common spelling *magic*, to point out a difference. This distinguishes magickal practitioners and others who practice supernatural methods from magicians who perform "stage magic" or who are "illusionists."

Mah jong A game the Chinese produced using tiles that resemble domino pieces involving four players. The players often used this game as a form of gambling. Different designs adorn these tiles. As the game is played, the pieces are drawn and discarded as in a card game. Eventually, one player wins with a particular hand of combinations.

meditation A deep level of concentration. Thoughts and messages may come to you from a higher power through meditation.

mental telepathy (telepathic communication) The ability to communicate information from mind to mind, without the benefit of any other form of communication. *See also* extrasensory perception (ESP).

nephomancy The technical word for cloud gazing.

nimbus clouds Commonly called rain clouds. They are associated with steady precipitation and often occur in dark gray, thick, continuous layers. They can also appear as puffy, vertically rising rain clouds.

numerology The ancient study and application of the meaning of numbers and how they can pertain and influence your life. Certain numbers have a special vibration that may affect your future.

Oracle at Delphi A priestess named Pynthia who supposedly got messages from Apollo while sitting on a tripod inhaling fumes, which put her in a trance state.

Ouija board The trademark name for the William Fuld/Parker Brothers board. The general name for this oracle is a "talking board." However, because of its popularity the trademark "Ouija board" became commonly used to describe any talking or spirit board. The board displays printed numbers, letters, and words. Participants place their fingers on the pointer, which moves around the board to spell out an answer.

palmistry (chiromancy) The practice of predicting future events through the study of one's palms. The lines, fingers, fingernails, and all sections of the hand can determine past, present, and future occurrences. All of these areas have meanings and give us an indication of a person's character.

pendulum A weighted object hanging from a string or chain.

phrenology The study of lumps and bumps on the head.

physiognomy (personology) The term we use in the West for the art of reading faces.

planchette A heart-shaped pointer that is used to point to the letters or words on the Ouija board. Placing the fingers gently on top of the planchette enables it to move across the board, spelling out messages. *See also* Ouija board.

precognition The ability to foretell a future event before it takes place.

prophecy The prediction of future events.

psychometry The ability to get information about an object or the people or things connected to it by touching it, holding it, or being close to it.

reading Another name for the practice of divination or fortune telling.

right-brained Using the part of your brain that dominates emotions, intuition, and creativeness. *See also* left-brained.

runes An ancient Germanic alphabet. The word *rune* derives from the Gothic for "mystery." These symbols were inscribed on rocks or wood as a form of writing. The runes were made up of straight lines, which apparently made the engraving easier. When individually inscribed on pieces of stones or wood, they became a form of divining and were used for magical practices. Runes have no lowercase letters and were read left to right as well as right to left.

scrying An act of divination using a reflective surface such as a mirror, crystal, polished stone, or even water to see images about the past, present, and future.

shamans Members of tribal societies who act as mediums between the real world and the world beyond the physical. They practice magic of sorts for divination, healing, and occurrences in nature.

spell A method of manifesting something you want into your life by using spoken, written, or chanted words. It does not refer to negative evil things; it is an appeal to a higher power.

Sphinx A renowned statue formed of sandstone depicting the head of a King and the body of a lion. It is believed to have been formed more than 4,500 years ago. Its location is not far from Cairo, Egypt.

spirit guides People (and sometimes, animals) who have made the transition into the death realms or into a higher dimensional plane, and who have come back to us to help us on this plane.

spondanomancy (spodomancy) Divination by examining ashes.

stratus clouds Clouds that appear in a thin, sheetlike formation covering large portions of the sky.

sweat lodge A type of sauna used as a ceremonial tool. Sometimes teepees or dome-shaped structures made of branches and blankets are used. Fires or hot stones put on the ground heat the lodge.

tablets of fate Pamphlets or papers peddled by seventeenth- and nineteenth-century street venders addressing daily matters according to daily planetary influences, like daily horoscopes. Other tablets of fate were standard and did not change daily. *See also* chapbooks.

Taoism Considered "the path or the way," it is said to be a philosophy more than a religion. However, Taoism was still labeled a religion, and along with Buddhism and Confucianism, became one of the most notable religions of China.

target card Used with a pendulum, any piece of paper or cardboard with a circle drawn on it.

Tarot cards A deck of 78 cards with varied pictures and symbolic images. They are used as a form of divination and as a tool for spiritual guidance.

tasseography (tasseomancy) The art of reading tea leaves or coffee grounds to forecast the future. The term *tasse* (cup) comes from the French, which, in turn, comes from the Arabic root word *tassa* (cup).

third eye The point on the forehead between our eyes, sometimes referred to as the mind's eye or a mystical center from where psychic impressions may arise.

three hit rule Pertains to seeing people you have lost communication with for a long time. You start thinking about them a lot in any form, including daydreaming, nighttime dreams, or reminders in places you visit. Things like photos falling off shelves, songs that bring back memories, other people talking about them, and similar reminders or any kind of suggestion of them count as a "hit." If you can count three (without forcing them), you will most likely see that person or hear news of him or her that will benefit you in some form.

threefold law The law that says "what goes around, comes around." Project kindness (harm no one), and it will come back to you three times over. Project hurtful intentions, and you will get back misfortune three times over.

trick dice Dice that are usually weighted on one side to always throw a 7 or 11. These are also referred to as "loaded" dice. They are often used in magic tricks.

trigrams The two three-line components to each hexagram.

yarrow An herb said to have many medicinal uses. Its tall stalks were traditionally used to "throw" the *I Ching*—in other words, to randomly create the hexagrams that would be read to prophesy.

yin and **yang** Yin is the feminine part of the energy that makes up the universe. It is also described as open and receiving. Yang is the masculine part of the energy that makes up the universe. It is also described as creative and forceful.

Resources

Books

Many of the forms of fortune telling cited in this book can be investigated to a fuller degree. After experimenting with the different techniques of divination, you will be drawn to some more than others. Additionally, you may want to delve into other intriguing mystical pursuits. In that event, I recommend the following books as a source to help you further your study in fortune telling and the things not of the physical.

Ideas and concepts will differ from one author to another, including myself. One isn't necessarily better than the other—they're just different. Therefore, research, read, and contemplate. You will find a way that works best with your rhythm using a little bit of this and a little bit of that!

Ahlquist, Diane. *Moon Spells*. Adams Media, 2002.

———. *White Light: The Complete Guide to Spells and Rituals for Psychic Protection*. Citadel Press Books, 2002.

Budilovsky, Joan, and Eve Adamson. *Complete Idiot's Guide to Meditation, Second Edition, The*. Alpha Books, 2002.

Butler, W. E. *How to Read the Aura and Practice Psychometry, Telepathy, and Clairvoyance*. Destiny Books, 1987.

Denning, Melita, and Osborne Phillips. *Creative Visualization.* Llewellyn Publishing, 1992.

Dunwich, Gerina. *The Magick of Candle Burning.* Carol Publishing Group, 1992.

Fenton, Sasha. *Tea Cup Reading: A Quick and Easy Guide to Tasseography.* Weiser Books, 2002.

Harary, Keith, and Pamela Weintraub. *Lucid Dreams in 30 Days: The Creative Sleep Program.* St. Martin's Griffen, 1989.

Knight, Sirona. *Empowering Your Life with Natural Magic.* Alpha Books, 2004.

———. *Little Giant Encyclopedia of Runes, The.* Sterling, 2000.

McClain, Gary R., and Carolyn Flynn. *Complete Idiot's Guide to Oracles, The.* Alpha Books, 2006.

Moran, Elizabeth, and Master Joseph Yu. *Complete Idiot's Guide to the I Ching, The.* Alpha Books, 2002.

Sullivan, Kevin. *The Crystal Handbook: Put Crystal Consciousness to Work!* Signet Books, 1987.

Tognetti, Arlene, and Carolyn Flynn. *Complete Idiot's Guide to Tarot Spreads Illustrated, The.* Alpha Books, 2006.

Webster, Richard. *Palm Reading for Beginners.* Llewellyn Publications, 2000.

Websites

So many interesting websites, and so little space! However, here are some that provide information, merchandise, and advice for your fortune-telling endeavors. While writing this book, the following websites were active. However, bear in mind that often websites change or are no longer available.

- **almanac.com** offers information about astronomy, including moon names and phases.

- **bestcrystals.com** is an extensive website about crystals and minerals.

- **bytheplanet.com** provides articles and products that may assist you in your divination.

◆ **dianeahlquist.com** offers information about the author, classes, and free information about metaphysics and spiritual endeavors.

◆ **facade.com** is devoted to several forms of divination and offers free online readings.

◆ **grandpasgeneral.com** sells metaphysical supplies and shares free information about etheric practices.

◆ **rainbowcrystal.com** assists you with useful tools for fortune telling, along with various information about divination and metaphysics.

◆ **realmusic.com** is a source of relaxation where you can order the latest releases, including New Age music.

◆ **spiritofangels.com** offers tips and information along with classes, products, and readings.

◆ **theherbsplace.com** is a source for herbs, supplements, and essential oils, as well as information on classes, consultations, and newsletters.

Fortune-Telling Journal

This ready-made guide will help you stay organized as you keep your fortune-telling journal. It identifies some of the major factors that can make a difference in your success. They may not seem important at the time, but later, after you've made some notes, you might see interesting correlations between what made a reading successful or not so successful.

Method of Divination

The type of divination you choose is important. If you attempt to use more than one method in the same day, make a different entry in your journal for each one. Note any details. For example, if you used tea leaves, what type of cup did you use? Don't get too specific, though: this is not the time to go into the details concerning results or how you did it. This is merely what form of fortune telling you used and what the tools looked like. This way, later you can remember, for example, whether you did better using playing cards with plain backs or playing cards with a pattern on the back.

Check the type of divination you used here, and make any notes in the space provided.

❑ Reading tea leaves/coffee grounds: _____

_____

❑ Ice rendering: _____

_____

❑ Spondanomancy (reading ashes): _____

_____

❑ Divining by sand and smoke: _____

_____

❑ Candle wax divination: _____

_____

❑ Using a Ouija board: _____

_____

❑ Cartomancy (reading playing cards): _____

_____

❑ Throwing dice or dominoes: _____

_____

❑ Knife prophecies: _____

_____

❑ Tablets of fate: _____

_____

❑ Reading facial features and bumps: _____

_____

❑ Cloud prophecies: _____

_____

❑ Crystal gazing and scrying: _____

_____

❑ Palmistry: _____

_____